THE COLLECTED POEMS

OF

WALLACE STEVENS

B Y

Wallace Stevens

P O E T R Y

Opus Posthumous   1957
The Collected Poems of Wallace Stevens   1954
The Auroras of Autumn   1950
Transport to Summer   1947
Parts of a World   1942, 1951
The Man with the Blue Guitar (including Ideas of
Order)   1936, 1937; in one volume, 1952
Harmonium   1923, 1931, 1937

P R O S E

The Necessary Angel: *Essays on Reality and the Imagination*   1951

These are BORZOI BOOKS
published by Alfred A. Knopf in New York

THE

COLLECTED POEMS

OF

WALLACE STEVENS

ALFRED A. KNOPF NEW YORK 1957

L. C. catalog card number: 54–11750

THIS IS A BORZOI BOOK,
PUBLISHED BY ALFRED A. KNOPF, INC.

First Collected Edition Published October 1, 1954
Second Printing, February 1955
Third Printing, May 1955
Fourth Printing, November 1957

Contents

HARMONIUM

vii

IDEAS OF ORDER

THE MAN WITH THE BLUE GUITAR

PARTS OF A WORLD

ix

TRANSPORT TO SUMMER

xi

THE AURORAS OF AUTUMN

THE ROCK

HARMONIUM

EARTHY ANECDOTE

Every time the bucks went clattering
Over Oklahoma
A firecat bristled in the way.

Wherever they went,
They went clattering,
Until they swerved
In a swift, circular line
To the right,
Because of the firecat.

Or until they swerved
In a swift, circular line
To the left,
Because of the firecat.

The bucks clattered.
The firecat went leaping,
To the right, to the left,
And
Bristled in the way.

Later, the firecat closed his bright eyes
And slept.

INVECTIVE AGAINST SWANS

The soul, O ganders, flies beyond the parks
And far beyond the discords of the wind.

A bronze rain from the sun descending marks
The death of summer, which that time endures

Like one who scrawls a listless testament
Of golden quirks and Paphian caricatures,

Bequeathing your white feathers to the moon
And giving your bland motions to the air.

Behold, already on the long parades
The crows anoint the statues with their dirt.

And the soul, O ganders, being lonely, flies
Beyond your chilly chariots, to the skies.

IN THE CAROLINAS

The lilacs wither in the Carolinas.
Already the butterflies flutter above the cabins.
Already the new-born children interpret love
In the voices of mothers.

4

Timeless mother,
How is it that your aspic nipples
For once vent honey?

The pine-tree sweetens my body
The white iris beautifies me.

◇◇

THE PALTRY NUDE
STARTS ON A SPRING VOYAGE

But not on a shell, she starts,
Archaic, for the sea.
But on the first-found weed
She scuds the glitters,
Noiselessly, like one more wave.

She too is discontent
And would have purple stuff upon her arms,
Tired of the salty harbors,
Eager for the brine and bellowing
Of the high interiors of the sea.

The wind speeds her,
Blowing upon her hands
And watery back.
She touches the clouds, where she goes
In the circle of her traverse of the sea.

Yet this is meagre play
In the scrurry and water-shine,
As her heels foam—
Not as when the goldener nude
Of a later day

Will go, like the centre of sea-green pomp,
In an intenser calm,
Scullion of fate,
Across the spick torrent, ceaselessly,
Upon her irretrievable way.

✤✧✤✧✤✧✤✧✤✧✤✧✤✧✤✧✤✧✤✧✤✧✤✧✤✧✤✧✤✧✤✧✤✧✤✧✤✧✤

THE PLOT AGAINST THE GIANT

First Girl

When this yokel comes maundering,
Whetting his hacker,
I shall run before him,
Diffusing the civilest odors
Out of geraniums and unsmelled flowers.
It will check him.

Second Girl

I shall run before him,
Arching cloths besprinkled with colors

6

As small as fish-eggs.
The threads
Will abash him.

Third Girl

Oh, la . . . le pauvre!
I shall run before him,
With a curious puffing.
He will bend his ear then.
I shall whisper
Heavenly labials in a world of gutturals.
It will undo him.

❂❂❂❂❂❂❂❂❂❂❂❂❂❂❂❂❂❂❂❂❂❂❂❂❂❂❂

INFANTA MARINA

Her terrace was the sand
And the palms and the twilight.

She made of the motions of her wrist
The grandiose gestures
Of her thought.

The rumpling of the plumes
Of this creature of the evening
Came to be sleights of sails
Over the sea.

7

And thus she roamed
In the roamings of her fan,
Partaking of the sea,
And of the evening,
As they flowed around
And uttered their subsiding sound.

◇◇◇

DOMINATION OF BLACK

At night, by the fire,
The colors of the bushes
And of the fallen leaves,
Repeating themselves,
Turned in the room,
Like the leaves themselves
Turning in the wind.
Yes: but the color of the heavy hemlocks
Came striding.
And I remembered the cry of the peacocks.

The colors of their tails
Were like the leaves themselves
Turning in the wind,
In the twilight wind.
They swept over the room,
Just as they flew from the boughs of the
    hemlocks

8

Down to the ground.
I heard them cry—the peacocks.
Was it a cry against the twilight
Or against the leaves themselves
Turning in the wind,
Turning as the flames
Turned in the fire,
Turning as the tails of the peacocks
Turned in the loud fire,
Loud as the hemlocks
Full of the cry of the peacocks?
Or was it a cry against the hemlocks?

Out of the window,
I saw how the planets gathered
Like the leaves themselves
Turning in the wind.
I saw how the night came,
Came striding like the color of the heavy
    hemlocks
I felt afraid.
And I remembered the cry of the peacocks.

◈◇

THE SNOW MAN

One must have a mind of winter
To regard the frost and the boughs
Of the pine-trees crusted with snow;

And have been cold a long time
To behold the junipers shagged with ice,
The spruces rough in the distant glitter

Of the January sun; and not to think
Of any misery in the sound of the wind,
In the sound of a few leaves,

Which is the sound of the land
Full of the same wind
That is blowing in the same bare place

For the listener, who listens in the snow,
And, nothing himself, beholds
Nothing that is not there and the nothing that is.

ᛤᛤᛤᛤᛤᛤᛤᛤᛤᛤᛤᛤᛤᛤᛤᛤᛤᛤᛤᛤᛤᛤᛤ

THE ORDINARY WOMEN

Then from their poverty they rose,
From dry catarrhs, and to guitars
They flitted
Through the palace walls.

They flung monotony behind,
Turned from their want, and, nonchalant,
They crowded
The nocturnal halls.

10

The lacquered loges huddled there
Mumbled zay-zay and a-zay, a-zay.
The moonlight
Fubbed the girandoles.

And the cold dresses that they wore,
In the vapid haze of the window-bays,
Were tranquil
As they leaned and looked

From the window-sills at the alphabets,
At beta b and gamma g,
To study
The canting curlicues

Of heaven and of the heavenly script.
And there they read of marriage-bed.
Ti-lill-o!
And they read right long.

The gaunt guitarists on the strings
Rumbled a-day and a-day, a-day.
The moonlight
Rose on the beachy floors.

How explicit the coiffures became,
The diamond point, the sapphire point,
The sequins
Of the civil fans!

Insinuations of desire,
Puissant speech, alike in each,

Cried quittance
To the wickless halls.

Then from their poverty they rose,
From dry guitars, and to catarrhs
They flitted
Through the palace walls.

◆◇◆

THE LOAD OF SUGAR–CANE

The going of the glade-boat
Is like water flowing;

Like water flowing
Through the green saw-grass,
Under the rainbows;

Under the rainbows
That are like birds,
Turning, bedizened,

While the wind still whistles
As kildeer do,

When they rise
At the red turban
Of the boatman.

LE MONOCLE DE MON ONCLE

"Mother of heaven, regina of the clouds,
O sceptre of the sun, crown of the moon,
There is not nothing, no, no, never nothing,
Like the clashed edges of two words that kill."
And so I mocked her in magnificent measure.
Or was it that I mocked myself alone?
I wish that I might be a thinking stone.
The sea of spuming thought foists up again
The radiant bubble that she was. And then
A deep up-pouring from some saltier well
Within me, bursts its watery syllable.

II

A red bird flies across the golden floor.
It is a red bird that seeks out his choir
Among the choirs of wind and wet and wing.
A torrent will fall from him when he finds.
Shall I uncrumple this much-crumpled thing?
I am a man of fortune greeting heirs;
For it has come that thus I greet the spring.
These choirs of welcome choir for me farewell.
No spring can follow past meridian.
Yet you persist with anecdotal bliss
To make believe a starry *connaissance*.

13

III

Is it for nothing, then, that old Chinese
Sat tittivating by their mountain pools
Or in the Yangtse studied out their beards?
I shall not play the flat historic scale.
You know how Utamaro's beauties sought
The end of love in their all-speaking braids.
You know the mountainous coiffures of Bath.
Alas! Have all the barbers lived in vain
That not one curl in nature has survived?
Why, without pity on these studious ghosts,
Do you come dripping in your hair from sleep?

IV

This luscious and impeccable fruit of life
Falls, it appears, of its own weight to earth.
When you were Eve, its acrid juice was sweet,
Untasted, in its heavenly, orchard air.
An apple serves as well as any skull
To be the book in which to read a round,
And is as excellent, in that it is composed
Of what, like skulls, comes rotting back to ground.
But it excels in this, that as the fruit
Of love, it is a book too mad to read
Before one merely reads to pass the time.

V

In the high west there burns a furious star.
It is for fiery boys that star was set
And for sweet-smelling virgins close to them.
The measure of the intensity of love
Is measure, also, of the verve of earth.

14

For me, the firefly's quick, electric stroke
Ticks tediously the time of one more year.
And you? Remember how the crickets came
Out of their mother grass, like little kin,
In the pale nights, when your first imagery
Found inklings of your bond to all that dust.

VI

If men at forty will be painting lakes
The ephemeral blues must merge for them in one,
The basic slate, the universal hue.
There is a substance in us that prevails.
But in our amours amorists discern
Such fluctuations that their scrivening
Is breathless to attend each quirky turn.
When amorists grow bald, then amours shrink
Into the compass and curriculum
Of introspective exiles, lecturing.
It is a theme for Hyacinth alone.

VII

The mules that angels ride come slowly down
The blazing passes, from beyond the sun.
Descensions of their tinkling bells arrive.
These muleteers are dainty of their way.
Meantime, centurions guffaw and beat
Their shrilling tankards on the table-boards.
This parable, in sense, amounts to this:
The honey of heaven may or may not come,
But that of earth both comes and goes at once.
Suppose these couriers brought amid their train
A damsel heightened by eternal bloom.

15

VIII

Like a dull scholar, I behold, in love,
An ancient aspect touching a new mind.
It comes, it blooms, it bears its fruit and dies.
This trivial trope reveals a way of truth.
Our bloom is gone. We are the fruit thereof.
Two golden gourds distended on our vines,
Into the autumn weather, splashed with frost,
Distorted by hale fatness, turned grotesque.
We hang like warty squashes, streaked and rayed,
The laughing sky will see the two of us
Washed into rinds by rotting winter rains.

IX

In verses wild with motion, full of din,
Loudened by cries, by clashes, quick and sure
As the deadly thought of men accomplishing
Their curious fates in war, come, celebrate
The faith of forty, ward of Cupido.
Most venerable heart, the lustiest conceit
Is not too lusty for your broadening.
I quiz all sounds, all thoughts, all everything
For the music and manner of the paladins
To make oblation fit. Where shall I find
Bravura adequate to this great hymn?

X

The fops of fancy in their poems leave
Memorabilia of the mystic spouts,
Spontaneously watering their gritty soils.
I am a yeoman, as such fellows go.
I know no magic trees, no balmy boughs,

16

No silver-ruddy, gold-vermilion fruits.
But, after all, I know a tree that bears
A semblance to the thing I have in mind.
It stands gigantic, with a certain tip
To which all birds come sometime in their time.
But when they go that tip still tips the tree.

XI

If sex were all, then every trembling hand
Could make us squeak, like dolls, the wished-for
    words.
But note the unconscionable treachery of fate,
That makes us weep, laugh, grunt and groan, and
    shout
Doleful heroics, pinching gestures forth
From madness or delight, without regard
To that first, foremost law. Anguishing hour!
Last night, we sat beside a pool of pink,
Clippered with lilies scudding the bright chromes,
Keen to the point of starlight, while a frog
Boomed from his very belly odious chords.

XII

A blue pigeon it is, that circles the blue sky,
On sidelong wing, around and round and round.
A white pigeon it is, that flutters to the ground,
Grown tired of flight. Like a dark rabbi, I
Observed, when young, the nature of mankind,
In lordly study. Every day, I found
Man proved a gobbet in my mincing world.
Like a rose rabbi, later, I pursued,

17

And still pursue, the origin and course
Of love, but until now I never knew
That fluttering things have so distinct a shade.

❖❖❖❖❖❖❖❖❖❖❖❖❖❖❖❖❖❖❖❖❖❖❖❖❖❖❖❖❖❖❖❖

NUANCES OF A THEME BY WILLIAMS

It's a strange courage
you give me, ancient star:

Shine alone in the sunrise
toward which you lend no part!

I

Shine alone, shine nakedly, shine like bronze,
that reflects neither my face nor any inner part
of my being, shine like fire, that mirrors nothing.

II

Lend no part to any humanity that suffuses
you in its own light.
Be not chimera of morning,
Half-man, half-star.
Be not an intelligence,
Like a widow's bird
Or an old horse.

18

METAPHORS OF A MAGNIFICO

Twenty men crossing a bridge,
Into a village,
Are twenty men crossing twenty bridges,
Into twenty villages,
Or one man
Crossing a single bridge into a village.

This is old song
That will not declare itself . . .

Twenty men crossing a bridge,
Into a village,
Are
Twenty men crossing a bridge
Into a village.

That will not declare itself
Yet is certain as meaning . . .

The boots of the men clump
On the boards of the bridge.
The first white wall of the village
Rises through fruit-trees.
Of what was it I was thinking?
So the meaning escapes.

The first white wall of the village . . .
The fruit-trees. . . .

19

PLOUGHING ON SUNDAY

The white cock's tail
Tosses in the wind.
The turkey-cock's tail
Glitters in the sun.

Water in the fields.
The wind pours down.
The feathers flare
And bluster in the wind.

Remus, blow your horn!
I'm ploughing on Sunday,
Ploughing North America.
Blow your horn!

Tum-ti-tum,
Ti-tum-tum-tum!
The turkey-cock's tail
Spreads to the sun.

The white cock's tail
Streams to the moon.
Water in the fields.
The wind pours down.

CY EST POURTRAICTE, MADAME STE URSULE, ET LES UNZE MILLE VIERGES

Ursula, in a garden, found
A bed of radishes.
She kneeled upon the ground
And gathered them,
With flowers around,
Blue, gold, pink, and green.

She dressed in red and gold brocade
And in the grass an offering made
Of radishes and flowers.

She said, "My dear,
Upon your altars,
I have placed
The marguerite and coquelicot,
And roses
Frail as April snow;
But here," she said,
"Where none can see,
I make an offering, in the grass,
Of radishes and flowers."
And then she wept
For fear the Lord would not accept.
The good Lord in His garden sought
New leaf and shadowy tinct,

And they were all His thought.
He heard her low accord,
Half prayer and half ditty,
And He felt a subtle quiver,
That was not heavenly love,
Or pity.

This is not writ
In any book.

<><><><><><><><><><><><><><><><><><><><><><><><><><><><><><><><><>

HIBISCUS ON THE SLEEPING SHORES

I say now, Fernando, that on that day
The mind roamed as a moth roams,
Among the blooms beyond the open sand;

And that whatever noise the motion of the waves
Made on the sea-weeds and the covered stones
Disturbed not even the most idle ear.

Then it was that that monstered moth
Which had lain folded against the blue
And the colored purple of the lazy sea,

And which had drowsed along the bony shores,
Shut to the blather that the water made,
Rose up besprent and sought the flaming red

Dabbled with yellow pollen—red as red
As the flag above the old café—
And roamed there all the stupid afternoon.

❀◈

FABLIAU OF FLORIDA

Barque of phosphor
On the palmy beach,

Move outward into heaven,
Into the alabasters
And night blues.

Foam and cloud are one.
Sultry moon-monsters
Are dissolving.

Fill your black hull
With white moonlight.

There will never be an end
To this droning of the surf.

THE DOCTOR OF GENEVA

The doctor of Geneva stamped the sand
That lay impounding the Pacific swell,
Patted his stove-pipe hat and tugged his shawl.

Lacustrine man had never been assailed
By such long-rolling opulent cataracts,
Unless Racine or Bossuet held the like.

He did not quail. A man so used to plumb
The multifarious heavens felt no awe
Before these visible, voluble delugings,

Which yet found means to set his simmering mind
Spinning and hissing with oracular
Notations of the wild, the ruinous waste,

Until the steeples of his city clanked and sprang
In an unburgherly apocalypse.
The doctor used his handkerchief and sighed.

ANOTHER WEEPING WOMAN

Pour the unhappiness out
From your too bitter heart,
Which grieving will not sweeten.

Poison grows in this dark.
It is in the water of tears
Its black blooms rise.

The magnificent cause of being,
The imagination, the one reality
In this imagined world

Leaves you
With him for whom no phantasy moves,
And you are pierced by a death.

HOMUNCULUS ET LA BELLE ÉTOILE

In the sea, Biscayne, there prinks
The young emerald, evening star,
Good light for drunkards, poets, widows,
And ladies soon to be married.

By this light the salty fishes
Arch in the sea like tree-branches,
Going in many directions
Up and down.

This light conducts
The thoughts of drunkards, the feelings
Of widows and trembling ladies,
The movements of fishes.

How pleasant an existence it is
That this emerald charms philosophers,
Until they become thoughtlessly willing
To bathe their hearts in later moonlight,

Knowing that they can bring back thought
In the night that is still to be silent,
Reflecting this thing and that,
Before they sleep!

It is better that, as scholars,
They should think hard in the dark cuffs
Of voluminous cloaks,
And shave their heads and bodies.

It might well be that their mistress
Is no gaunt fugitive phantom.
She might, after all, be a wanton,
Abundantly beautiful, eager,

Fecund,
From whose being by starlight, on sea-coast,

The innermost good of their seeking
Might come in the simplest of speech.

It is a good light, then, for those
That know the ultimate Plato,
Tranquillizing with this jewel
The torments of confusion.

◊⊁

THE COMEDIAN AS THE LETTER C

I

The World without Imagination

Nota: man is the intelligence of his soil,
The sovereign ghost. As such, the Socrates
Of snails, musician of pears, principium
And lex. Sed quæritur: is this same wig
Of things, this nincompated pedagogue,
Preceptor to the sea? Crispin at sea
Created, in his day, a touch of doubt.
An eye most apt in gelatines and jupes,
Berries of villages, a barber's eye,
An eye of land, of simple salad-beds,
Of honest quilts, the eye of Crispin, hung
On porpoises, instead of apricots,
And on silentious porpoises, whose snouts
Dibbled in waves that were mustachios,
Inscrutable hair in an inscrutable world.

27

One eats one paté, even of salt, quotha.
It was not so much the lost terrestrial,
The snug hibernal from that sea and salt,
That century of wind in a single puff.
What counted was mythology of self,
Blotched out beyond unblotching. Crispin,
The lutanist of fleas, the knave, the thane,
The ribboned stick, the bellowing breeches, cloak
Of China, cap of Spain, imperative haw
Of hum, inquisitorial botanist,
And general lexicographer of mute
And maidenly greenhorns, now beheld himself,
A skinny sailor peering in the sea-glass.
What word split up in clickering syllables
And storming under multitudinous tones
Was name for this short-shanks in all that brunt?
Crispin was washed away by magnitude.
The whole of life that still remained in him
Dwindled to one sound strumming in his ear,
Ubiquitous concussion, slap and sigh,
Polyphony beyond his baton's thrust.

Could Crispin stem verboseness in the sea,
The old age of a watery realist,
Triton, dissolved in shifting diaphanes
Of blue and green? A wordy, watery age
That whispered to the sun's compassion, made
A convocation, nightly, of the sea-stars,
And on the clopping foot-ways of the moon
Lay grovelling. Triton incomplicate with that
Which made him Triton, nothing left of him,

28

Except in faint, memorial gesturings,
That were like arms and shoulders in the waves,
Here, something in the rise and fall of wind
That seemed hallucinating horn, and here,
A sunken voice, both of remembering
And of forgetfulness, in alternate strain.

Just so an ancient Crispin was dissolved.
The valet in the tempest was annulled.
Bordeaux to Yucatan, Havana next,
And then to Carolina. Simple jaunt.
Crispin, merest minuscule in the gales,
Dejected his manner to the turbulence.
The salt hung on his spirit like a frost,
The dead brine melted in him like a dew
Of winter, until nothing of himself
Remained, except some starker, barer self
In a starker, barer world, in which the sun
Was not the sun because it never shone
With bland complaisance on pale parasols,
Beetled, in chapels, on the chaste bouquets.
Against his pipping sounds a trumpet cried
Celestial sneering boisterously. Crispin
Became an introspective voyager.

Here was the veritable ding an sich, at last,
Crispin confronting it, a vocable thing,
But with a speech belched out of hoary darks
Noway resembling his, a visible thing,
And excepting negligible Triton, free
From the unavoidable shadow of himself

29

That lay elsewhere around him. Severance
Was clear. The last distortion of romance
Forsook the insatiable egotist. The sea
Severs not only lands but also selves.
Here was no help before reality.
Crispin beheld and Crispin was made new.
The imagination, here, could not evade,
In poems of plums, the strict austerity
Of one vast, subjugating, final tone.
The drenching of stale lives no more fell down.
What was this gaudy, gusty panoply?
Out of what swift destruction did it spring?
It was caparison of wind and cloud
And something given to make whole among
The ruses that were shattered by the large.

II

Concerning the Thunderstorms of Yucatan

In Yucatan, the Maya sonneteers
Of the Caribbean amphitheatre,
In spite of hawk and falcon, green toucan
And jay, still to the night-bird made their plea,
As if raspberry tanagers in palms,
High up in orange air, were barbarous.
But Crispin was too destitute to find
In any commonplace the sought-for aid.
He was a man made vivid by the sea,
A man come out of luminous traversing,
Much trumpeted, made desperately clear,
Fresh from discoveries of tidal skies,
To whom oracular rockings gave no rest.
Into a savage color he went on.

30

How greatly had he grown in his demesne,
This auditor of insects! He that saw
The stride of vanishing autumn in a park
By way of decorous melancholy; he
That wrote his couplet yearly to the spring,
As dissertation of profound delight,
Stopping, on voyage, in a land of snakes,
Found his vicissitudes had much enlarged
His apprehension, made him intricate
In moody rucks, and difficult and strange
In all desires, his destitution's mark.
He was in this as other freemen are,
Sonorous nutshells rattling inwardly.
His violence was for aggrandizement
And not for stupor, such as music makes
For sleepers halfway waking. He perceived
That coolness for his heat came suddenly,
And only, in the fables that he scrawled
With his own quill, in its indigenous dew,
Of an æsthetic tough, diverse, untamed,
Incredible to prudes, the mint of dirt,
Green barbarism turning paradigm.
Crispin foresaw a curious promenade
Or, nobler, sensed an elemental fate,
And elemental potencies and pangs,
And beautiful barenesses as yet unseen,
Making the most of savagery of palms,
Of moonlight on the thick, cadaverous bloom
That yuccas breed, and of the panther's tread.
The fabulous and its intrinsic verse
Came like two spirits parleying, adorned
In radiance from the Atlantic coign,
For Crispin and his quill to catechize.

But they came parleying of such an earth,
So thick with sides and jagged lops of green,
So intertwined with serpent-kin encoiled
Among the purple tufts, the scarlet crowns,
Scenting the jungle in their refuges,
So streaked with yellow, blue and green and red
In beak and bud and fruity gobbet-skins,
That earth was like a jostling festival
Of seeds grown fat, too juicily opulent,
Expanding in the gold's maternal warmth.
So much for that. The affectionate emigrant found
A new reality in parrot-squawks.
Yet let that trifle pass. Now, as this odd
Discoverer walked through the harbor streets
Inspecting the cabildo, the façade
Of the cathedral, making notes, he heard
A rumbling, west of Mexico, it seemed,
Approaching like a gasconade of drums.
The white cabildo darkened, the façade,
As sullen as the sky, was swallowed up
In swift, successive shadows, dolefully.
The rumbling broadened as it fell. The wind,
Tempestuous clarion, with heavy cry,
Came bluntly thundering, more terrible
Than the revenge of music on bassoons.
Gesticulating lightning, mystical,
Made pallid flitter. Crispin, here, took flight.
An annotator has his scruples, too.
He knelt in the cathedral with the rest,
This connoisseur of elemental fate,
Aware of exquisite thought. The storm was one
Of many proclamations of the kind,

32

Proclaiming something harsher than he learned
From hearing signboards whimper in cold nights
Or seeing the midsummer artifice
Of heat upon his pane. This was the span
Of force, the quintessential fact, the note
Of Vulcan, that a valet seeks to own,
The thing that makes him envious in phrase.

And while the torrent on the roof still droned
He felt the Andean breath. His mind was free
And more than free, elate, intent, profound
And studious of a self possessing him,
That was not in him in the crusty town
From which he sailed. Beyond him, westward, lay
The mountainous ridges, purple balustrades,
In which the thunder, lapsing in its clap,
Let down gigantic quavers of its voice,
For Crispin to vociferate again.

III

Approaching Carolina

The book of moonlight is not written yet
Nor half begun, but, when it is, leave room
For Crispin, fagot in the lunar fire,
Who, in the hubbub of his pilgrimage
Through sweating changes, never could forget
That wakefulness or meditating sleep,
In which the sulky strophes willingly
Bore up, in time, the somnolent, deep songs.
Leave room, therefore, in that unwritten book
For the legendary moonlight that once burned

33

In Crispin's mind above a continent.
America was always north to him,
A northern west or western north, but north,
And thereby polar, polar-purple, chilled
And lank, rising and slumping from a sea
Of hardy foam, receding flatly, spread
In endless ledges, glittering, submerged
And cold in a boreal mistiness of the moon.
The spring came there in clinking pannicles
Of half-dissolving frost, the summer came,
If ever, whisked and wet, not ripening,
Before the winter's vacancy returned.
The myrtle, if the myrtle ever bloomed,
Was like a glacial pink upon the air.
The green palmettoes in crepuscular ice
Clipped frigidly blue-black meridians,
Morose chiaroscuro, gauntly drawn.

How many poems he denied himself
In his observant progress, lesser things
Than the relentless contact he desired;
How many sea-masks he ignored; what sounds
He shut out from his tempering ear; what thoughts,
Like jades affecting the sequestered bride;
And what descants, he sent to banishment!
Perhaps the Arctic moonlight really gave
The liaison, the blissful liaison,
Between himself and his environment,
Which was, and if, chief motive, first delight,
For him, and not for him alone. It seemed
Illusive, faint, more mist than moon, perverse,
Wrong as a divagation to Peking,

To him that postulated as his theme
The vulgar, as his theme and hymn and flight,
A passionately niggling nightingale.
Moonlight was an evasion, or, if not,
A minor meeting, facile, delicate.

Thus he conceived his voyaging to be
An up and down between two elements,
A fluctuating between sun and moon,
A sally into gold and crimson forms,
As on this voyage, out of goblinry,
And then retirement like a turning back
And sinking down to the indulgences
That in the moonlight have their habitude.
But let these backward lapses, if they would,
Grind their seductions on him, Crispin knew
It was a flourishing tropic he required
For his refreshment, an abundant zone,
Prickly and obdurate, dense, harmonious,
Yet with a harmony not rarefied
Nor fined for the inhibited instruments
Of over-civil stops. And thus he tossed
Between a Carolina of old time,
A little juvenile, an ancient whim,
And the visible, circumspect presentment drawn
From what he saw across his vessel's prow.

He came. The poetic hero without palms
Or jugglery, without regalia.
And as he came he saw that it was spring,
A time abhorrent to the nihilist
Or searcher for the fecund minimum.

35

The moonlight fiction disappeared. The spring,
Although contending featly in its veils,
Irised in dew and early fragrancies,
Was gemmy marionette to him that sought
A sinewy nakedness. A river bore
The vessel inward. Tilting up his nose,
He inhaled the rancid rosin, burly smells
Of dampened lumber, emanations blown
From warehouse doors, the gustiness of ropes,
Decays of sacks, and all the arrant stinks
That helped him round his rude æsthetic out.
He savored rankness like a sensualist.
He marked the marshy ground around the dock,
The crawling railroad spur, the rotten fence,
Curriculum for the marvelous sophomore.
It purified. It made him see how much
Of what he saw he never saw at all.
He gripped more closely the essential prose
As being, in a world so falsified,
The one integrity for him, the one
Discovery still possible to make,
To which all poems were incident, unless
That prose should wear a poem's guise at last.

IV

The Idea of a Colony

Nota: his soil is man's intelligence.
That's better. That's worth crossing seas to find.
Crispin in one laconic phrase laid bare
His cloudy drift and planned a colony.
Exit the mental moonlight, exit lex,

36

Rex and principium, exit the whole
Shebang. Exeunt omnes. Here was prose
More exquisite than any tumbling verse:
A still new continent in which to dwell.
What was the purpose of his pilgrimage,
Whatever shape it took in Crispin's mind,
If not, when all is said, to drive away
The shadow of his fellows from the skies,
And, from their stale intelligence released,
To make a new intelligence prevail?
Hence the reverberations in the words
Of his first central hymns, the celebrants
Of rankest trivia, tests of the strength
Of his æsthetic, his philosophy,
The more invidious, the more desired:
The florist asking aid from cabbages,
The rich man going bare, the paladin
Afraid, the blind man as astronomer,
The appointed power unwielded from disdain.
His western voyage ended and began.
The torment of fastidious thought grew slack,
Another, still more bellicose, came on.
He, therefore, wrote his prolegomena,
And, being full of the caprice, inscribed
Commingled souvenirs and prophecies.
He made a singular collation. Thus:
The natives of the rain are rainy men.
Although they paint effulgent, azure lakes,
And April hillsides wooded white and pink,
Their azure has a cloudy edge, their white
And pink, the water bright that dogwood bears.
And in their music showering sounds intone.

37

On what strange froth does the gross Indian dote,
What Eden sapling gum, what honeyed gore,
What pulpy dram distilled of innocence,
That streaking gold should speak in him
Or bask within his images and words?
If these rude instances impeach themselves
By force of rudeness, let the principle
Be plain. For application Crispin strove,
Abhorring Turk as Esquimau, the lute
As the marimba, the magnolia as rose.

Upon these premises propounding, he
Projected a colony that should extend
To the dusk of a whistling south below the south,
A comprehensive island hemisphere.
The man in Georgia waking among pines
Should be pine-spokesman. The responsive man,
Planting his pristine cores in Florida,
Should prick thereof, not on the psaltery,
But on the banjo's categorical gut,
Tuck, tuck, while the flamingoes flapped his bays.
Sepulchral señors, bibbling pale mescal,
Oblivious to the Aztec almanacs,
Should make the intricate Sierra scan.
And dark Brazilians in their cafés,
Musing immaculate, pampean dits,
Should scrawl a vigilant anthology,
To be their latest, lucent paramour.
These are the broadest instances. Crispin,
Progenitor of such extensive scope,
Was not indifferent to smart detail.

38

The melon should have apposite ritual,
Performed in verd apparel, and the peach,
When its black branches came to bud, belle day,
Should have an incantation. And again,
When piled on salvers its aroma steeped
The summer, it should have a sacrament
And celebration. Shrewd novitiates
Should be the clerks of our experience.
These bland excursions into time to come,
Related in romance to backward flights,
However prodigal, however proud,
Contained in their afflatus the reproach
That first drove Crispin to his wandering.
He could not be content with counterfeit,
With masquerade of thought, with hapless words
That must belie the racking masquerade,
With fictive flourishes that preordained
His passion's permit, hang of coat, degree
Of buttons, measure of his salt. Such trash
Might help the blind, not him, serenely sly.
It irked beyond his patience. Hence it was,
Preferring text to gloss, he humbly served
Grotesque apprenticeship to chance event,
A clown, perhaps, but an aspiring clown.
There is a monotonous babbling in our dreams
That makes them our dependent heirs, the heirs
Of dreamers buried in our sleep, and not
The oncoming fantasies of better birth.
The apprentice knew these dreamers. If he dreamed
Their dreams, he did it in a gingerly way.
All dreams are vexing. Let them be expunged.
But let the rabbit run, the cock declaim.

39

Trinket pasticcio, flaunting skyey sheets,
With Crispin as the tiptoe cozener?
No, no: veracious page on page, exact.

A Nice Shady Home

Crispin as hermit, pure and capable,
Dwelt in the land. Perhaps if discontent
Had kept him still the prickling realist,
Choosing his element from droll confect
Of was and is and shall or ought to be,
Beyond Bordeaux, beyond Havana, far
Beyond carked Yucatan, he might have come
To colonize his polar planterdom
And jig his chits upon a cloudy knee.
But his emprize to that idea soon sped.
Crispin dwelt in the land and dwelling there
Slid from his continent by slow recess
To things within his actual eye, alert
To the difficulty of rebellious thought
When the sky is blue. The blue infected will.
It may be that the yarrow in his fields
Sealed pensive purple under its concern.
But day by day, now this thing and now that
Confined him, while it cosseted, condoned,
Little by little, as if the suzerain soil
Abashed him by carouse to humble yet
Attach. It seemed haphazard denouement.
He first, as realist, admitted that
Whoever hunts a matinal continent
May, after all, stop short before a plum
And be content and still be realist.

The words of things entangle and confuse.
The plum survives its poems. It may hang
In the sunshine placidly, colored by ground
Obliquities of those who pass beneath,
Harlequined and mazily dewed and mauved
In bloom. Yet it survives in its own form,
Beyond these changes, good, fat, guzzly fruit.
So Crispin hasped on the surviving form,
For him, of shall or ought to be in is.

Was he to bray this in profoundest brass
Arointing his dreams with fugal requiems?
Was he to company vastest things defunct
With a blubber of tom-toms harrowing the sky?
Scrawl a tragedian's testament? Prolong
His active force in an inactive dirge,
Which, let the tall musicians call and call,
Should merely call him dead? Pronounce amen
Through choirs infolded to the outmost clouds?
Because he built a cabin who once planned
Loquacious columns by the ructive sea?
Because he turned to salad-beds again?
Jovial Crispin, in calamitous crape?
Should he lay by the personal and make
Of his own fate an instance of all fate?
What is one man among so many men?
What are so many men in such a world?
Can one man think one thing and think it long?
Can one man be one thing and be it long?
The very man despising honest quilts
Lies quilted to his poll in his despite.
For realist, what is is what should be.

41

And so it came, his cabin shuffled up,
His trees were planted, his duenna brought
Her prismy blonde and clapped her in his hands,
The curtains flittered and the door was closed.
Crispin, magister of a single room,
Latched up the night. So deep a sound fell down
It was as if the solitude concealed
And covered him and his congenial sleep.
So deep a sound fell down it grew to be
A long soothsaying silence down and down.
The crickets beat their tambours in the wind,
Marching a motionless march, custodians.

In the presto of the morning, Crispin trod,
Each day, still curious, but in a round
Less prickly and much more condign than that
He once thought necessary. Like Candide,
Yeoman and grub, but with a fig in sight,
And cream for the fig and silver for the cream,
A blonde to tip the silver and to taste
The rapey gouts. Good star, how that to be
Annealed them in their cabin ribaldries!
Yet the quotidian saps philosophers
And men like Crispin like them in intent,
If not in will, to track the knaves of thought.
But the quotidian composed as his,
Of breakfast ribands, fruits laid in their leaves,
The tomtit and the cassia and the rose,
Although the rose was not the noble thorn
Of crinoline spread, but of a pining sweet,
Composed of evenings like cracked shutters flung
Upon the rumpling bottomness, and nights

In which those frail custodians watched,
Indifferent to the tepid summer cold,
While he poured out upon the lips of her
That lay beside him, the quotidian
Like this, saps like the sun, true fortuner.
For all it takes it gives a humped return
Exchequering from piebald fiscs unkeyed.

VI

And Daughters with Curls

Portentous enunciation, syllable
To blessed syllable affined, and sound
Bubbling felicity in cantilene,
Prolific and tormenting tenderness
Of music, as it comes to unison,
Forgather and bell boldly Crispin's last
Deduction. Thrum with a proud douceur
His grand pronunciamento and devise.
The chits came for his jigging, bluet-eyed,
Hands without touch yet touching poignantly,
Leaving no room upon his cloudy knee,
Prophetic joint, for its diviner young.
The return to social nature, once begun,
Anabasis or slump, ascent or chute,
Involved him in midwifery so dense
His cabin counted as phylactery,
Then place of vexing palankeens, then haunt
Of children nibbling at the sugared void,
Infants yet eminently old, then dome
And halidom for the unbraided femes,
Green crammers of the green fruits of the world,

43

Bidders and biders for its ecstasies,
True daughters both of Crispin and his clay.
All this with many mulctings of the man,
Effective colonizer sharply stopped
In the door-yard by his own capacious bloom.
But that this bloom grown riper, showing nibs
Of its eventual roundness, puerile tints
Of spiced and weathery rouges, should complex
The stopper to indulgent fatalist
Was unforeseen. First Crispin smiled upon
His goldenest demoiselle, inhabitant,
She seemed, of a country of the capuchins,
So delicately blushed, so humbly eyed,
Attentive to a coronal of things
Secret and singular. Second, upon
A second similar counterpart, a maid
Most sisterly to the first, not yet awake
Excepting to the motherly footstep, but
Marvelling sometimes at the shaken sleep.
Then third, a thing still flaxen in the light,
A creeper under jaunty leaves. And fourth,
Mere blusteriness that gewgaws jollified,
All din and gobble, blasphemously pink.
A few years more and the vermeil capuchin
Gave to the cabin, lordlier than it was,
The dulcet omen fit for such a house.
The second sister dallying was shy
To fetch the one full-pinioned one himself
Out of her botches, hot embosomer.
The third one gaping at the orioles
Lettered herself demurely as became
A pearly poetess, peaked for rhapsody.

44

The fourth, pent now, a digit curious.
Four daughters in a world too intricate
In the beginning, four blithe instruments
Of differing struts, four voices several
In couch, four more personæ, intimate
As buffo, yet divers, four mirrors blue
That should be silver, four accustomed seeds
Hinting incredible hues, four selfsame lights
That spread chromatics in hilarious dark,
Four questioners and four sure answerers.

Crispin concocted doctrine from the rout.
The world, a turnip once so readily plucked,
Sacked up and carried overseas, daubed out
Of its ancient purple, pruned to the fertile main,
And sown again by the stiffest realist,
Came reproduced in purple, family font,
The same insoluble lump. The fatalist
Stepped in and dropped the chuckling down his craw,
Without grace or grumble. Score this anecdote
Invented for its pith, not doctrinal
In form though in design, as Crispin willed,
Disguised pronunciamento, summary,
Autumn's compendium, strident in itself
But muted, mused, and perfectly revolved
In those portentous accents, syllables,
And sounds of music coming to accord
Upon his lap, like their inherent sphere,
Seraphic proclamations of the pure
Delivered with a deluging onwardness.
Or if the music sticks, if the anecdote
Is false, if Crispin is a profitless

45

Philosopher, beginning with green brag,
Concluding fadedly, if as a man
Prone to distemper he abates in taste,
Fickle and fumbling, variable, obscure,
Glozing his life with after-shining flicks,
Illuminating, from a fancy gorged
By apparition, plain and common things,
Sequestering the fluster from the year,
Making gulped potions from obstreperous drops,
And so distorting, proving what he proves
Is nothing, what can all this matter since
The relation comes, benignly, to its end?

So may the relation of each man be clipped.

❖❖❖

FROM THE MISERY OF DON JOOST

I have finished my combat with the sun;
And my body, the old animal,
Knows nothing more.

The powerful seasons bred and killed,
And were themselves the genii
Of their own ends.

Oh, but the very self of the storm
Of sun and slaves, breeding and death,
The old animal,

46

The senses and feeling, the very sound
And sight, and all there was of the storm,
Knows nothing more.

❖❖❖❖❖❖❖❖❖❖❖❖❖❖❖❖❖❖❖❖❖❖❖❖❖❖❖❖❖❖❖❖❖❖❖

O FLORIDA, VENEREAL SOIL

A few things for themselves,
Convolvulus and coral,
Buzzards and live-moss,
Tiestas from the keys,
A few things for themselves,
Florida, venereal soil,
Disclose to the lover.

The dreadful sundry of this world,
The Cuban, Polodowsky,
The Mexican women,
The negro undertaker
Killing the time between corpses
Fishing for crayfish . . .
Virgin of boorish births,

Swiftly in the nights,
In the porches of Key West,
Behind the bougainvilleas,
After the guitar is asleep,

47

Lasciviously as the wind,
You come tormenting,
Insatiable,

When you might sit,
A scholar of darkness,
Sequestered over the sea,
Wearing a clear tiara
Of red and blue and red,
Sparkling, solitary, still,
In the high sea-shadow.

Donna, donna, dark,
Stooping in indigo gown
And cloudy constellations,
Conceal yourself or disclose
Fewest things to the lover—
A hand that bears a thick-leaved fruit,
A pungent bloom against your shade.

LAST LOOKS AT THE LILACS

To what good, in the alleys of the lilacs,
O caliper, do you scratch your buttocks
And tell the divine ingénue, your companion,
That this bloom is the bloom of soap
And this fragrance the fragrance of vegetal?

Do you suppose that she cares a tick,
In this hymeneal air, what it is
That marries her innocence thus,
So that her nakedness is near,
Or that she will pause at scurrilous words?

Poor buffo! Look at the lavender
And look your last and look still steadily,
And say how it comes that you see
Nothing but trash and that you no longer feel
Her body quivering in the Floréal

Toward the cool night and its fantastic star,
Prime paramour and belted paragon,
Well-booted, rugged, arrogantly male,
Patron and imager of the gold Don John,
Who will embrace her before summer comes.

❖◇❖

THE WORMS AT HEAVEN'S GATE

Out of the tomb, we bring Badroulbadour,
Within our bellies, we her chariot.
Here is an eye. And here are, one by one,
The lashes of that eye and its white lid.
Here is the cheek on which that lid declined,
And, finger after finger, here, the hand,

49

The genius of that cheek. Here are the lips,
The bundle of the body and the feet.

.   .   .   .

Out of the tomb we bring Badroulbadour.

THE JACK–RABBIT

In the morning,
The jack-rabbit sang to the Arkansaw.
He carolled in caracoles
On the feat sandbars.

The black man said,
"Now, grandmother,
Crochet me this buzzard
On your winding-sheet,
And do not forget his wry neck
After the winter."

The black man said,
"Look out, O caroller,
The entrails of the buzzard
Are rattling."

VALLEY CANDLE

My candle burned alone in an immense valley.
Beams of the huge night converged upon it,
Until the wind blew.
Then beams of the huge night
Converged upon its image,
Until the wind blew.

ANECDOTE OF MEN BY THE THOUSAND

The soul, he said, is composed
Of the external world.

There are men of the East, he said,
Who are the East.
There are men of a province
Who are that province.
There are men of a valley
Who are that valley.

There are men whose words
Are as natural sounds
Of their places

51

As the cackle of toucans
In the place of toucans.

The mandoline is the instrument
Of a place.

Are there mandolines of western mountains?
Are there mandolines of northern moonlight?

The dress of a woman of Lhassa,
In its place,
Is an invisible element of that place
Made visible.

❀◇

THE APOSTROPHE TO VINCENTINE

I

I figured you as nude between
Monotonous earth and dark blue sky.
It made you seem so small and lean
And nameless,
Heavenly Vincentine.

II

I saw you then, as warm as flesh,
Brunette,
But yet not too brunette,
As warm, as clean.

Your dress was green,
Was whited green,
Green Vincentine.

III

Then you came walking,
In a group
Of human others,
Voluble.
Yes: you came walking,
Vincentine.
Yes: you came talking.

IV

And what I knew you felt
Came then.
Monotonous earth I saw become
Illimitable spheres of you,
And that white animal, so lean,
Turned Vincentine,
Turned heavenly Vincentine,
And that white animal, so lean,
Turned heavenly, heavenly Vincentine.

FLORAL DECORATIONS FOR BANANAS

Well, nuncle, this plainly won't do.
These insolent, linear peels
And sullen, hurricane shapes

53

Won't do with your eglantine.
They require something serpentine.
Blunt yellow in such a room!

You should have had plums tonight,
In an eighteenth-century dish,
And pettifogging buds,
For the women of primrose and purl,
Each one in her decent curl.
Good God! What a precious light!

But bananas hacked and hunched . . .
The table was set by an ogre,
His eye on an outdoor gloom
And a stiff and noxious place.
Pile the bananas on planks.
The women will be all shanks
And bangles and slatted eyes.

And deck the bananas in leaves
Plucked from the Carib trees,
Fibrous and dangling down,
Oozing cantankerous gum
Out of their purple maws,
Darting out of their purple craws
Their musky and tingling tongues.

ANECDOTE OF CANNA

Huge are the canna in the dreams of
X, the mighty thought, the mighty man.
They fill the terrace of his capitol.

His thought sleeps not. Yet thought that wakes
In sleep may never meet another thought
Or thing. . . . Now day-break comes. . .

X promenades the dewy stones,
Observes the canna with a clinging eye,
Observes and then continues to observe.

ON THE MANNER OF ADDRESSING
CLOUDS

Gloomy grammarians in golden gowns,
Meekly you keep the mortal rendezvous,
Eliciting the still sustaining pomps
Of speech which are like music so profound
They seem an exaltation without sound.
Funest philosophers and ponderers,
Their evocations are the speech of clouds.

55

So speech of your processionals returns
In the casual evocations of your tread
Across the stale, mysterious seasons. These
Are the music of meet resignation; these
The responsive, still sustaining pomps for you
To magnify, if in that drifting waste
You are to be accompanied by more
Than mute bare splendors of the sun and moon.

OF HEAVEN CONSIDERED AS A TOMB

What word have you, interpreters, of men
Who in the tomb of heaven walk by night,
The darkened ghosts of our old comedy?
Do they believe they range the gusty cold,
With lanterns borne aloft to light the way,
Freemen of death, about and still about
To find whatever it is they seek? Or does
That burial, pillared up each day as porte
And spiritous passage into nothingness,
Foretell each night the one abysmal night,
When the host shall no more wander, nor the
        light
Of the steadfast lanterns creep across the dark?
Make hue among the dark comedians,
Halloo them in the topmost distances
For answer from their icy Élysée.

OF THE SURFACE OF THINGS

I

In my room, the world is beyond my understanding;
But when I walk I see that it consists of three or four
    hills and a cloud.

II

From my balcony, I survey the yellow air,
Reading where I have written,
"The spring is like a belle undressing."

III

The gold tree is blue.
The singer has pulled his cloak over his head.
The moon is in the folds of the cloak.

ANECDOTE OF THE PRINCE OF
PEACOCKS

In the moonlight
I met Berserk,
In the moonlight
On the bushy plain.

Oh, sharp he was
As the sleepless!

And, "Why are you red
In this milky blue?"
I said.
"Why sun-colored,
As if awake
In the midst of sleep?"

"You that wander,"
So he said,
"On the bushy plain,
Forget so soon.
But I set my traps
In the midst of dreams."

I knew from this
That the blue ground
Was full of blocks
And blocking steel.
I knew the dread
Of the bushy plain,
And the beauty
Of the moonlight
Falling there,
Falling
As sleep falls
In the innocent air.

A HIGH–TONED OLD CHRISTIAN WOMAN

Poetry is the supreme fiction, madame.
Take the moral law and make a nave of it
And from the nave build haunted heaven. Thus,
The conscience is converted into palms,
Like windy citherns hankering for hymns.
We agree in principle. That's clear. But take
The opposing law and make a peristyle,
And from the peristyle project a masque
Beyond the planets. Thus, our bawdiness,
Unpurged by epitaph, indulged at last,
Is equally converted into palms,
Squiggling like saxophones. And palm for palm,
Madame, we are where we began. Allow,
Therefore, that in the planetary scene
Your disaffected flagellants, well-stuffed,
Smacking their muzzy bellies in parade,
Proud of such novelties of the sublime,
Such tink and tank and tunk-a-tunk-tunk,
May, merely may, madame, whip from themselves
A jovial hullabaloo among the spheres.
This will make widows wince. But fictive things
Wink as they will. Wink most when widows wince.

THE PLACE OF THE SOLITAIRES

Let the place of the solitaires
Be a place of perpetual undulation.

Whether it be in mid-sea
On the dark, green water-wheel,
Or on the beaches,
There must be no cessation
Of motion, or of the noise of motion,
The renewal of noise
And manifold continuation;

And, most, of the motion of thought
And its restless iteration,

In the place of the solitaires,
Which is to be a place of perpetual undulation.

THE WEEPING BURGHER

It is with a strange malice
That I distort the world.

Ah! that ill humors
Should mask as white girls.
And ah! that Scaramouche
Should have a black barouche.

The sorry verities!
Yet in excess, continual,
There is cure of sorrow.

Permit that if as ghost I come
Among the people burning in me still,
I come as belle design
Of foppish line.

And I, then, tortured for old speech,
A white of wildly woven rings;
I, weeping in a calcined heart,
My hands such sharp, imagined things.

THE CURTAINS IN THE HOUSE
OF THE METAPHYSICIAN

It comes about that the drifting of these curtains
Is full of long motions; as the ponderous
Deflations of distance; or as clouds
Inseparable from their afternoons;
Or the changing of light, the dropping
Of the silence, wide sleep and solitude
Of night, in which all motion
Is beyond us, as the firmament,
Up-rising and down-falling, bares
The last largeness, bold to see.

BANAL SOJOURN

Two wooden tubs of blue hydrangeas stand at the foot of the
    stone steps.
The sky is a blue gum streaked with rose. The trees are black.
The grackles crack their throats of bone in the smooth air.
Moisture and heat have swollen the garden into a slum of
    bloom.
Pardie! Summer is like a fat beast, sleepy in mildew,
Our old bane, green and bloated, serene, who cries,

"That bliss of stars, that princox of evening heaven!" remind-
    ing of seasons,
When radiance came running down, slim through the bare-
    ness.
And so it is one damns that green shade at the bottom of the
    land.
For who can care at the wigs despoiling the Satan ear?
And who does not seek the sky unfuzzed, soaring to the prin-
    cox?
One has a malady, here, a malady. One feels a malady.

❦◇

DEPRESSION BEFORE SPRING

The cock crows
But no queen rises.

The hair of my blonde
Is dazzling,
As the spittle of cows
Threading the wind.

Ho! Ho!

But ki-ki-ri-ki
Brings no rou-cou,
No rou-cou-cou.

But no queen comes
In slipper green.

63

THE EMPEROR OF ICE–CREAM

Call the roller of big cigars,
The muscular one, and bid him whip
In kitchen cups concupiscent curds.
Let the wenches dawdle in such dress
As they are used to wear, and let the boys
Bring flowers in last month's newspapers.
Let be be finale of seem.
The only emperor is the emperor of ice-cream.

Take from the dresser of deal.
Lacking the three glass knobs, that sheet
On which she embroidered fantails once
And spread it so as to cover her face.
If her horny feet protrude, they come
To show how cold she is, and dumb.
Let the lamp affix its beam.
The only emperor is the emperor of ice-cream.

THE CUBAN DOCTOR

I went to Egypt to escape
The Indian, but the Indian struck
Out of his cloud and from his sky.

This was no worm bred in the moon,
Wriggling far down the phantom air,
And on a comfortable sofa dreamed.

The Indian struck and disappeared.
I knew my enemy was near—I,
Drowsing in summer's sleepiest horn.

❖◇

TEA AT THE PALAZ OF HOON

Not less because in purple I descended
The western day through what you called
The loneliest air, not less was I myself.

What was the ointment sprinkled on my beard?
What were the hymns that buzzed beside my ears?
What was the sea whose tide swept through me there?

Out of my mind the golden ointment rained,
And my ears made the blowing hymns they heard.
I was myself the compass of that sea:

I was the world in which I walked, and what I saw
Or heard or felt came not but from myself;
And there I found myself more truly and more strange.

DISILLUSIONMENT OF TEN O'CLOCK

The houses are haunted
By white night-gowns.
None are green,
Or purple with green rings,
Or green with yellow rings,
Or yellow with blue rings.
None of them are strange,
With socks of lace
And beaded ceintures.
People are not going
To dream of baboons and periwinkles.
Only, here and there, an old sailor,
Drunk and asleep in his boots,
Catches tigers
In red weather.

SUNDAY MORNING

I

Complacencies of the peignoir, and late
Coffee and oranges in a sunny chair,
And the green freedom of a cockatoo
Upon a rug mingle to dissipate

The holy hush of ancient sacrifice.
She dreams a little, and she feels the dark
Encroachment of that old catastrophe,
As a calm darkens among water-lights.
The pungent oranges and bright, green wings
Seem things in some procession of the dead,
Winding across wide water, without sound.
The day is like wide water, without sound,
Stilled for the passing of her dreaming feet
Over the seas, to silent Palestine,
Dominion of the blood and sepulchre.

II

Why should she give her bounty to the dead?
What is divinity if it can come
Only in silent shadows and in dreams?
Shall she not find in comforts of the sun,
In pungent fruit and bright, green wings, or else
In any balm or beauty of the earth,
Things to be cherished like the thought of heaven?
Divinity must live within herself:
Passions of rain, or moods in falling snow;
Grievings in loneliness, or unsubdued
Elations when the forest blooms; gusty
Emotions on wet roads on autumn nights;
All pleasures and all pains, remembering
The bough of summer and the winter branch.
These are the measures destined for her soul.

III

Jove in the clouds had his inhuman birth.
No mother suckled him, no sweet land gave
Large-mannered motions to his mythy mind
He moved among us, as a muttering king,

Magnificent, would move among his hinds,
Until our blood, commingling, virginal,
With heaven, brought such requital to desire
The very hinds discerned it, in a star.
Shall our blood fail? Or shall it come to be
The blood of paradise? And shall the earth
Seem all of paradise that we shall know?
The sky will be much friendlier then than now,
A part of labor and a part of pain,
And next in glory to enduring love,
Not this dividing and indifferent blue.

IV

She says, "I am content when wakened birds,
Before they fly, test the reality
Of misty fields, by their sweet questionings;
But when the birds are gone, and their warm fields
Return no more, where, then, is paradise?"
There is not any haunt of prophecy,
Nor any old chimera of the grave,
Neither the golden underground, nor isle
Melodious, where spirits gat them home,
Nor visionary south, nor cloudy palm
Remote on heaven's hill, that has endured
As April's green endures; or will endure
Like her remembrance of awakened birds,
Or her desire for June and evening, tipped
By the consummation of the swallow's wings.

V

She says, "But in contentment I still feel
The need of some imperishable bliss."
Death is the mother of beauty; hence from her,

Alone, shall come fulfilment to our dreams
And our desires. Although she strews the leaves
Of sure obliteration on our paths,
The path sick sorrow took, the many paths
Where triumph rang its brassy phrase, or love
Whispered a little out of tenderness,
She makes the willow shiver in the sun
For maidens who were wont to sit and gaze
Upon the grass, relinquished to their feet.
She causes boys to pile new plums and pears
On disregarded plate. The maidens taste
And stray impassioned in the littering leaves.

VI

Is there no change of death in paradise?
Does ripe fruit never fall? Or do the boughs
Hang always heavy in that perfect sky,
Unchanging, yet so like our perishing earth,
With rivers like our own that seek for seas
They never find, the same receding shores
That never touch with inarticulate pang?
Why set the pear upon those river-banks
Or spice the shores with odors of the plum?
Alas, that they should wear our colors there,
The silken weavings of our afternoons,
And pick the strings of our insipid lutes!
Death is the mother of beauty, mystical,
Within whose burning bosom we devise
Our earthly mothers waiting, sleeplessly.

VII

Supple and turbulent, a ring of men
Shall chant in orgy on a summer morn

69

Their boisterous devotion to the sun,
Not as a god, but as a god might be,
Naked among them, like a savage source.
Their chant shall be a chant of paradise,
Out of their blood, returning to the sky;
And in their chant shall enter, voice by voice,
The windy lake wherein their lord delights,
The trees, like serafin, and echoing hills,
That choir among themselves long afterward.
They shall know well the heavenly fellowship
Of men that perish and of summer morn.
And whence they came and whither they shall go
The dew upon their feet shall manifest.

VIII

She hears, upon that water without sound,
A voice that cries, "The tomb in Palestine
Is not the porch of spirits lingering.
It is the grave of Jesus, where he lay."
We live in an old chaos of the sun,
Or old dependency of day and night,
Or island solitude, unsponsored, free,
Of that wide water, inescapable.
Deer walk upon our mountains, and the quail
Whistle about us their spontaneous cries;
Sweet berries ripen in the wilderness;
And, in the isolation of the sky,
At evening, casual flocks of pigeons make
Ambiguous undulations as they sink,
Downward to darkness, on extended wings.

THE VIRGIN CARRYING A LANTERN

There are no bears among the roses,
Only a negress who supposes
Things false and wrong

About the lantern of the beauty
Who walks there, as a farewell duty,
Walks long and long.

The pity that her pious egress
Should fill the vigil of a negress
With heat so strong!

STARS AT TALLAPOOSA

The lines are straight and swift between the stars.
The night is not the cradle that they cry,
The criers, undulating the deep-oceaned phrase.
The lines are much too dark and much too sharp.

The mind herein attains simplicity.
There is no moon, on single, silvered leaf.
The body is no body to be seen
But is an eye that studies its black lid.

71

Let these be your delight, secretive hunter,
Wading the sea-lines, moist and ever-mingling,
Mounting the earth-lines, long and lax, lethargic.
These lines are swift and fall without diverging.

The melon-flower nor dew nor web of either
Is like to these. But in yourself is like:
A sheaf of brilliant arrows flying straight,
Flying and falling straightway for their pleasure,

Their pleasure that is all bright-edged and cold;
Or, if not arrows, then the nimblest motions,
Making recoveries of young nakedness
And the lost vehemence the midnights hold.

EXPLANATION

Ach, Mutter,
This old, black dress,
I have been embroidering
French flowers on it.

Not by way of romance,
Here is nothing of the ideal,
Nein,
Nein.

It would have been different,
Liebchen,

If I had imagined myself,
In an orange gown,
Drifting through space,
Like a figure on the church-wall.

❖❖❖❖❖❖❖❖❖❖❖❖❖❖❖❖❖❖❖❖❖❖❖❖❖❖❖❖❖❖❖❖

SIX SIGNIFICANT LANDSCAPES

I

An old man sits
In the shadow of a pine tree
In China.
He sees larkspur,
Blue and white,
At the edge of the shadow,
Move in the wind.
His beard moves in the wind.
The pine tree moves in the wind.
Thus water flows
Over weeds.

II

The night is of the color
Of a woman's arm:
Night, the female,
Obscure,
Fragrant and supple,
Conceals herself.

73

A pool shines,
Like a bracelet
Shaken in a dance.

III

I measure myself
Against a tall tree.
I find that I am much taller,
For I reach right up to the sun,
With my eye;
And I reach to the shore of the sea
With my ear.
Nevertheless, I dislike
The way the ants crawl
In and out of my shadow.

IV

When my dream was near the moon,
The white folds of its gown
Filled with yellow light.
The soles of its feet
Grew red.
Its hair filled
With certain blue crystallizations
From stars,
Not far off.

V

Not all the knives of the lamp-posts,
Nor the chisels of the long streets,
Nor the mallets of the domes
And high towers,

74

Can carve
What one star can carve,
Shining through the grape-leaves.

VI

Rationalists, wearing square hats,
Think, in square rooms,
Looking at the floor,
Looking at the ceiling.
They confine themselves
To right-angled triangles.
If they tried rhomboids,
Cones, waving lines, ellipses—
As, for example, the ellipse of the half-
    moon—
Rationalists would wear sombreros.

BANTAMS IN PINE–WOODS

Chieftain Iffucan of Azcan in caftan
Of tan with henna hackles, halt!

Damned universal cock, as if the sun
Was blackamoor to bear your blazing tail.

Fat! Fat! Fat! Fat! I am the personal.
Your world is you. I am my world.

75

You ten-foot poet among inchlings. Fat!
Begone! An inchling bristles in these pines,

Bristles, and points their Appalachian tangs,
And fears not portly Azcan nor his hoos.

ANECDOTE OF THE JAR

I placed a jar in Tennessee,
And round it was, upon a hill.
It made the slovenly wilderness
Surround that hill.

The wilderness rose up to it,
And sprawled around, no longer wild.
The jar was round upon the ground
And tall and of a port in air.

It took dominion everywhere.
The jar was gray and bare.
It did not give of bird or bush,
Like nothing else in Tennessee.

PALACE OF THE BABIES

The disbeliever walked the moonlit place,
Outside of gates of hammered serafin,
Observing the moon-blotches on the walls.

The yellow rocked across the still façades,
Or else sat spinning on the pinnacles,
While he imagined humming sounds and sleep.

The walker in the moonlight walked alone,
And each blank window of the building balked
His loneliness and what was in his mind:

If in a shimmering room the babies came,
Drawn close by dreams of fledgling wing,
It was because night nursed them in its fold.

Night nursed not him in whose dark mind
The clambering wings of birds of black revolved,
Making harsh torment of the solitude.

The walker in the moonlight walked alone,
And in his heart his disbelief lay cold.
His broad-brimmed hat came close upon his eyes.

FROGS EAT BUTTERFLIES. SNAKES EAT FROGS. HOGS EAT SNAKES. MEN EAT HOGS

It is true that the rivers went nosing like swine,
Tugging at banks, until they seemed
Bland belly-sounds in somnolent troughs,

That the air was heavy with the breath of these swine,
The breath of turgid summer, and
Heavy with thunder's rattapallax,

That the man who erected this cabin, planted
This field, and tended it awhile,
Knew not the quirks of imagery,

That the hours of his indolent, arid days,
Grotesque with this nosing in banks,
This somnolence and rattapallax,

Seemed to suckle themselves on his arid being,
As the swine-like rivers suckled themselves
While they went seaward to the sea-mouths.

JASMINE'S BEAUTIFUL THOUGHTS
UNDERNEATH THE WILLOW

My titillations have no foot-notes
And their memorials are the phrases
Of idiosyncratic music.

The love that will not be transported
In an old, frizzled, flambeaued manner,
But muses on its eccentricity,

Is like a vivid apprehension
Of bliss beyond the mutes of plaster,
Or paper souvenirs of rapture,

Of bliss submerged beneath appearance,
In an interior ocean's rocking
Of long, capricious fugues and chorals.

CORTÈGE FOR ROSENBLOOM

Now, the wry Rosenbloom is dead
And his finical carriers tread,
On a hundred legs, the tread
Of the dead.
Rosenbloom is dead.

They carry the wizened one
Of the color of horn
To the sullen hill,
Treading a tread
In unison for the dead.

Rosenbloom is dead.
The tread of the carriers does not halt
On the hill, but turns
Up the sky.
They are bearing his body into the sky.

It is the infants of misanthropes
And the infants of nothingness
That tread
The wooden ascents
Of the ascending of the dead.

It is turbans they wear
And boots of fur
As they tread the boards
In a region of frost,
Viewing the frost;

To a chirr of gongs
And a chitter of cries
And the heavy thrum
Of the endless tread
That they tread;

To a jangle of doom
And a jumble of words

80

Of the intense poem
Of the strictest prose
Of Rosenbloom.

And they bury him there,
Body and soul,
In a place in the sky.
The lamentable tread!
Rosenbloom is dead.

❀❀❀❀❀❀❀❀❀❀❀❀❀❀❀❀❀❀❀❀❀❀❀❀❀❀❀❀

TATTOO

The light is like a spider.
It crawls over the water.
It crawls over the edges of the snow.
It crawls under your eyelids
And spreads its webs there—
Its two webs.

The webs of your eyes
Are fastened
To the flesh and bones of you
As to rafters or grass.

There are filaments of your eyes
On the surface of the water
And in the edges of the snow.

THE BIRD WITH THE COPPERY, KEEN CLAWS

Above the forest of the parakeets,
A parakeet of parakeets prevails,
A pip of life amid a mort of tails.

(The rudiments of tropics are around,
Aloe of ivory, pear of rusty rind.)
His lids are white because his eyes are blind.

He is not paradise of parakeets,
Of his gold ether, golden alguazil,
Except because he broods there and is still.

Panache upon panache, his tails deploy
Upward and outward, in green-vented forms,
His tip a drop of water full of storms.

But though the turbulent tinges undulate
As his pure intellect applies its laws,
He moves not on his coppery, keen claws.

He munches a dry shell while he exerts
His will, yet never ceases, perfect cock,
To flare, in the sun-pallor of his rock.

LIFE IS MOTION

In Oklahoma,
Bonnie and Josie,
Dressed in calico,
Danced around a stump.
They cried,
"Ohoyaho,
Ohoo" . . .
Celebrating the marriage
Of flesh and air.

THE WIND SHIFTS

This is how the wind shifts:
Like the thoughts of an old human,
Who still thinks eagerly
And despairingly.
The wind shifts like this:
Like a human without illusions,
Who still feels irrational things within her.
The wind shifts like this:
Like humans approaching proudly,
Like humans approaching angrily.

This is how the wind shifts:
Like a human, heavy and heavy,
Who does not care.

◇◇

COLLOQUY WITH A POLISH AUNT

*Elle savait toutes les légendes
du Paradis et tous les contes de
la Pologne.*
REVUE DES DEUX MONDES

SHE

How is it that my saints from Voragine,
In their embroidered slippers, touch your spleen?

HE

Old pantaloons, duenna of the spring!

SHE

Imagination is the will of things. . . .
Thus, on the basis of the common drudge,
You dream of women, swathed in indigo,
Holding their books toward the nearer stars,
To read, in secret, burning secrecies. . . .

84

GUBBINAL

That strange flower, the sun,
Is just what you say.
Have it your way.

The world is ugly,
And the people are sad.

That tuft of jungle feathers,
That animal eye,
Is just what you say.

That savage of fire,
That seed,
Have it your way.

The world is ugly,
And the people are sad.

TWO FIGURES IN DENSE VIOLET NIGHT

I had as lief be embraced by the porter at the hotel
As to get no more from the moonlight
Than your moist hand.

Be the voice of night and Florida in my ear.
Use dusky words and dusky images.
Darken your speech.

Speak, even, as if I did not hear you speaking,
But spoke for you perfectly in my thoughts,
Conceiving words,

As the night conceives the sea-sounds in silence,
And out of their droning sibilants makes
A serenade.

Say, puerile, that the buzzards crouch on the ridge-pole
And sleep with one eye watching the stars fall
Below Key West.

Say that the palms are clear in a total blue,
Are clear and are obscure; that it is night;
That the moon shines.

<hr />

THEORY

I am what is around me.

Women understand this.
One is not duchess
A hundred yards from a carriage.

These, then are portraits:
A black vestibule;
A high bed sheltered by curtains.

These are merely instances.

◈◇

TO THE ONE OF FICTIVE MUSIC

Sister and mother and diviner love,
And of the sisterhood of the living dead
Most near, most clear, and of the clearest bloom,
And of the fragrant mothers the most dear
And queen, and of diviner love the day
And flame and summer and sweet fire, no thread
Of cloudy silver sprinkles in your gown
Its venom of renown, and on your head
No crown is simpler than the simple hair.

Now, of the music summoned by the birth
That separates us from the wind and sea,
Yet leaves us in them, until earth becomes,
By being so much of the things we are,
Gross effigy and simulacrum, none
Gives motion to perfection more serene
Than yours, out of our imperfections wrought,
Most rare, or ever of more kindred air
In the laborious weaving that you wear.

87

For so retentive of themselves are men
That music is intensest which proclaims
The near, the clear, and vaunts the clearest bloom,
And of all vigils musing the obscure,
That apprehends the most which sees and names,
As in your name, an image that is sure,
Among the arrant spices of the sun,
O bough and bush and scented vine, in whom
We give ourselves our likest issuance.

Yet not too like, yet not so like to be
Too near, too clear, saving a little to endow
Our feigning with the strange unlike, whence
    springs
The difference that heavenly pity brings.
For this, musician, in your girdle fixed
Bear other perfumes. On your pale head wear
A band entwining, set with fatal stones.
Unreal, give back to us what once you gave:
The imagination that we spurned and crave.

HYMN FROM A WATERMELON PAVILION

You dweller in the dark cabin,
To whom the watermelon is always purple,
Whose garden is wind and moon,

Of the two dreams, night and day,
What lover, what dreamer, would choose
The one obscured by sleep?

Here is the plantain by your door
And the best cock of red feather
That crew before the clocks.

A feme may come, leaf-green,
Whose coming may give revel
Beyond revelries of sleep,

Yes, and the blackbird spread its tail,
So that the sun may speckle,
While it creaks hail.

You dweller in the dark cabin,
Rise, since rising will not waken,
And hail, cry hail, cry hail.

PETER QUINCE AT THE CLAVIER

I

Just as my fingers on these keys
Make music, so the selfsame sounds
On my spirit make a music, too.

Music is feeling, then, not sound;
And thus it is that what I feel,
Here in this room, desiring you,

Thinking of your blue-shadowed silk,
Is music. It is like the strain
Waked in the elders by Susanna.

Of a green evening, clear and warm,
She bathed in her still garden, while
The red-eyed elders watching, felt

The basses of their beings throb
In witching chords, and their thin blood
Pulse pizzicati of Hosanna.

II

In the green water, clear and warm,
Susanna lay.
She searched
The touch of springs,
And found
Concealed imaginings.
She sighed,
For so much melody.

Upon the bank, she stood
In the cool
Of spent emotions.
She felt, among the leaves,
The dew
Of old devotions.

She walked upon the grass,
Still quavering.
The winds were like her maids,
On timid feet,
Fetching her woven scarves,
Yet wavering.

A breath upon her hand
Muted the night.
She turned—
A cymbal crashed,
And roaring horns.

III

Soon, with a noise like tambourines,
Came her attendant Byzantines.

They wondered why Susanna cried
Against the elders by her side;

And as they whispered, the refrain
Was like a willow swept by rain.

Anon, their lamps' uplifted flame
Revealed Susanna and her shame.

And then, the simpering Byzantines
Fled, with a noise like tambourines.

IV

Beauty is momentary in the mind—
The fitful tracing of a portal;
But in the flesh it is immortal.

The body dies; the body's beauty lives.
So evenings die, in their green going,
A wave, interminably flowing.
So gardens die, their meek breath scenting
The cowl of winter, done repenting.
So maidens die, to the auroral
Celebration of a maiden's choral.
Susanna's music touched the bawdy strings
Of those white elders; but, escaping,
Left only Death's ironic scraping.
Now, in its immortality, it plays
On the clear viol of her memory,
And makes a constant sacrament of praise.

❀◇

THIRTEEN WAYS OF LOOKING
AT A BLACKBIRD

I

Among twenty snowy mountains,
The only moving thing
Was the eye of the blackbird.

II

I was of three minds,
Like a tree
In which there are three blackbirds.

III

The blackbird whirled in the autumn winds.
It was a small part of the pantomime.

IV

A man and a woman
Are one.
A man and a woman and a blackbird
Are one.

V

I do not know which to prefer,
The beauty of inflections
Or the beauty of innuendoes,
The blackbird whistling
Or just after.

VI

Icicles filled the long window
With barbaric glass.
The shadow of the blackbird
Crossed it, to and fro.
The mood
Traced in the shadow
An indecipherable cause.

VII

O thin men of Haddam,
Why do you imagine golden birds?
Do you not see how the blackbird
Walks around the feet
Of the women about you?

VIII

I know noble accents
And lucid, inescapable rhythms;
But I know, too,
That the blackbird is involved
In what I know.

IX

When the blackbird flew out of sight,
It marked the edge
Of one of many circles.

X

At the sight of blackbirds
Flying in a green light,
Even the bawds of euphony
Would cry out sharply.

XI

He rode over Connecticut
In a glass coach.
Once, a fear pierced him,
In that he mistook
The shadow of his equipage
For blackbirds.

XII

The river is moving.
The blackbird must be flying.

It was evening all afternoon.
It was snowing
And it was going to snow.
The blackbird sat
In the cedar-limbs.

O₊O₊O₊O₊O₊O₊O₊O₊O₊O₊O₊O₊O₊O₊O₊O₊O₊O₊O₊O₊O₊O₊O₊O₊O₊O₊O₊O₊

NOMAD EXQUISITE

As the immense dew of Florida
Brings forth
The big-finned palm
And green vine angering for life,

As the immense dew of Florida
Brings forth hymn and hymn
From the beholder,
Beholding all these green sides
And gold sides of green sides,

And blessed mornings,
Meet for the eye of the young alligator,
And lightning colors
So, in me, come flinging
Forms, flames, and the flakes of flames.

THE MAN WHOSE PHARYNX WAS BAD

The time of year has grown indifferent.
Mildew of summer and the deepening snow
Are both alike in the routine I know.
I am too dumbly in my being pent.

The wind attendant on the solstices
Blows on the shutters of the metropoles,
Stirring no poet in his sleep, and tolls
The grand ideas of the villages.

The malady of the quotidian. . . .
Perhaps, if winter once could penetrate
Through all its purples to the final slate,
Persisting bleakly in an icy haze,

One might in turn become less diffident,
Out of such mildew plucking neater mould
And spouting new orations of the cold.
One might. One might. But time will not relent.

THE DEATH OF A SOLDIER

Life contracts and death is expected,
As in a season of autumn.
The soldier falls.

He does not become a three-days personage,
Imposing his separation,
Calling for pomp.

Death is absolute and without memorial,
As in a season of autumn,
When the wind stops,

When the wind stops and, over the heavens,
The clouds go, nevertheless,
In their direction.

NEGATION

Hi! The creator too is blind,
Struggling toward his harmonious whole,
Rejecting intermediate parts,
Horrors and falsities and wrongs;
Incapable master of all force,

97

Too vague idealist, overwhelmed
By an afflatus that persists.
For this, then, we endure brief lives,
The evanescent symmetries
From that meticulous potter's thumb.

THE SURPRISES OF THE SUPERHUMAN

The palais de justice of chambermaids
Tops the horizon with its colonnades.

If it were lost in Übermenschlichkeit,
Perhaps our wretched state would soon come right.

For somehow the brave dicta of its kings
Make more awry our faulty human things.

SEA SURFACE FULL OF CLOUDS

I

In that November off Tehuantepec,
The slopping of the sea grew still one night
And in the morning summer hued the deck

98

And made one think of rosy chocolate
And gilt umbrellas. Paradisal green
Gave suavity to the perplexed machine

Of ocean, which like limpid water lay.
Who, then, in that ambrosial latitude
Out of the light evolved the moving blooms,

Who, then, evolved the sea-blooms from the clouds
Diffusing balm in that Pacific calm?
C'était mon enfant, mon bijou, mon âme.

The sea-clouds whitened far below the calm
And moved, as blooms move, in the swimming green
And in its watery radiance, while the hue

Of heaven in an antique reflection rolled
Round those flotillas. And sometimes the sea
Poured brilliant iris on the glistening blue.

II

In that November off Tehuantepec
The slopping of the sea grew still one night.
At breakfast jelly yellow streaked the deck

And made one think of chop-house chocolate
And sham umbrellas. And a sham-like green
Capped summer-seeming on the tense machine

Of ocean, which in sinister flatness lay.
Who, then, beheld the rising of the clouds
That strode submerged in that malevolent sheen,

Who saw the mortal massives of the blooms
Of water moving on the water-floor?
C'était mon frère du ciel, ma vie, mon or.

The gongs rang loudly as the windy booms
Hoo-hooed it in the darkened ocean-blooms.
The gongs grew still. And then blue heaven spread

Its crystalline pendentives on the sea
And the macabre of the water-glooms
In an enormous undulation fled.

III

In that November off Tehuantepec,
The slopping of the sea grew still one night
And a pale silver patterned on the deck

And made one think of porcelain chocolate
And pied umbrellas. An uncertain green,
Piano-polished, held the tranced machine

Of ocean, as a prelude holds and holds.
Who, seeing silver petals of white blooms
Unfolding in the water, feeling sure

Of the milk within the saltiest spurge, heard, then,
The sea unfolding in the sunken clouds?
Oh! C'était mon extase et mon amour.

So deeply sunken were they that the shrouds,
The shrouding shadows, made the petals black
Until the rolling heaven made them blue,

A blue beyond the rainy hyacinth,
And smiting the crevasses of the leaves
Deluged the ocean with a sapphire blue.

IV

In that November off Tehuantepec
The night-long slopping of the sea grew still.
A mallow morning dozed upon the deck

And made one think of musky chocolate
And frail umbrellas. A too-fluent green
Suggested malice in the dry machine

Of ocean, pondering dank stratagem.
Who then beheld the figures of the clouds
Like blooms secluded in the thick marine?

Like blooms? Like damasks that were shaken off
From the loosed girdles in the spangling must.
C'était ma foi, la nonchalance divine.

The nakedness would rise and suddenly turn
Salt masks of beard and mouths of bellowing,
Would—But more suddenly the heaven rolled

Its bluest sea-clouds in the thinking green,
And the nakedness became the broadest blooms,
Mile-mallows that a mallow sun cajoled.

V

In that November off Tehuantepec
Night stilled the slopping of the sea. The day
Came, bowing and voluble, upon the deck,

Good clown. . . . One thought of Chinese chocolate
And large umbrellas. And a motley green
Followed the drift of the obese machine

Of ocean, perfected in indolence.
What pistache one, ingenious and droll,
Beheld the sovereign clouds as jugglery

And the sea as turquoise-turbaned Sambo, neat
At tossing saucers—cloudy-conjuring sea?
C'était mon esprit bâtard, l'ignominie.

The sovereign clouds came clustering. The conch
Of loyal conjuration trumped. The wind
Of green blooms turning crisped the motley hue

To clearing opalescence. Then the sea
And heaven rolled as one and from the two
Came fresh transfigurings of freshest blue.

THE REVOLUTIONISTS STOP FOR
ORANGEADE

Capitán profundo, capitán geloso,
Ask us not to sing standing in the sun,
Hairy-backed and hump-armed,
Flat-ribbed and big-bagged.

There is no pith in music
Except in something false.

Bellissimo, pomposo,
Sing a song of serpent-kin,
Necks among the thousand leaves,
Tongues around the fruit.
Sing in clownish boots
Strapped and buckled bright.

Wear the breeches of a mask,
Coat half-flare and half galloon;
Wear a helmet without reason,
Tufted, tilted, twirled, and twisted.
Start the singing in a voice
Rougher than a grinding shale.

Hang a feather by your eye,
Nod and look a little sly.
This must be the vent of pity,
Deeper than a truer ditty
Of the real that wrenches,
Of the quick that's wry.

NEW ENGLAND VERSES

I

The Whole World Including the Speaker

Why nag at the ideas of Hercules, Don Don?
Widen your sense. All things in the sun are sun.

II

The Whole World Excluding the Speaker

I found between moon-rising and moon-setting
The world was round. But not from my begetting.

III

Soupe Aux Perles

Health-o, when ginger and fromage bewitch
The vile antithesis of poor and rich.

IV

Soupe Sans Perles

I crossed in '38 in the *Western Head*.
It depends which way you crossed, the tea-belle said.

V

Boston with a Note-book

Lean encyclopædists, inscribe an Iliad.
There's a weltanschauung of the penny pad.

VI

Boston without a Note-book

Let us erect in the Basin a lofty fountain.
Suckled on ponds, the spirit craves a watery mountain.

VII

Artist in Tropic

Of Phœbus Apothicaire the first beatitude:
Blessed, who is his nation's multitude.

VIII

Artist in Arctic

And of Phœbus the Tailor the second saying goes:
Blessed, whose beard is cloak against the snows.

IX

Statue against a Clear Sky

Ashen man on ashen cliff above the salt halloo,
O ashen admiral of the hale, hard blue. . . .

X

Statue against a Cloudy Sky

Scaffolds and derricks rise from the reeds to the clouds
Meditating the will of men in formless crowds.

XI

Land of Locust

Patron and patriarch of couplets, walk
In fragrant leaves heat-heavy yet nimble in talk.

105

XII

Land of Pine and Marble

Civilization must be destroyed. The hairy saints
Of the North have earned this crumb by their com-
plaints.

XIII

The Male Nude

Dark cynic, strip and bathe and bask at will.
Without cap or strap, you are the cynic still.

XIV

The Female Nude

Ballatta dozed in the cool on a straw divan
At home, a bit like the slenderest courtesan.

XV

Scène Flétrie

The purple dress in autumn and the belfry breath
Hinted autumnal farewells of academic death.

XVI

Scène Fleurie

A perfect fruit in perfect atmosphere.
Nature as Pinakothek. Whist! Chanticleer. . . .

LUNAR PARAPHRASE

The moon is the mother of pathos and pity.

When, at the wearier end of November,
Her old light moves along the branches,
Feebly, slowly, depending upon them;
When the body of Jesus hangs in a pallor,
Humanly near, and the figure of Mary,
Touched on by hoar-frost, shrinks in a shelter
Made by the leaves, that have rotted and fallen;
When over the houses, a golden illusion
Brings back an earlier season of quiet
And quieting dreams in the sleepers in darkness—

The moon is the mother of pathos and pity.

ANATOMY OF MONOTONY

I

If from the earth we came, it was an earth
That bore us as a part of all the things
It breeds and that was lewder than it is.
Our nature is her nature. Hence it comes,

Since by our nature we grow old, earth grows
The same. We parallel the mother's death.
She walks an autumn ampler than the wind
Cries up for us and colder than the frost
Pricks in our spirits at the summer's end,
And over the bare spaces of our skies
She sees a barer sky that does not bend.

II

The body walks forth naked in the sun
And, out of tenderness or grief, the sun
Gives comfort, so that other bodies come,
Twinning our phantasy and our device,
And apt in versatile motion, touch and sound
To make the body covetous in desire
Of the still finer, more implacable chords.
So be it. Yet the spaciousness and light
In which the body walks and is deceived,
Falls from that fatal and that barer sky,
And this the spirit sees and is aggrieved.

THE PUBLIC SQUARE

A slash of angular blacks
Like a fractured edifice
That was buttressed by blue slants
In a coma of the moon.

A slash and the edifice fell,
Pylon and pier fell down.
A mountain-blue cloud arose
Like a thing in which they fell,

Fell slowly as when at night
A languid janitor bears
His lantern through colonnades
And the architecture swoons.

It turned cold and silent. Then
The square began to clear.
The bijou of Atlas, the moon,
Was last with its porcelain leer.

❖◇

SONATINA TO HANS CHRISTIAN

If any duck in any brook,
Fluttering the water
For your crumb,
Seemed the helpless daughter

Of a mother
Regretful that she bore her;
Or of another,
Barren, and longing for her;

What of the dove,
Or thrush, or any singing mysteries?
What of the trees
And intonations of the trees?

What of the night
That lights and dims the stars?
Do you know, Hans Christian,
Now that you see the night?

❀❀❀❀❀❀❀❀❀❀❀❀❀❀❀❀❀❀❀❀❀❀❀❀❀❀❀❀❀❀❀

IN THE CLEAR SEASON OF GRAPES

The mountains between our lands and the sea—
This conjunction of mountains and sea and our lands—
Have I stopped and thought of its point before?

When I think of our lands I think of the house
And the table that holds a platter of pears,
Vermilion smeared over green, arranged for show.

But this gross blue under rolling bronzes
Belittles those carefully chosen daubs.
Flashier fruits! A flip for the sun and moon,

If they mean no more than that. But they do.
And mountains and the sea do. And our lands.
And the welter of frost and the fox cries do.

110

Much more than that. Autumnal passages
Are overhung by the shadows of the rocks
And his nostrils blow out salt around each man.

◇◇

TWO AT NORFOLK

Mow the grass in the cemetery, darkies,
Study the symbols and the requiescats,
But leave a bed beneath the myrtles.
This skeleton had a daughter and that, a son.

In his time, this one had little to speak of,
The softest word went gurrituck in his skull.
For him the moon was always in Scandinavia
And his daughter was a foreign thing.

And that one was never a man of heart.
The making of his son was one more duty.
When the music of the boy fell like a fountain,
He praised Johann Sebastian, as he should.

The dark shadows of the funereal magnolias
Are full of the songs of Jamanda and Carlotta;
The son and the daughter, who come to the darkness,
He for her burning breast and she for his arms.

And these two never meet in the air so full of
     summer

III

And touch each other, even touching closely,
Without an escape in the lapses of their kisses.
Make a bed and leave the iris in it.

<hr>

INDIAN RIVER

The trade-wind jingles the rings in the nets around the racks
    by the docks on Indian River.
It is the same jingle of the water among the roots under the
    banks of the palmettoes,
It is the same jingle of the red-bird breasting the orange-trees
    out of the cedars.
Yet there is no spring in Florida, neither in boskage perdu, nor
    on the nunnery beaches.

<hr>

TEA

When the elephant's-ear in the park
Shrivelled in frost,
And the leaves on the paths
Ran like rats,
Your lamp-light fell

On shining pillows,
Of sea-shades and sky-shades,
Like umbrellas in Java.

<hr />

TO THE ROARING WIND

What syllable are you seeking,
Vocalissimus,
In the distances of sleep?
Speak it.

IDEAS OF ORDER

FAREWELL TO FLORIDA

I

Go on, high ship, since now, upon the shore,
The snake has left its skin upon the floor.
Key West sank downward under massive clouds
And silvers and greens spread over the sea. The moon
Is at the mast-head and the past is dead.
Her mind will never speak to me again.
I am free. High above the mast the moon
Rides clear of her mind and the waves make a refrain
Of this: that the snake has shed its skin upon
The floor. Go on through the darkness. The waves
    fly back.

II

Her mind had bound me round. The palms were hot
As if I lived in ashen ground, as if
The leaves in which the wind kept up its sound
From my North of cold whistled in a sepulchral
    South,
Her South of pine and coral and coraline sea,
Her home, not mine, in the ever-freshened Keys,
Her days, her oceanic nights, calling
For music, for whisperings from the reefs.
How content I shall be in the North to which I sail
And to feel sure and to forget the bleaching
    sand . . .

117

III

I hated the weathery yawl from which the pools
Disclosed the sea floor and the wilderness
Of waving weeds. I hated the vivid blooms
Curled over the shadowless hut, the rust and bones,
The trees likes bones and the leaves half sand, half
    sun.
To stand here on the deck in the dark and say
Farewell and to know that that land is forever gone
And that she will not follow in any word
Or look, nor ever again in thought, except
That I loved her once . . . Farewell. Go on, high
    ship.

IV

My North is leafless and lies in a wintry slime
Both of men and clouds, a slime of men in crowds.
The men are moving as the water moves,
This darkened water cloven by sullen swells
Against your sides, then shoving and slithering,
The darkness shattered, turbulent with foam.
To be free again, to return to the violent mind
That is their mind, these men, and that will bind
Me round, carry me, misty deck, carry me
To the cold, go on, high ship, go on, plunge on.

GHOSTS AS COCOONS

The grass is in seed. The young birds are flying.
Yet the house is not built, not even begun.

The vetch has turned purple. But where is the bride?
It is easy to say to those bidden—But where,

Where, butcher, seducer, bloodman, reveller,
Where is sun and music and highest heaven's lust,

For which more than any words cries deeplier?
This mangled, smutted semi-world hacked out

Of dirt . . . It is not possible for the moon
To blot this with its dove-winged blendings.

She must come now. The grass is in seed and high.
Come now. Those to be born have need

Of the bride, love being a birth, have need to see
And to touch her, have need to say to her,

"The fly on the rose prevents us, O season
Excelling summer, ghost of fragrance falling

On dung." Come now, pearled and pasted, bloomy-
        leafed,
While the domes resound with chant involving chant.

119

SAILING AFTER LUNCH

It is the word *pejorative* that hurts.
My old boat goes round on a crutch
And doesn't get under way.
It's the time of the year
And the time of the day.

Perhaps it's the lunch that we had
Or the lunch that we should have had.
But I am, in any case,
A most inappropriate man
In a most unpropitious place.

Mon Dieu, hear the poet's prayer.
The romantic should be here.
The romantic should be there.
It ought to be everywhere.
But the romantic must never remain,

Mon Dieu, and must never again return.
This heavy historical sail
Through the mustiest blue of the lake
In a really vertiginous boat
Is wholly the vapidest fake. . . .

It is least what one ever sees.
It is only the way one feels, to say
Where my spirit is I am,

To say the light wind worries the sail,
To say the water is swift today,

To expunge all people and be a pupil
Of the gorgeous wheel and so to give
That slight transcendence to the dirty sail,
By light, the way one feels, sharp white,
And then rush brightly through the summer
     air.

❁◈

SAD STRAINS OF A GAY WALTZ

The truth is that there comes a time
When we can mourn no more over music
That is so much motionless sound.

There comes a time when the waltz
Is no longer a mode of desire, a mode
Of revealing desire and is empty of shadows.

Too many waltzes have ended. And then
There's that mountain-minded Hoon,
For whom desire was never that of the waltz,

Who found all form and order in solitude,
For whom the shapes were never the figures of men.
Now, for him, his forms have vanished.

There is order in neither sea nor sun.
The shapes have lost their glistening.
There are these sudden mobs of men,

These sudden clouds of faces and arms,
An immense suppression, freed,
These voices crying without knowing for what,

Except to be happy, without knowing how,
Imposing forms they cannot describe,
Requiring order beyond their speech.

Too many waltzes have ended. Yet the shapes
For which the voices cry, these, too, may be
Modes of desire, modes of revealing desire.

Too many waltzes—The epic of disbelief
Blares oftener and soon, will soon be constant.
Some harmonious skeptic soon in a skeptical music

Will unite these figures of men and their shapes
Will glisten again with motion, the music
Will be motion and full of shadows.

DANCE OF THE MACABRE MICE

In the land of turkeys in turkey weather
At the base of the statue, we go round and round.
What a beautiful history, beautiful surprise!
Monsieur is on horseback. The horse is covered with
      mice.

This dance has no name. It is a hungry dance.
We dance it out to the tip of Monsieur's sword,
Reading the lordly language of the inscription,
Which is like zithers and tambourines combined:

The Founder of the State. Whoever founded
A state that was free, in the dead of winter, from mice?
What a beautiful tableau tinted and towering,
The arm of bronze outstretched against all evil!

◇◆◇

MEDITATION CELESTIAL & TERRESTRIAL

The wild warblers are warbling in the jungle
Of life and spring and of the lustrous inundations,
Flood on flood, of our returning sun.

123

Day after day, throughout the winter,
We hardened ourselves to live by bluest reason
In a world of wind and frost,

And by will, unshaken and florid
In mornings of angular ice,
That passed beyond us through the narrow sky.

But what are radiant reason and radiant will
To warblings early in the hilarious trees
Of summer, the drunken mother?

❀◇

LIONS IN SWEDEN

No more phrases, Swenson: I was once
A hunter of those sovereigns of the soul
And savings banks, Fides, the sculptor's prize,
All eyes and size, and galled Justitia,
Trained to poise the tables of the law,
Patientia, forever soothing wounds,
And mighty Fortitudo, frantic bass.
But these shall not adorn my souvenirs,
These lions, these majestic images.
If the fault is with the soul, the sovereigns
Of the soul must likewise be at fault, and first.

124

If the fault is with the souvenirs, yet these
Are the soul itself. And the whole of the soul,
    Swenson,
As every man in Sweden will concede,
Still hankers after lions, or, to shift,
Still hankers after sovereign images.
If the fault is with the lions, send them back
To Monsieur Dufy's Hamburg whence they came.
The vegetation still abounds with forms.

❦❧❦❧❦❧❦❧❦❧❦❧❦❧❦❧❦❧❦❧❦❧❦❧❦❧❦❧❦❧❦❧

HOW TO LIVE. WHAT TO DO

Last evening the moon rose above this rock
Impure upon a world unpurged.
The man and his companion stopped
To rest before the heroic height.

Coldly the wind fell upon them
In many majesties of sound:
They that had left the flame-freaked sun
To seek a sun of fuller fire.

Instead there was this tufted rock
Massively rising high and bare
Beyond all trees, the ridges thrown
Like giant arms among the clouds.

There was neither voice nor crested image,
No chorister, nor priest. There was
Only the great height of the rock
And the two of them standing still to rest.

There was the cold wind and the sound
It made, away from the muck of the land
That they had left, heroic sound
Joyous and jubilant and sure.

SOME FRIENDS FROM PASCAGOULA

Tell me more of the eagle, Cotton,
And you, black Sly,
Tell me how he descended
Out of the morning sky.

Describe with deepened voice
And noble imagery
His slowly-falling round
Down to the fishy sea.

Here was a sovereign sight,
Fit for a kinky clan.
Tell me again of the point
At which the flight began,

Say how his heavy wings,
Spread on the sun-bronzed air,
Turned tip and tip away,
Down to the sand, the glare

Of the pine trees edging the sand,
Dropping in sovereign rings
Out of his fiery lair.
Speak of the dazzling wings.

WAVING ADIEU, ADIEU, ADIEU

That would be waving and that would be crying,
Crying and shouting and meaning farewell,
Farewell in the eyes and farewell at the centre,
Just to stand still without moving a hand.

In a world without heaven to follow, the stops
Would be endings, more poignant than partings, profounder,
And that would be saying farewell, repeating farewell,
Just to be there and just to behold.

To be one's singular self, to despise
The being that yielded so little, acquired

So little, too little to care, to turn
To the ever-jubilant weather, to sip

One's cup and never to say a word,
Or to sleep or just to lie there still,
Just to be there, just to be beheld,
That would be bidding farewell, be bidding farewell.

One likes to practice the thing. They practice,
Enough, for heaven. Ever-jubilant,
What is there here but weather, what spirit
Have I except it comes from the sun?

❀❀❀❀❀❀❀❀❀❀❀❀❀❀❀❀❀❀❀❀❀❀❀❀❀❀❀❀❀

THE IDEA OF ORDER AT KEY WEST

She sang beyond the genius of the sea.
The water never formed to mind or voice,
Like a body wholly body, fluttering
Its empty sleeves; and yet its mimic motion
Made constant cry, caused constantly a cry,
That was not ours although we understood,
Inhuman, of the veritable ocean.

The sea was not a mask. No more was she.
The song and water were not medleyed sound
Even if what she sang was what she heard,
Since what she sang was uttered word by word.

128

It may be that in all her phrases stirred
The grinding water and the gasping wind;
But it was she and not the sea we heard.

For she was the maker of the song she sang.
The ever-hooded, tragic-gestured sea
Was merely a place by which she walked to sing.
Whose spirit is this? we said, because we knew
It was the spirit that we sought and knew
That we should ask this often as she sang.

If it was only the dark voice of the sea
That rose, or even colored by many waves;
If it was only the outer voice of sky
And cloud, of the sunken coral water-walled,
However clear, it would have been deep air,
The heaving speech of air, a summer sound
Repeated in a summer without end
And sound alone. But it was more than that,
More even than her voice, and ours, among
The meaningless plungings of water and the wind,
Theatrical distances, bronze shadows heaped
On high horizons, mountainous atmospheres
Of sky and sea.
                    It was her voice that made
The sky acutest at its vanishing.
She measured to the hour its solitude.
She was the single artificer of the world
In which she sang. And when she sang, the sea,
Whatever self it had, became the self
That was her song, for she was the maker. Then we,
As we beheld her striding there alone,

Knew that there never was a world for her
Except the one she sang and, singing, made.

Ramon Fernandez, tell me, if you know,
Why, when the singing ended and we turned
Toward the town, tell why the glassy lights,
The lights in the fishing boats at anchor there,
As the night descended, tilting in the air,
Mastered the night and portioned out the sea,
Fixing emblazoned zones and fiery poles,
Arranging, deepening, enchanting night.

Oh! Blessed rage for order, pale Ramon,
The maker's rage to order words of the sea,
Words of the fragrant portals, dimly-starred,
And of ourselves and of our origins,
In ghostlier demarcations, keener sounds.

◇◇

THE AMERICAN SUBLIME

How does one stand
To behold the sublime,
To confront the mockers,
The mickey mockers
And plated pairs?

When General Jackson
Posed for his statue

He knew how one feels.
Shall a man go barefoot
Blinking and blank?

But how does one feel?
One grows used to the weather,
The landscape and that;
And the sublime comes down
To the spirit itself,

The spirit and space,
The empty spirit
In vacant space.
What wine does one drink?
What bread does one eat?

✵◇◇

MOZART, 1935

Poet, be seated at the piano.
Play the present, its hoo-hoo-hoo,
Its shoo-shoo-shoo, its ric-a-nic,
Its envious cachinnation.

If they throw stones upon the roof
While you practice arpeggios,
It is because they carry down the stairs

A body in rags.
Be seated at the piano.

That lucid souvenir of the past,
The divertimento;
That airy dream of the future,
The unclouded concerto . . .
The snow is falling.
Strike the piercing chord.

Be thou the voice,
Not you. Be thou, be thou
The voice of angry fear,
The voice of this besieging pain.

Be thou that wintry sound
As of the great wind howling,
By which sorrow is released,
Dismissed, absolved
In a starry placating.

We may return to Mozart.
He was young, and we, we are old.
The snow is falling
And the streets are full of cries.
Be seated, thou.

SNOW AND STARS

The grackles sing avant the spring
Most spiss—oh! Yes, most spissantly.
They sing right puissantly.

This robe of snow and winter stars,
The devil take it, wear it, too.
It might become his hole of blue.

Let him remove it to his regions,
White and star-furred for his legions,
And make much bing, high bing.

It would be ransom for the willow
And fill the hill and fill it full
Of ding, ding, dong.

THE SUN THIS MARCH

The exceeding brightness of this early sun
Makes me conceive how dark I have become,

And re-illumines things that used to turn
To gold in broadest blue, and be a part

Of a turning spirit in an earlier self.
That, too, returns from out the winter's air,

Like an hallucination come to daze
The corner of the eye. Our element,

Cold is our element and winter's air
Brings voices as of lions coming down.

Oh! Rabbi, rabbi, fend my soul for me
And true savant of this dark nature be.

❀✧

BOTANIST ON ALP (NO. 1)

Panoramas are not what they used to be.
Claude has been dead a long time
And apostrophes are forbidden on the fu-
    nicular.
Marx has ruined Nature,
For the moment.

For myself, I live by leaves,
So that corridors of clouds,
Corridors of cloudy thoughts,
Seem pretty much one:
I don't know what.

134

But in Claude how near one was
(In a world that was resting on pillars,
That was seen through arches)
To the central composition,
The essential theme.

What composition is there in all this:
Stockholm slender in a slender light,
An Adriatic *riva* rising,
Statues and stars,
Without a theme?

The pillars are prostrate, the arches are hag-
    gard,
The hotel is boarded and bare.
Yet the panorama of despair
Cannot be the specialty
Of this ecstatic air.

☙☙☙☙☙☙☙☙☙☙☙☙☙☙☙☙☙☙☙☙☙☙☙☙☙☙☙☙☙☙☙

BOTANIST ON ALP (NO. 2)

The crosses on the convent roofs
Gleam sharply as the sun comes up.

What's down below is in the past
Like last night's crickets, far below.

And what's above is in the past
As sure as all the angels are.

Why should the future leap the clouds
The bays of heaven, brighted, blued?

Chant, O ye faithful, in your paths
The poem of long celestial death;

For who could tolerate the earth
Without that poem, or without

An earthier one, tum, tum-ti-tum,
As of those crosses, glittering,

And merely of their glittering,
A mirror of a mere delight?

◇◇◇

EVENING WITHOUT ANGELS

> the great interests of man: air
> and light, the joy of having a
> body, the voluptuousness of
> looking.
>
> MARIO ROSSI

Why seraphim like lutanists arranged
Above the trees? And why the poet as
Eternal *chef d'orchestre*?

                    Air is air,
Its vacancy glitters round us everywhere.
Its sounds are not angelic syllables
But our unfashioned spirits realized
More sharply in more furious selves.

                            And light
That fosters seraphim and is to them
Coiffeur of haloes, fecund jeweller—
Was the sun concoct for angels or for men?
Sad men made angels of the sun, and of
The moon they made their own attendant ghosts,
Which led them back to angels, after death.

Let this be clear that we are men of sun
And men of day and never of pointed night,
Men that repeat antiquest sounds of air
In an accord of repetitions. Yet,
If we repeat, it is because the wind
Encircling us, speaks always with our speech.

Light, too, encrusts us making visible
The motions of the mind and giving form
To moodiest nothings, as, desire for day
Accomplished in the immensely flashing East,
Desire for rest, in that descending sea
Of dark, which in its very darkening
Is rest and silence spreading into sleep.

. . . Evening, when the measure skips a beat
And then another, one by one, and all
To a seething minor swiftly modulate.
Bare night is best. Bare earth is best. Bare, bare,

Except for our own houses, huddled low
Beneath the arches and their spangled air,
Beneath the rhapsodies of fire and fire,
Where the voice that is in us makes a true re-
    sponse,
Where the voice that is great within us rises up,
As we stand gazing at the rounded moon.

❖✿❖

THE BRAVE MAN

The sun, that brave man,
Comes through boughs that lie in wait,
That brave man.

Green and gloomy eyes
In dark forms of the grass
Run away.

The good stars,
Pale helms and spiky spurs,
Run away.

Fears of my bed,
Fears of life and fears of death,
Run away.

That brave man comes up
From below and walks without meditation,
That brave man.

138

A FADING OF THE SUN

Who can think of the sun costuming clouds
When all people are shaken
Or of night endazzled, proud,
When people awaken
And cry and cry for help?

The warm antiquity of self,
Everyone, grows suddenly cold.
The tea is bad, bread sad.
How can the world so old be so mad
That the people die?

If joy shall be without a book
It lies, themselves within themselves,
If they will look
Within themselves
And cry and cry for help?

Within as pillars of the sun,
Supports of night. The tea,
The wine is good. The bread,
The meat is sweet.
And they will not die.

GRAY STONES AND GRAY PIGEONS

The archbishop is away. The church is gray.
He has left his robes folded in camphor
And, dressed in black, he walks
Among fireflies.

The bony buttresses, the bony spires
Arranged under the stony clouds
Stand in a fixed light.
The bishop rests.

He is away. The church is gray.
This is his holiday.
The sexton moves with a sexton's stare
In the air.

A dithery gold falls everywhere.
It wets the pigeons,
It goes and the birds go,
Turn dry,

Birds that never fly
Except when the bishop passes by,
Globed in today and tomorrow,
Dressed in his colored robes.

WINTER BELLS

The Jew did not go to his synagogue
To be flogged.
But it was solemn,
That church without bells.

He preferred the brightness of bells,
The *mille fiori* of vestments,
The voice of centuries
On the priestly gramophones.

It was the custom
For his rage against chaos
To abate on the way to church,
In regulations of his spirit.
How good life is, on the basis of propriety,
To be followed by a platter of capon!

Yet he kept promising himself
To go to Florida one of these days,
And in one of the little arrondissements
Of the sea there,
To give this further thought.

ACADEMIC DISCOURSE AT HAVANA

I

Canaries in the morning, orchestras
In the afternoon, balloons at night. That is
A difference, at least, from nightingales,
Jehovah and the great sea-worm. The air
Is not so elemental nor the earth
So near.
　　　　　But the sustenance of the wilderness
Does not sustain us in the metropoles.

II

Life is an old casino in a park.
The bills of the swans are flat upon the ground.
A most desolate wind has chilled Rouge-Fatima
And a grand decadence settles down like cold.

III

The swans . . . Before the bills of the swans fell
　　　flat
Upon the ground, and before the chronicle
Of affected homage foxed so many books,
They warded the blank waters of the lakes
And island canopies which were entailed
To that casino. Long before the rain
Swept through its boarded windows and the leaves
Filled its encrusted fountains, they arrayed
The twilights of the mythy goober khan.

142

The centuries of excellence to be
Rose out of promise and became the sooth
Of trombones floating in the trees.

The toil
Of thought evoked a peace eccentric to
The eye and tinkling to the ear. Gruff drums
Could beat, yet not alarm the populace.
The indolent progressions of the swans
Made earth come right; a peanut parody
For peanut people.

And serener myth
Conceiving from its perfect plenitude,
Lusty as June, more fruitful than the weeks
Of ripest summer, always lingering
To touch again the hottest bloom, to strike
Once more the longest resonance, to cap
The clearest woman with apt weed, to mount
The thickest man on thickest stallion-back,
This urgent, competent, serener myth
Passed like a circus.

Politic man ordained
Imagination as the fateful sin.
Grandmother and her basketful of pears
Must be the crux for our compendia.
That's world enough, and more, if one includes
Her daughters to the peached and ivory wench
For whom the towers are built. The burgher's
        breast,

143

And not a delicate ether star-impaled,
Must be the place for prodigy, unless
Prodigious things are tricks. The world is not
The bauble of the sleepless nor a word
That should import a universal pith
To Cuba. Jot these milky matters down.
They nourish Jupiters. Their casual pap
Will drop like sweetness in the empty nights
When too great rhapsody is left annulled
And liquorish prayer provokes new sweats: so, so:
Life is an old casino in a wood.

IV

Is the function of the poet here mere sound,
Subtler than the ornatest prophecy,
To stuff the ear? It causes him to make
His infinite repetition and alloys
Of pick of ebon, pick of halcyon.
It weights him with nice logic for the prim.
As part of nature he is part of us.
His rarities are ours: may they be fit
And reconcile us to our selves in those
True reconcilings, dark, pacific words,
And the adroiter harmonies of their fall.
Close the cantina. Hood the chandelier.
The moonlight is not yellow but a white
That silences the ever-faithful town.
How pale and how possessed a night it is,
How full of exhalations of the sea . . .
All this is older than its oldest hymn,
Has no more meaning than tomorrow's bread.
But let the poet on his balcony

144

Speak and the sleepers in their sleep shall move,
Waken, and watch the moonlight on their floors.
This may be benediction, sepulcher,
And epitaph. It may, however, be
An incantation that the moon defines
By mere example opulently clear.
And the old casino likewise may define
An infinite incantation of our selves
In the grand decadence of the perished swans.

NUDITY AT THE CAPITAL

But nakedness, woolen massa, concerns an innermost atom.
If that remains concealed, what does the bottom matter?

NUDITY IN THE COLONIES

Black man, bright nouveautés leave one, at best, pseudony-
    mous.
Thus one is most disclosed when one is most anonymous.

RE–STATEMENT OF ROMANCE

The night knows nothing of the chants of night.
It is what it is as I am what I am:
And in perceiving this I best perceive myself

And you. Only we two may interchange
Each in the other what each has to give.
Only we two are one, not you and night,

Nor night and I, but you and I, alone,
So much alone, so deeply by ourselves,
So far beyond the casual solitudes,

That night is only the background of our selves,
Supremely true each to its separate self,
In the pale light that each upon the other throws.

THE READER

All night I sat reading a book,
Sat reading as if in a book
Of sombre pages.

146

It was autumn and falling stars
Covered the shrivelled forms
Crouched in the moonlight.

No lamp was burning as I read,
A voice was mumbling, "Everything
Falls back to coldness,

Even the musky muscadines,
The melons, the vermilion pears
Of the leafless garden."

The sombre pages bore no print
Except the trace of burning stars
In the frosty heaven.

❀❖

MUD MASTER

The muddy rivers of spring
Are snarling
Under muddy skies.
The mind is muddy.

As yet, for the mind, new banks
Of bulging green
Are not;

147

Sky-sides of gold
Are not.
The mind snarls.

Blackest of pickanines,
There is a master of mud.
The shaft of light
Falling, far off, from sky to land,
That is he—

The peach-bud maker,
The mud master,
The master of the mind.

ANGLAIS MORT À FLORENCE

A little less returned for him each spring.
Music began to fail him. Brahms, although
His dark familiar, often walked apart.

His spirit grew uncertain of delight,
Certain of its uncertainty, in which
That dark companion left him unconsoled

For a self returning mostly memory.
Only last year he said that the naked moon
Was not the moon he used to see, to feel

148

(In the pale coherences of moon and mood
When he was young), naked and alien,
More leanly shining from a lankier sky.

Its ruddy pallor had grown cadaverous.
He used his reason, exercised his will,
Turning in time to Brahms as alternate

In speech. He has that music and himself.
They were particles of order, a single majesty:
But he remembered the time when he stood alone.

He stood at last by God's help and the police;
But he remembered the time when he stood alone.
He yielded himself to that single majesty;

But he remembered the time when he stood alone,
When to be and delight to be seemed to be one,
Before the colors deepened and grew small.

◇◇◇

THE PLEASURES OF MERELY CIRCULATING

The garden flew round with the angel,
The angel flew round with the clouds,
And the clouds flew round and the clouds flew
          round
And the clouds flew round with the clouds.

149

Is there any secret in skulls,
The cattle skulls in the woods?
Do the drummers in black hoods
Rumble anything out of their drums?

Mrs. Anderson's Swedish baby
Might well have been German or Spanish,
Yet that things go round and again go round
Has rather a classical sound.

❀◇❀◇❀◇❀◇❀◇❀◇❀◇❀◇❀◇❀◇❀◇❀◇❀◇❀◇❀◇❀◇❀◇❀◇

LIKE DECORATIONS IN A NIGGER CEMETERY

[for Arthur Powell]

I

In the far South the sun of autumn is passing
Like Walt Whitman walking along a ruddy shore.
He is singing and chanting the things that are part of him,
The worlds that were and will be, death and day.
Nothing is final, he chants. No man shall see the end.
His beard is of fire and his staff is a leaping flame.

II

Sigh for me, night-wind, in the noisy leaves of the oak.
I am tired. Sleep for me, heaven over the hill.
Shout for me, loudly and loudly, joyful sun, when you
    rise.

150

III

It was when the trees were leafless first in November
And their blackness became apparent, that one first
Knew the eccentric to be the base of design.

IV

Under the mat of frost and over the mat of clouds.
But in between lies the sphere of my fortune
And the fortunes of frost and of clouds,
All alike, except for the rules of the rabbis,
Happy men, distinguishing frost and clouds.

V

If ever the search for a tranquil belief should end,
The future might stop emerging out of the past,
Out of what is full of us; yet the search
And the future emerging out of us seem to be one.

VI

We should die except for Death
In his chalk and violet robes.
Not to die a parish death.

VII

How easily the feelings flow this afternoon
Over the simplest words:
It is too cold for work, now, in the fields.

VIII

Out of the spirit of the holy temples,
Empty and grandiose, let us make hymns
And sing them in secrecy as lovers do.

IX

In a world of universal poverty
The philosophers alone will be fat
Against the autumn winds
In an autumn that will be perpetual.

X

Between farewell and the absence of farewell,
The final mercy and the final loss,
The wind and the sudden falling of the wind.

XI

The cloud rose upward like a heavy stone
That lost its heaviness through that same will,
Which changed light green to olive then to blue.

XII

The sense of the serpent in you, Ananke,
And your averted stride
Add nothing to the horror of the frost
That glistens on your face and hair.

XIII

The birds are singing in the yellow patios,
Pecking at more lascivious rinds than ours,
From sheer Gemütlichkeit.

XIV

The leaden pigeon on the entrance gate
Must miss the symmetry of a leaden mate,
Must see her fans of silver undulate.

XV

Serve the rouged fruits in early snow.
They resemble a page of Toulet
Read in the ruins of a new society,
Furtively, by candle and out of need.

XVI

If thinking could be blown away
Yet this remain the dwelling-place
Of those with a sense for simple space.

XVII

The sun of Asia creeps above the horizon
Into this haggard and tenuous air,
A tiger lamed by nothingness and frost.

XVIII

Shall I grapple with my destroyers
In the muscular poses of the museums?
But my destroyers avoid the museums.

XIX

An opening of portals when night ends,
A running forward, arms stretched out as drilled.
Act I, Scene i, at a German Staats-Oper.

XX

Ah, but the meaningless, natural effigy!
The revealing aberration should appear,
The agate in the eye, the tufted ear,
The rabbit fat, at last, in glassy grass.

153

XXI

She was a shadow as thin in memory
As an autumn ancient underneath the snow,
Which one recalls at a concert or in a café.

XXII

The comedy of hollow sounds derives
From truth and not from satire on our lives.
Clog, therefore, purple Jack and crimson Jill.

XXIII

The fish are in the fishman's window,
The grain is in the baker's shop,
The hunter shouts as the pheasant falls.
Consider the odd morphology of regret.

XXIV

A bridge above the bright and blue of water
And the same bridge when the river is frozen.
Rich Tweedle-dum, poor Tweedle-dee.

XXV

From oriole to crow, note the decline
In music. Crow is realist. But, then,
Oriole, also, may be realist.

XXVI

This fat pistache of Belgian grapes exceeds
The total gala of auburn aureoles.
Cochon! Master, the grapes are here and now.

XXVII

John Constable they could never quite transplant
And our streams rejected the dim Academy.

Granted the Picts impressed us otherwise
In the taste for iron dogs and iron deer.

XXVIII

A pear should come to the table popped with juice,
Ripened in warmth and served in warmth. On terms
Like these, autumn beguiles the fatalist.

XXIX

Choke every ghost with acted violence,
Stamp down the phosphorescent toes, tear off
The spittling tissues tight across the bones.
The heavy bells are tolling rowdy-dow.

XXX

The hen-cock crows at midnight and lays no egg,
The cock-hen crows all day. But cockerel shrieks,
Hen shudders: the copious egg is made and laid.

XXXI

A teeming millpond or a furious mind.
Gray grasses rolling windily away
And bristling thorn-trees spinning on the bank
The actual is a deft beneficence.

XXXII

Poetry is a finikin thing of air
That lives uncertainly and not for long
Yet radiantly beyond much lustier blurs.

XXXIII

For all his purple, the purple bird must have
Notes for his comfort that he may repeat
Through the gross tedium of being rare.

155

XXXIV

A calm November. Sunday in the fields.
A reflection stagnant in a stagnant stream.
Yet invisible currents clearly circulate.

XXXV

Men and the affairs of men seldom concerned
This pundit of the weather, who never ceased
To think of man the abstraction, the comic sum.

XXXVI

The children will be crying on the stair,
Half-way to bed, when the phrase will be spoken,
The starry voluptuary will be born.

XXXVII

Yesterday the roses were rising upward,
Pushing their buds above the dark green leaves,
Noble in autumn, yet nobler than autumn.

XXXVIII

The album of Corot is premature.
A little later when the sky is black.
Mist that is golden is not wholly mist.

XXXIX

Not the ocean of the virtuosi
But the ugly alien, the mask that speaks
Things unintelligible, yet understood.

XL

Always the standard repertoire in line
And that would be perfection, if each began
Not by beginning but at the last man's end.

XLI

The chrysanthemums' astringent fragrance comes
Each year to disguise the clanking mechanism
Of machine within machine within machine.

XLII

God of the sausage-makers, sacred guild,
Or possibly, the merest patron saint
Ennobled as in a mirror to sanctity.

XLIII

It is curious that the density of life
On a given plane is ascertainable
By dividing the number of legs one sees by two.
At least the number of people may thus be fixed.

XLIV

Freshness is more than the east wind blowing round one.
There is no such thing as innocence in autumn,
Yet, it may be, innocence is never lost.

XLV

Encore un instant de bonheur. The words
Are a woman's words, unlikely to satisfy
The taste of even a country connoisseur.

XLVI

Everything ticks like a clock. The cabinet
Of a man gone mad, after all, for time, in spite
Of the cuckoos, a man with a mania for clocks.

XLVII

The sun is seeking something bright to shine on.
The trees are wooden, the grass is yellow and thin.

The ponds are not the surfaces it seeks.
It must create its colors out of itself.

XLVIII

Music is not yet written but is to be.
The preparation is long and of long intent
For the time when sound shall be subtler than we our-
   selves.

XLIX

It needed the heavy nights of drenching weather
To make him return to people, to find among them
Whatever it was that he found in their absence,
A pleasure, an indulgence, an infatuation.

L

Union of the weakest develops strength
Not wisdom. Can all men, together, avenge
One of the leaves that have fallen in autumn?
But the wise man avenges by building his city in snow.

❉❉❉❉❉❉❉❉❉❉❉❉❉❉❉❉❉❉❉❉❉❉❉❉❉❉❉❉❉❉❉❉❉❉❉

A POSTCARD FROM THE VOLCANO

Children picking up our bones
Will never know that these were once
As quick as foxes on the hill;

And that in autumn, when the grapes
Made sharp air sharper by their smell
These had a being, breathing frost;

And least will guess that with our bones
We left much more, left what still is
The look of things, left what we felt

At what we saw. The spring clouds blow
Above the shuttered mansion-house,
Beyond our gate and the windy sky

Cries out a literate despair.
We knew for long the mansion's look
And what we said of it became

A part of what it is . . . Children,
Still weaving budded aureoles,
Will speak our speech and never know,

Will say of the mansion that it seems
As if he that lived there left behind
A spirit storming in blank walls,

A dirty house in a gutted world,
A tatter of shadows peaked to white,
Smeared with the gold of the opulent sun.

AUTUMN REFRAIN

The skreak and skritter of evening gone
And grackles gone and sorrows of the sun,
The sorrows of sun, too, gone . . . the moon and
    moon,
The yellow moon of words about the nightingale
In measureless measures, not a bird for me
But the name of a bird and the name of a nameless air
I have never—shall never hear. And yet beneath
The stillness of everything gone, and being still,
Being and sitting still, something resides,
Some skreaking and skrittering residuum,
And grates these evasions of the nightingale
Though I have never—shall never hear that bird.
And the stillness is in the key, all of it is,
The stillness is all in the key of that desolate sound.

A FISH–SCALE SUNRISE

Melodious skeletons, for all of last night's music
Today is today and the dancing is done.

Dew lies on the instruments of straw that you were playing,
The ruts in your empty road are red.

You Jim and you Margaret and you singer of La Paloma,
The cocks are crowing and crowing loud,

And although my mind perceives the force behind the mo-
      ment,
The mind is smaller than the eye.

The sun rises green and blue in the fields and in the heavens.
The clouds foretell a swampy rain.

GALLANT CHÂTEAU

Is it bad to have come here
And to have found the bed empty?

One might have found tragic hair,
Bitter eyes, hands hostile and cold.

There might have been a light on a book
Lighting a pitiless verse or two.

There might have been the immense solitude
Of the wind upon the curtains.

Pitiless verse? A few words tuned
And tuned and tuned and tuned.

It is good. The bed is empty,
The curtains are stiff and prim and still.

DELIGHTFUL EVENING

A very felicitous eve,
Herr Doktor, and that's enough,
Though the brow in your palm may grieve

At the vernacular of light
(Omitting reefs of cloud):
Empurpled garden grass;

The spruces' outstretched hands;
The twilight overfull
Of wormy metaphors.

THE MAN
WITH THE BLUE GUITAR

THE MAN WITH THE BLUE GUITAR

I

The man bent over his guitar,
A shearsman of sorts. The day was green.

They said, "You have a blue guitar,
You do not play things as they are."

The man replied, "Things as they are
Are changed upon the blue guitar."

And they said then, "But play, you must,
A tune beyond us, yet ourselves,

A tune upon the blue guitar
Of things exactly as they are."

II

I cannot bring a world quite round,
Although I patch it as I can.

I sing a hero's head, large eye
And bearded bronze, but not a man,

Although I patch him as I can
And reach through him almost to man.

If to serenade almost to man
Is to miss, by that, things as they are,

165

Say that it is the serenade
Of a man that plays a blue guitar.

III

Ah, but to play man number one,
To drive the dagger in his heart,

To lay his brain upon the board
And pick the acrid colors out,

To nail his thought across the door,
Its wings spread wide to rain and snow,

To strike his living hi and ho,
To tick it, tock it, turn it true,

To bang it from a savage blue,
Jangling the metal of the strings . . .

IV

So that's life, then: things as they are?
It picks its way on the blue guitar.

A million people on one string?
And all their manner in the thing,

And all their manner, right and wrong,
And all their manner, weak and strong?

The feelings crazily, craftily call,
Like a buzzing of flies in autumn air,

And that's life, then: things as they are,
This buzzing of the blue guitar.

V

Do not speak to us of the greatness of poetry,
Of the torches wisping in the underground,

Of the structure of vaults upon a point of light.
There are no shadows in our sun,

Day is desire and night is sleep.
There are no shadows anywhere.

The earth, for us, is flat and bare.
There are no shadows. Poetry

Exceeding music must take the place
Of empty heaven and its hymns,

Ourselves in poetry must take their place,
Even in the chattering of your guitar.

VI

A tune beyond us as we are,
Yet nothing changed by the blue guitar;

Ourselves in the tune as if in space,
Yet nothing changed, except the place

Of things as they are and only the place
As you play them, on the blue guitar,

167

Placed, so, beyond the compass of change,
Perceived in a final atmosphere;

For a moment final, in the way
The thinking of art seems final when

The thinking of god is smoky dew.
The tune is space. The blue guitar

Becomes the place of things as they are,
A composing of senses of the guitar.

VII

It is the sun that shares our works.
The moon shares nothing. It is a sea.

When shall I come to say of the sun,
It is a sea; it shares nothing;

The sun no longer shares our works
And the earth is alive with creeping men,

Mechanical beetles never quite warm?
And shall I then stand in the sun, as now

I stand in the moon, and call it good,
The immaculate, the merciful good,

Detached from us, from things as they are?
Not to be part of the sun? To stand

Remote and call it merciful?
The strings are cold on the blue guitar.

The vivid, florid, turgid sky,
The drenching thunder rolling by,

The morning deluged still by night,
The clouds tumultuously bright

And the feeling heavy in cold chords
Struggling toward impassioned choirs,

Crying among the clouds, enraged
By gold antagonists in air—

I know my lazy, leaden twang
Is like the reason in a storm;

And yet it brings the storm to bear.
I twang it out and leave it there.

IX
And the color, the overcast blue
Of the air, in which the blue guitar

Is a form, described but difficult,
And I am merely a shadow hunched

Above the arrowy, still strings,
The maker of a thing yet to be made;

The color like a thought that grows
Out of a mood, the tragic robe

169

Of the actor, half his gesture, half
His speech, the dress of his meaning, silk

Sodden with his melancholy words,
The weather of his stage, himself.

x

Raise reddest columns. Toll a bell
And clap the hollows full of tin.

Throw papers in the streets, the wills
Of the dead, majestic in their seals.

And the beautiful trombones—behold
The approach of him whom none believes,

Whom all believe that all believe,
A pagan in a varnished car.

Roll a drum upon the blue guitar.
Lean from the steeple. Cry aloud,

"Here am I, my adversary, that
Confront you, hoo-ing the slick trombones,

Yet with a petty misery
At heart, a petty misery,

Ever the prelude to your end,
The touch that topples men and rock."

XI

Slowly the ivy on the stones
Becomes the stones. Women become

170

The cities, children become the fields
And men in waves become the sea.

It is the chord that falsifies.
The sea returns upon the men,

The fields entrap the children, brick
Is a weed and all the flies are caught,

Wingless and withered, but living alive.
The discord merely magnifies.

Deeper within the belly's dark
Of time, time grows upon the rock.

XII

Tom-tom, c'est moi. The blue guitar
And I are one. The orchestra

Fills the high hall with shuffling men
High as the hall. The whirling noise

Of a multitude dwindles, all said,
To his breath that lies awake at night.

I know that timid breathing. Where
Do I begin and end? And where,

As I strum the thing, do I pick up
That which momentously declares

Itself not to be I and yet
Must be. It could be nothing else.

171

XIII

The pale intrusions into blue
Are corrupting pallors . . . ay di mi,

Blue buds or pitchy blooms. Be content—
Expansions, diffusions—content to be

The unspotted imbecile revery,
The heraldic center of the world

Of blue, blue sleek with a hundred chins,
The amorist Adjective aflame . . .

XIV

First one beam, then another, then
A thousand are radiant in the sky.

Each is both star and orb; and day
Is the riches of their atmosphere.

The sea appends its tattery hues.
The shores are banks of muffling mist.

One says a German chandelier—
A candle is enough to light the world.

It makes it clear. Even at noon
It glistens in essential dark.

At night, it lights the fruit and wine,
The book and bread, things as they are,

In a chiaroscuro where
One sits and plays the blue guitar.

172

XV

Is this picture of Picasso's, this "hoard
Of destructions," a picture of ourselves,

Now, an image of our society?
Do I sit, deformed, a naked egg,

Catching at Good-bye, harvest moon,
Without seeing the harvest or the moon?

Things as they are have been destroyed.
Have I? Am I a man that is dead

At a table on which the food is cold?
Is my thought a memory, not alive?

Is the spot on the floor, there, wine or blood
And whichever it may be, is it mine?

XVI

The earth is not earth but a stone,
Not the mother that held men as they fell

But stone, but like a stone, no: not
The mother, but an oppressor, but like

An oppressor that grudges them their death,
As it grudges the living that they live.

To live in war, to live at war,
To chop the sullen psaltery,

173

To improve the sewers in Jerusalem,
To electrify the nimbuses—

Place honey on the altars and die,
You lovers that are bitter at heart.

XVII

The person has a mould. But not
Its animal. The angelic ones

Speak of the soul, the mind. It is
An animal. The blue guitar—

On that its claws propound, its **fangs**
Articulate its desert days.

The blue guitar a mould? That shell?
Well, after all, the north wind blows

A horn, on which its victory
Is a worm composing on a straw.

XVIII

A dream (to call it a dream) in which
I can believe, in face of the object,

A dream no longer a dream, a thing,
Of things as they are, as the blue guitar

After long strumming on certain nights
Gives the touch of the senses, not of the hand,

174

But the very senses as they touch
The wind-gloss. Or as daylight comes,

Like light in a mirroring of cliffs,
Rising upward from a sea of ex.

XIX

That I may reduce the monster to
Myself, and then may be myself

In face of the monster, be more than part
Of it, more than the monstrous player of

One of its monstrous lutes, not be
Alone, but reduce the monster and be,

Two things, the two together as one,
And play of the monster and of myself,

Or better not of myself at all,
But of that as its intelligence,

Being the lion in the lute
Before the lion locked in stone.

XX

What is there in life except one's ideas,
Good air, good friend, what is there in life?

Is it ideas that I believe?
Good air, my only friend, believe,

Believe would be a brother full
Of love, believe would be a friend,

175

Friendlier than my only friend,
Good air. Poor pale, poor pale guitar . . .

XXI
A substitute for all the gods:
This self, not that gold self aloft,

Alone, one's shadow magnified,
Lord of the body, looking down,

As now and called most high,
The shadow of Chocorua

In an immenser heaven, aloft,
Alone, lord of the land and lord

Of the men that live in the land, high lord.
One's self and the mountains of one's land,

Without shadows, without magnificence,
The flesh, the bone, the dirt, the stone.

XXII
Poetry is the subject of the poem,
From this the poem issues and

To this returns. Between the two,
Between issue and return, there is

An absence in reality,
Things as they are. Or so we say.

176

But are these separate? Is it
An absence for the poem, which acquires

Its true appearances there, sun's green,
Cloud's red, earth feeling, sky that thinks?

From these it takes. Perhaps it gives,
In the universal intercourse.

XXIII

A few final solutions, like a duet
With the undertaker: a voice in the clouds,

Another on earth, the one a voice
Of ether, the other smelling of drink,

The voice of ether prevailing, the swell
Of the undertaker's song in the snow

Apostrophizing wreaths, the voice
In the clouds serene and final, next

The grunted breath serene and final,
The imagined and the real, thought

And the truth, Dichtung und Wahrheit, all
Confusion solved, as in a refrain

One keeps on playing year by year,
Concerning the nature of things as they are.

XXIV

A poem like a missal found
In the mud, a missal for that young man,

177

That scholar hungriest for that book,
The very book, or, less, a page

Or, at the least, a phrase, that phrase,
A hawk of life, that latined phrase:

To know; a missal for brooding-sight.
To meet that hawk's eye and to flinch

Not at the eye but at the joy of it.
I play. But this is what I think.

xxv

He held the world upon his nose
And this-a-way he gave a fling.

His robes and symbols, ai-yi-yi—
And that-a-way he twirled the thing.

Sombre as fir-trees, liquid cats
Moved in the grass without a sound.

They did not know the grass went round.
The cats had cats and the grass turned gray

And the world had worlds, ai, this-a-way:
The grass turned green and the grass turned gray.

And the nose is eternal, that-a-way.
Things as they were, things as they are,

Things as they will be by and by . . .
A fat thumb beats out ai-yi-yi.

XXVI

The world washed in his imagination,
The world was a shore, whether sound or form

Or light, the relic of farewells,
Rock, of valedictory echoings,

To which his imagination returned,
From which it sped, a bar in space,

Sand heaped in the clouds, giant that fought
Against the murderous alphabet:

The swarm of thoughts, the swarm of dreams
Of inaccessible Utopia.

A mountainous music always seemed
To be falling and to be passing away.

XXVII

It is the sea that whitens the roof.
The sea drifts through the winter air.

It is the sea that the north wind makes.
The sea is in the falling snow.

This gloom is the darkness of the sea.
Geographers and philosophers,

Regard. But for that salty cup,
But for the icicles on the eaves—

The sea is a form of ridicule.
The iceberg settings satirize

The demon that cannot be himself,
That tours to shift the shifting scene.

XXVIII

I am a native in this world
And think in it as a native thinks,

Gesu, not native of a mind
Thinking the thoughts I call my own,

Native, a native in the world
And like a native think in it.

It could not be a mind, the wave
In which the watery grasses flow

And yet are fixed as a photograph,
The wind in which the dead leaves blow.

Here I inhale profounder strength
And as I am, I speak and move

And things are as I think they are
And say they are on the blue guitar.

XXIX

In the cathedral, I sat there, and read,
Alone, a lean Review and said,

"These degustations in the vaults
Oppose the past and the festival,

What is beyond the cathedral, outside,
Balances with nuptial song.

So it is to sit and to balance things
To and to and to the point of still,

To say of one mask it is like,
To say of another it is like,

To know that the balance does not quite rest,
That the mask is strange, however like."

The shapes are wrong and the sounds are false.
The bells are the bellowing of bulls.

Yet Franciscan don was never more
Himself than in this fertile glass.

xxx

From this I shall evolve a man.
This is his essence: the old fantoche

Hanging his shawl upon the wind,
Like something on the stage, puffed out,

His strutting studied through centuries.
At last, in spite of his manner, his eye

A-cock at the cross-piece on a pole
Supporting heavy cables, slung

181

Through Oxidia, banal suburb,
One-half of all its installments paid.

Dew-dapper clapper-traps, blazing
From crusty stacks above machines.

Ecce, Oxidia is the seed
Dropped out of this amber-ember pod,

Oxidia is the soot of fire,
Oxidia is Olympia.

XXXI

How long and late the pheasant sleeps . . .
The employer and employee contend,

Combat, compose their droll affair.
The bubbling sun will bubble up,

Spring sparkle and the cock-bird shriek.
The employer and employee will hear

And continue their affair. The shriek
Will rack the thickets. There is no place,

Here, for the lark fixed in the mind,
In the museum of the sky. The cock

Will claw sleep. Morning is not sun,
It is this posture of the nerves,

As if a blunted player clutched
The nuances of the blue guitar.

It must be this rhapsody or none,
The rhapsody of things as they are.

XXXII

Throw away the lights, the definitions,
And say of what you see in the dark

That it is this or that it is that,
But do not use the rotted names.

How should you walk in that space and know
Nothing of the madness of space,

Nothing of its jocular procreations?
Throw the lights away. Nothing must stand

Between you and the shapes you take
When the crust of shape has been destroyed.

You as you are? You are yourself.
The blue guitar surprises you.

XXXIII

That generation's dream, aviled
In the mud, in Monday's dirty light,

That's it, the only dream they knew,
Time in its final block, not time

To come, a wrangling of two dreams.
Here is the bread of time to come,

Here is its actual stone. The bread
Will be our bread, the stone will be

Our bed and we shall sleep by night.
We shall forget by day, except

The moments when we choose to play
The imagined pine, the imagined jay.

❁❁❁❁❁❁❁❁❁❁❁❁❁❁❁❁❁❁❁❁❁❁❁❁❁❁❁

A THOUGHT REVOLVED

I

The Mechanical Optimist

A lady dying of diabetes
Listened to the radio,
Catching the lesser dithyrambs.
So heaven collects its bleating lambs.

Her useless bracelets fondly fluttered,
Paddling the melodic swirls,
The idea of god no longer sputtered
At the roots of her indifferent curls.

The idea of the Alps grew large,
Not yet, however, a thing to die in.
It seemed serener just to die,
To float off in the floweriest barge,

Accompanied by the exegesis
Of familiar things in a cheerful voice,
Like the night before Christmas and all the carols.
Dying lady, rejoice, rejoice!

II

Mystic Garden & Middling Beast

The poet striding among the cigar stores,
Ryan's lunch, hatters, insurance and medicines,
Denies that abstraction is a vice except
To the fatuous. These are his infernal walls,
A space of stone, of inexplicable base
And peaks outsoaring possible adjectives.
One man, the idea of man, that is the space,
The true abstract in which he promenades.
The era of the idea of man, the cloak
And speech of Virgil dropped, that's where he walks,
That's where his hymns come crowding, hero-hymns,
Chorals for mountain voices and the moral chant,
Happy rather than holy but happy-high,
Day hymns instead of constellated rhymes,
Hymns of the struggle of the idea of god
And the idea of man, the mystic garden and
The middling beast, the garden of paradise
And he that created the garden and peopled it.

III

Romanesque Affabulation

He sought an earthly leader who could stand
Without panache, without cockade,
Son only of man and sun of men,
The outer captain, the inner saint,

The pine, the pillar and the priest,
The voice, the book, the hidden well,
The faster's feast and heavy-fruited star,
The father, the beater of the rigid drums,

He that at midnight touches the guitar,
The solitude, the barrier, the Pole
In Paris, celui qui chante et pleure,
Winter devising summer in its breast,

Summer assaulted, thundering, illumed,
Shelter yet thrower of the summer spear,
With all his attributes no god but man
Of men whose heaven is in themselves,

Or else whose hell, foamed with their blood
And the long echo of their dying cry,
A fate intoned, a death before they die,
The race that sings and weeps and knows not why.

IV

The Leader

Behold the moralist hidalgo
Whose whore is Morning Star
Dressed in metal, silk and stone,
Syringa, cicada, his flea.

In how severe a book he read,
Until his nose grew thin and taut
And knowledge dropped upon his heart
Its pitting poison, half the night.

186

He liked the nobler works of man,
The gold façade round early squares,
The bronzes liquid through gay light.
He hummed to himself at such a plan.

He sat among beggars wet with dew,
Heard the dogs howl at barren bone,
Sat alone, his great toe like a horn,
The central flaw in the solar morn.

◇◇◇

THE MEN THAT ARE FALLING

God and all angels sing the world to sleep,
Now that the moon is rising in the heat

And crickets are loud again in the grass. The moon
Burns in the mind on lost remembrances.

He lies down and the night wind blows upon him
    here.
The bells grow longer. This is not sleep. This is
    desire.

Ah! Yes, desire . . . this leaning on his bed,
This leaning on his elbows on his bed,

Staring, at midnight, at the pillow that is black
In the catastrophic room . . . beyond despair,

Like an intenser instinct. What is it he desires?
But this he cannot know, the man that thinks,

Yet life itself, the fulfilment of desire
In the grinding ric-rac, staring steadily

At a head upon the pillow in the dark,
More than sudarium, speaking the speech

Of absolutes, bodiless, a head
Thick-lipped from riot and rebellious cries,

The head of one of the men that are falling, placed
Upon the pillow to repose and speak,

Speak and say the immaculate syllables
That he spoke only by doing what he did.

God and all angels, this was his desire,
Whose head lies blurring here, for this he died.

Taste of the blood upon his martyred lips,
O pensioners, O demagogues and pay-men!

This death was his belief though death is a stone.
This man loved earth, not heaven, enough to die.

The night wind blows upon the dreamer, bent
Over words that are life's voluble utterance.

PARTS OF A WORLD

PAROCHIAL THEME

Long-tailed ponies go nosing the pine-lands,
Ponies of Parisians shooting on the hill.

The wind blows. In the wind, the voices
Have shapes that are not yet fully themselves,

Are sounds blown by a blower into shapes,
The blower squeezed to the thinnest *mi* of falsetto.

The hunters run to and fro. The heavy trees,
The grunting, shuffling branches, the robust,

The nocturnal, the antique, the blue-green pines
Deepen the feelings to inhuman depths.

These are the forest. This health is holy,
This halloo, halloo, halloo heard over the cries

Of those for whom a square room is a fire,
Of those whom the statues torture and keep down.

This health is holy, this descant of a self,
This barbarous chanting of what is strong, this blare.

But salvation here? What about the rattle of sticks
On tins and boxes? What about horses eaten by wind?

When spring comes and the skeletons of the hunters
Stretch themselves to rest in their first summer's sun,

The spring will have a health of its own, with none
Of autumn's halloo in its hair. So that closely, then,

Health follows after health. Salvation there:
There's no such thing as life; or if there is,

It is faster than the weather, faster than
Any character. It is more than any scene:

Of the guillotine or of any glamorous hanging.
Piece the world together, boys, but not with your
    hands.

POETRY IS A DESTRUCTIVE FORCE

That's what misery is,
Nothing to have at heart.
It is to have or nothing.

It is a thing to have,
A lion, an ox in his breast,
To feel it breathing there.

Corazon, stout dog,
Young ox, bow-legged bear,
He tastes its blood, not spit.

192

He is like a man
In the body of a violent beast.
Its muscles are his own . . .

The lion sleeps in the sun.
Its nose is on its paws.
It can kill a man.

◇◇

THE POEMS OF OUR CLIMATE

I

Clear water in a brilliant bowl,
Pink and white carnations. The light
In the room more like a snowy air,
Reflecting snow. A newly-fallen snow
At the end of winter when afternoons return.
Pink and white carnations—one desires
So much more than that. The day itself
Is simplified: a bowl of white,
Cold, a cold porcelain, low and round,
With nothing more than the carnations there.

II

Say even that this complete simplicity
Stripped one of all one's torments, concealed
The evilly compounded, vital I
And made it fresh in a world of white,

193

A world of clear water, brilliant-edged,
Still one would want more, one would need more,
More than a world of white and snowy scents.

III

There would still remain the never-resting mind,
So that one would want to escape, come back
To what had been so long composed.
The imperfect is our paradise.
Note that, in this bitterness, delight,
Since the imperfect is so hot in us,
Lies in flawed words and stubborn sounds.

❀◇

PRELUDE TO OBJECTS

I

If he will be heaven after death,
If, while he lives, he hears himself
Sounded in music, if the sun,
Stormer, is the color of a self
As certainly as night is the color
Of a self, if, without sentiment,
He is what he hears and sees and if,
Without pathos, he feels what he hears
And sees, being nothing otherwise,
Having nothing otherwise, he has not
To go to the Louvre to behold himself.

Granted each picture is a glass,
That the walls are mirrors multiplied,
That the marbles are gluey pastiches, the stairs
The sweep of an impossible elegance,
And the notorious views from the windows
Wax wasted, monarchies beyond
The S.S. *Normandie*, granted
One is always seeing and feeling oneself,
That's not by chance. It comes to this:
That the guerilla I should be booked
And bound. Its nigger mystics should change
Foolscap for wigs. Academies
As of a tragic science should rise.

II

Poet, patting more nonsense foamed
From the sea, conceive for the courts
Of these academies, the diviner health
Disclosed in common forms. Set up
The rugged black, the image. Design
The touch. Fix quiet. Take the place
Of parents, lewdest of ancestors.
We are conceived in your conceits.

195

STUDY OF TWO PEARS

I

Opusculum paedagogum.
The pears are not viols,
Nudes or bottles.
They resemble nothing else.

II

They are yellow forms
Composed of curves
Bulging toward the base.
They are touched red.

III

They are not flat surfaces
Having curved outlines.
They are round
Tapering toward the top.

IV

In the way they are modelled
There are bits of blue.
A hard dry leaf hangs
From the stem.

V

The yellow glistens.
It glistens with various yellows,

Citrons, oranges and greens
Flowering over the skin.

VI

The shadows of the pears
Are blobs on the green cloth.
The pears are not seen
As the observer wills.

◇◇

THE GLASS OF WATER

That the glass would melt in heat,
That the water would freeze in cold,
Shows that this object is merely a state,
One of many, between two poles. So,
In the metaphysical, there are these poles.

Here in the centre stands the glass. Light
Is the lion that comes down to drink. There
And in that state, the glass is a pool.
Ruddy are his eyes and ruddy are his claws
When light comes down to wet his frothy jaws

And in the water winding weeds move round.
And there and in another state—the refractions,
The *metaphysica*, the plastic parts of poems
Crash in the mind—But, fat Jocundus, worrying
About what stands here in the centre, not the glass,

197

But in the centre of our lives, this time, this day,
It is a state, this spring among the politicians
Playing cards. In a village of the indigenes,
One would have still to discover. Among the dogs
     and dung,
One would continue to contend with one's ideas.

❀◇

ADD THIS TO RHETORIC

It is posed and it is posed.
But in nature it merely grows.
Stones pose in the falling night;
And beggars dropping to sleep,
They pose themselves and their rags.
Shucks . . . lavender moonlight falls.
The buildings pose in the sky
And, as you paint, the clouds,
Grisaille, impearled, profound,
Pftt. . . . In the way you speak
You arrange, the thing is posed,
What in nature merely grows.

To-morrow when the sun,
For all your images,
Comes up as the sun, bull fire,
Your images will have left
No shadow of themselves.

198

The poses of speech, of paint,
Of music—Her body lies
Worn out, her arm falls down,
Her fingers touch the ground.
Above her, to the left,
A brush of white, the obscure,
The moon without a shape,
A fringed eye in a crypt.
The sense creates the pose.
In this it moves and speaks.
This is the figure and not
An evading metaphor.

Add this. It is to add.

DRY LOAF

It is equal to living in a tragic land
To live in a tragic time.
Regard now the sloping, mountainous rocks
And the river that batters its way over stones,
Regard the hovels of those that live in this land.

That was what I painted behind the loaf,
The rocks not even touched by snow,
The pines along the river and the dry men blown

Brown as the bread, thinking of birds
Flying from burning countries and brown sand
    shores,

Birds that came like dirty water in waves
Flowing above the rocks, flowing over the sky,
As if the sky was a current that bore them along,
Spreading them as waves spread flat on the shore,
One after another washing the mountains bare.

It was the battering of drums I heard
It was hunger, it was the hungry that cried
And the waves, the waves were soldiers moving,
Marching and marching in a tragic time
Below me, on the asphalt, under the trees.

It was soldiers went marching over the rocks
And still the birds came, came in watery flocks,
Because it was spring and the birds had to come.
No doubt that soldiers had to be marching
And that drums had to be rolling, rolling, rolling.

◇◇

IDIOM OF THE HERO

I heard two workers say, "This chaos
Will soon be ended."

This chaos will not be ended,
The red and the blue house blended,

Not ended, never and never ended,
The weak man mended,

The man that is poor at night
Attended

Like the man that is rich and right.
The great men will not be blended . . .

I am the poorest of all.
I know that I cannot be mended,

Out of the clouds, pomp of the air,
By which at least I am befriended.

✿◇

THE MAN ON THE DUMP

Day creeps down. The moon is creeping up.
The sun is a corbeil of flowers the moon Blanche
Places there, a bouquet. Ho-ho . . . The dump is full
Of images. Days pass like papers from a press.
The bouquets come here in the papers. So the sun,
And so the moon, both come, and the janitor's poems
Of every day, the wrapper on the can of pears,
The cat in the paper-bag, the corset, the box
From Esthonia: the tiger chest, for tea.

The freshness of night has been fresh a long time.
The freshness of morning, the blowing of day, one says
That it puffs as Cornelius Nepos reads, it puffs
More than, less than or it puffs like this or that.
The green smacks in the eye, the dew in the green
Smacks like fresh water in a can, like the sea
On a cocoanut—how many men have copied dew
For buttons, how many women have covered them-
    selves
With dew, dew dresses, stones and chains of dew, heads
Of the floweriest flowers dewed with the dewiest dew.
One grows to hate these things except on the dump.

Now, in the time of spring (azaleas, trilliums,
Myrtle, viburnums, daffodils, blue phlox),
Between that disgust and this, between the things
That are on the dump (azaleas and so on)
And those that will be (azaleas and so on),
One feels the purifying change. One rejects
The trash.

        That's the moment when the moon creeps up
To the bubbling of bassoons. That's the time
One looks at the elephant-colorings of tires.
Everything is shed; and the moon comes up as the moon
(All its images are in the dump) and you see
As a man (not like an image of a man),
You see the moon rise in the empty sky.

One sits and beats an old tin can, lard pail.
One beats and beats for that which one believes.
That's what one wants to get near. Could it after all

Be merely oneself, as superior as the ear
To a crow's voice? Did the nightingale torture the ear,
Pack the heart and scratch the mind? And does the ear
Solace itself in peevish birds? Is it peace,
Is it a philosopher's honeymoon, one finds
On the dump? Is it to sit among mattresses of the dead,
Bottles, pots, shoes and grass and murmur *aptest eve:*
Is it to hear the blatter of grackles and say
Invisible priest; is it to eject, to pull
The day to pieces and cry *stanza my stone?*
Where was it one first heard of the truth? The the.

❀❀❀❀❀❀❀❀❀❀❀❀❀❀❀❀❀❀❀❀❀❀❀❀❀❀❀❀❀

ON THE ROAD HOME

It was when I said,
"There is no such thing as the truth,"
That the grapes seemed fatter.
The fox ran out of his hole.

You . . . You said,
"There are many truths,
But they are not parts of a truth."
Then the tree, at night, began to change,

Smoking through green and smoking blue.
We were two figures in a wood.
We said we stood alone.

It was when I said,
"Words are not forms of a single word.
In the sum of the parts, there are only the parts.
The world must be measured by eye";

It was when you said,
"The idols have seen lots of poverty,
Snakes and gold and lice,
But not the truth";

It was at that time, that the silence was largest
And longest, the night was roundest,
The fragrance of the autumn warmest,
Closest and strongest.

THE LATEST FREED MAN

Tired of the old descriptions of the world,
The latest freed man rose at six and sat
On the edge of his bed. He said,
                            "I suppose there is
A doctrine to this landscape. Yet, having just
Escaped from the truth, the morning is color and mist,
Which is enough: the moment's rain and sea,
The moment's sun (the strong man vaguely seen),
Overtaking the doctrine of this landscape. Of him
And of his works, I am sure. He bathes in the mist

Like a man without a doctrine. The light he gives—
It is how he gives his light. It is how he shines,
Rising upon the doctors in their beds
And on their beds. . . ."
                              And so the freed man said.
It was how the sun came shining into his room:
To be without a description of to be,
For a moment on rising, at the edge of the bed, to be,
To have the ant of the self changed to an ox
With its organic boomings, to be changed
From a doctor into an ox, before standing up,
To know that the change and that the ox-like struggle
Come from the strength that is the strength of the sun,
Whether it comes directly or from the sun.
It was how he was free. It was how his freedom came.
It was being without description, being an ox.
It was the importance of the trees outdoors,
The freshness of the oak-leaves, not so much
That they were oak-leaves, as the way they looked.
It was everything being more real, himself
At the centre of reality, seeing it.
It was everything bulging and blazing and big in itself,
The blue of the rug, the portrait of Vidal,
Qui fait fi des joliesses banales, the chairs.

UNITED DAMES OF AMERICA

*Je tâche, en restant exact,
d'être poète.*

JULES RENARD

There are not leaves enough to cover the face
It wears. This is the way the orator spoke:
"The mass is nothing. The number of men in a mass
Of men is nothing. The mass is no greater than

The singular man of the mass. Masses produce
Each one its paradigm." There are not leaves
Enough to hide away the face of the man
Of this dead mass and that. The wind might fill

With faces as with leaves, be gusty with mouths,
And with mouths crying and crying day by day.
Could all these be ourselves, sounding ourselves,
Our faces circling round a central face

And then nowhere again, away and away?
Yet one face keeps returning (never the one),
The face of the man of the mass, never the face
That hermit on reef sable would have seen,

Never the naked politician taught
By the wise. There are not leaves enough to crown,
To cover, to crown, to cover—let it go—
The actor that will at last declaim our end.

206

COUNTRY WORDS

I sang a canto in a canton,
Cunning-coo, O, cuckoo cock,
In a canton of Belshazzar
To Belshazzar, putrid rock,
Pillar of a putrid people,
Underneath a willow there
I stood and sang and filled the air.

It was an old rebellious song,
An edge of song that never clears;
But if it did . . . If the cloud that hangs
Upon the heart and round the mind
Cleared from the north and in that height
The sun appeared and reddened great
Belshazzar's brow, O, ruler, rude
With rubies then, attend me now.

What is it that my feeling seeks?
I know from all the things it touched
And left beside and left behind.
It wants the diamond pivot bright.
It wants Belshazzar reading right
The luminous pages on his knee,
Of being, more than birth or death.
It wants words virile with his breath.

207

THE DWARF

Now it is September and the web is woven.
The web is woven and you have to wear it.

The winter is made and you have to bear it,
The winter web, the winter woven, wind and wind,

For all the thoughts of summer that go with it
In the mind, pupa of straw, moppet of rags.

It is the mind that is woven, the mind that was jerked
And tufted in straggling thunder and shattered sun.

It is all that you are, the final dwarf of you,
That is woven and woven and waiting to be worn,

Neither as mask nor as garment but as a being,
Torn from insipid summer, for the mirror of cold,

Sitting beside your lamp, there citron to nibble
And coffee dribble . . . Frost is in the stubble.

A RABBIT AS KING OF THE GHOSTS

The difficulty to think at the end of day,
When the shapeless shadow covers the sun
And nothing is left except light on your fur—

There was the cat slopping its milk all day,
Fat cat, red tongue, green mind, white milk
And August the most peaceful month.

To be, in the grass, in the peacefullest time,
Without that monument of cat,
The cat forgotten in the moon;

And to feel that the light is a rabbit-light,
In which everything is meant for you
And nothing need be explained;

Then there is nothing to think of. It comes of it-
    self;
And east rushes west and west rushes down,
No matter. The grass is full

And full of yourself. The trees around are for you,
The whole of the wideness of night is for you,
A self that touches all edges,

You become a self that fills the four corners of
    night.
The red cat hides away in the fur-light
And there you are humped high, humped up,

You are humped higher and higher, black as
    stone—
You sit with your head like a carving in space
And the little green cat is a bug in the grass.

LONELINESS IN JERSEY CITY

The deer and the dachshund are one.
Well, the gods grow out of the weather.
The people grow out of the weather;
The gods grow out of the people.
Encore, encore, encore les dieux . . .

The distance between the dark steeple
And cobble ten thousand and three
Is more than a seven-foot inchworm
Could measure by moonlight in June.

Kiss, cats: for the deer and the dachshund
Are one. My window is twenty-nine three
And plenty of window for me.
The steeples are empty and so are the people,
There's nothing whatever to see
Except Polacks that pass in their motors
And play concertinas all night.
They think that things are all right,
Since the deer and the dachshund are one.

ANYTHING IS BEAUTIFUL IF YOU SAY IT IS

Under the eglantine
The fretful concubine
Said, "Phooey! Phoo!"
She whispered, "Pfui!"

The demi-monde
On the mezzanine
Said, "Phooey!" too,
And a "Hey-de-i-do!"

The bee may have all sweet
For his honey-hive-o,
From the eglantine-o.

And the chandeliers are neat . . .
But their mignon, marblish glare!
We are cold, the parrots cried,
In a place so debonair.

The Johannisberger, Hans.
I love the metal grapes,
The rusty, battered shapes
Of the pears and of the cheese

And the window's lemon light,
The very will of the nerves,
The crack across the pane,
The dirt along the sill.

211

A WEAK MIND IN THE MOUNTAINS

There was the butcher's hand.
He squeezed it and the blood
Spurted from between the fingers
And fell to the floor.
And then the body fell.

So afterward, at night,
The wind of Iceland and
The wind of Ceylon,
Meeting, gripped my mind,
Gripped it and grappled my thoughts.

The black wind of the sea
And the green wind
Whirled upon me.
The blood of the mind fell
To the floor. I slept.

Yet there was a man within me
Could have risen to the clouds,
Could have touched these winds,
Bent and broken them down,
Could have stood up sharply in the sky.

THE BAGATELLES THE MADRIGALS

Where do you think, serpent,
Where do you lie, beneath snow,
And with eyes closed
Breathe in a crevice of earth?

In what camera do you taste
Poison, in what darkness set
Glittering scales and point
The tipping tongue?

And where is it, you, people,
Where is it that you think, baffled
By the trash of life,
Through winter's meditative light?

In what crevice do you find
Forehead's cold, spite of the eye
Seeing that which is refused,
Vengeful, shadowed by gestures

Of the life that you will not live,
Of days that will be wasted,
Of nights that will not be more than
Surly masks and destroyers?

(This is one of the thoughts
Of the mind that forms itself
Out of all the minds,
One of the songs of that dominance.)

213

GIRL IN A NIGHTGOWN

Lights out. Shades up.
A look at the weather.
There has been a booming all the spring,
A refrain from the end of the boulevards.

This is the silence of night,
This is what could not be shaken,
Full of stars and the images of stars—
And that booming wintry and dull,

Like a tottering, a falling and an end,
Again and again, always there,
Massive drums and leaden trumpets,
Perceived by feeling instead of sense,

A revolution of things colliding.
Phrases! But of fear and of fate.
The night should be warm and fluters' fortune
Should play in the trees when morning comes.

Once it was, the repose of night,
Was a place, strong place, in which to sleep.
It is shaken now. It will burst into flames,
Either now or tomorrow or the day after that.

CONNOISSEUR OF CHAOS

I

A.   A violent order is disorder; and
B.   A great disorder is an order. These
Two things are one. (Pages of illustrations.)

II

If all the green of spring was blue, and it is;
If the flowers of South Africa were bright
On the tables of Connecticut, and they are;
If Englishmen lived without tea in Ceylon, and
        they do;
And if it all went on in an orderly way,
And it does; a law of inherent opposites,
Of essential unity, is as pleasant as port,
As pleasant as the brush-strokes of a bough,
An upper, particular bough in, say, Marchand.

III

After all the pretty contrast of life and death
Proves that these opposite things partake of one,
At least that was the theory, when bishops' books
Resolved the world. We cannot go back to that.
The squirming facts exceed the squamous mind,
If one may say so. And yet relation appears,
A small relation expanding like the shade
Of a cloud on sand, a shape on the side of a hill.

215

A.   Well, an old order is a violent one.
This proves nothing. Just one more truth, one more
Element in the immense disorder of truths.
B.   It is April as I write. The wind
Is blowing after days of constant rain.
All this, of course, will come to summer soon.
But suppose the disorder of truths should ever come
To an order, most Plantagenet, most fixed . . .
A great disorder is an order. Now, A
And B are not like statuary, posed
For a vista in the Louvre. They are things chalked
On the sidewalk so that the pensive man may see.

V

The pensive man . . . He sees that eagle float
For which the intricate Alps are a single nest.

THE BLUE BUILDINGS IN THE SUMMER AIR

I

Cotton Mather died when I was a boy. The books
He read, all day, all night and all the nights,
Had got him nowhere. There was always the doubt,
That made him preach the louder, long for a church
In which his voice would roll its cadences,
After the sermon, to quiet that mouse in the wall.

216

II

Over wooden Boston, the sparkling Byzantine
Was everything that Cotton Mather was
And more. Yet the eminent thunder from the mouse,
The grinding in the arches of the church,
The plaster dropping, even dripping, down,
The mouse, the moss, the woman on the shore . . .

III

If the mouse should swallow the steeple, in its
     time . . .
It was a theologian's needle, much
Too sharp for that. The shore, the sea, the sun,
Their brilliance through the lattices, crippled
The chandeliers, their morning glazes spread
In opal blobs along the walls and floor.

IV

Look down now, Cotton Mather, from the blank.
Was heaven where you thought? It must be there.
It must be where you think it is, in the light
On bed-clothes, in an apple on a plate.
It is the honey-comb of the seeing man.
It is the leaf the bird brings back to the boat.

V

Go, mouse, go nibble at Lenin in his tomb.
Are you not le plus pur, you ancient one?
Cut summer down to find the honey-comb.
You are one . . . Go hunt for honey in his hair.
You are one of the not-numberable mice
Searching all day, all night, for the honey-comb.

217

DEZEMBRUM

I

Tonight there are only the winter stars.
The sky is no longer a junk-shop,
Full of javelins and old fire-balls,
Triangles and the names of girls.

II

Over and over again you have said,
This great world, it divides itself in two,
One part is man, the other god:
Imagined man, the monkish mask, the face.

III

Tonight the stars are like a crowd of faces
Moving round the sky and singing
And laughing, a crowd of men,
Whose singing is a mode of laughter,

IV

Never angels, nothing of the dead,
Faces to people night's brilliancy,
Laughing and singing and being happy,
Filling the imagination's need.

V

In this rigid room, an intenser love,
Not toys, not thing-a-ma-jigs—
The reason can give nothing at all
Like the response to desire.

POEM WRITTEN AT MORNING

A sunny day's complete Poussiniana
Divide it from itself. It is this or that
And it is not.
            By metaphor you paint
A thing. Thus, the pineapple was a leather fruit,
A fruit for pewter, thorned and palmed and blue,
To be served by men of ice.
                       The senses paint
By metaphor. The juice was fragranter
Than wettest cinnamon. It was cribled pears
Dripping a morning sap.
                  The truth must be
That you do not see, you experience, you feel,
That the buxom eye brings merely its element
To the total thing, a shapeless giant forced
Upward.
            Green were the curls upon that head.

THUNDER BY THE MUSICIAN

Sure enough, moving, the thunder became men,
Ten thousand, men hewn and tumbling,
Mobs of ten thousand, clashing together,
This way and that.

Slowly, one man, savager than the rest,
Rose up, tallest, in the black sun,
Stood up straight in the air, struck off
The clutch of the others.

And, according to the composer, this butcher,
Held in his hand the suave egg-diamond
That had flashed (like vicious music that ends
In transparent accords).

It would have been better, the time conceived,
To have had him holding—what?
His arm would be trembling, he would be weak,
Even though he shouted.

The sky would be full of bodies like wood.
There would have been the cries of the dead
And the living would be speaking,
As a self that lives on itself.

It would have been better for his hands
To be convulsed, to have remained the hands
Of one wilder than the rest (like music blunted,
Yet the sound of that).

THE COMMON LIFE

That's the down-town frieze,
Principally the church steeple,
A black line beside a white line;
And the stack of the electric plant,
A black line drawn on flat air.

It is a morbid light
In which they stand,
Like an electric lamp
On a page of Euclid.

In this light a man is a result,
A demonstration, and a woman,
Without rose and without violet,
The shadows that are absent from Euclid,
Is not a woman for a man.

The paper is whiter
For these black lines.
It glares beneath the webs
Of wire, the designs of ink,
The planes that ought to have genius,
The volumes like marble ruins
Outlined and having alphabetical
Notations and footnotes.
The paper is whiter.
The men have no shadows
And the women have only one side.

THE SENSE OF THE SLEIGHT-OF-HAND MAN

One's grand flights, one's Sunday baths,
One's tootings at the weddings of the soul
Occur as they occur. So bluish clouds
Occurred above the empty house and the leaves
Of the rhododendrons rattled their gold,
As if someone lived there. Such floods of white
Came bursting from the clouds. So the wind
Threw its contorted strength around the sky.

Could you have said the bluejay suddenly
Would swoop to earth? It is a wheel, the rays
Around the sun. The wheel survives the myths.
The fire eye in the clouds survives the gods.
To think of a dove with an eye of grenadine
And pines that are cornets, so it occurs,
And a little island full of geese and stars:
It may be that the ignorant man, alone,
Has any chance to mate his life with life
That is the sensual, pearly spouse, the life
That is fluent in even the wintriest bronze.

THE CANDLE A SAINT

Green is the night, green kindled and apparelled.
It is she that walks among astronomers.

She strides above the rabbit and the cat,
Like a noble figure, out of the sky,

Moving among the sleepers, the men,
Those that lie chanting *green is the night*.

Green is the night and out of madness woven,
The self-same madness of the astronomers

And of him that sees, beyond the astronomers,
The topaz rabbit and the emerald cat,

That sees above them, that sees rise up above them,
The noble figure, the essential shadow,

Moving and being, the image at its source,
The abstract, the archaic queen. Green is the night.

A DISH OF PEACHES IN RUSSIA

With my whole body I taste these peaches,
I touch them and smell them. Who speaks?

I absorb them as the Angevine
Absorbs Anjou. I see them as a lover sees,

As a young lover sees the first buds of spring
And as the black Spaniard plays his guitar.

Who speaks? But it must be that I,
That animal, that Russian, that exile, for whom

The bells of the chapel pullulate sounds at
Heart. The peaches are large and round,

Ah! and red; and they have peach fuzz, ah!
They are full of juice and the skin is soft.

They are full of the colors of my village
And of fair weather, summer, dew, peace.

The room is quiet where they are.
The windows are open. The sunlight fills

The curtains. Even the drifting of the curtains,
Slight as it is, disturbs me. I did not know

That such ferocities could tear
One self from another, as these peaches do.

ARCADES OF PHILADELPHIA THE PAST

Only the rich remember the past,
The strawberries once in the Apennines,
Philadelphia that the spiders ate.

There they sit, holding their eyes in their hands.
Queer, in this Vallombrosa of ears,
That they never hear the past. To see,
To hear, to touch, to taste, to smell, that's now,
That's this. Do they touch the thing they see,
Feel the wind of it, smell the dust of it?
They do not touch it. Sounds never rise
Out of what they see. They polish their eyes
In their hands. The lilacs came long after.
But the town and the fragrance were never one,
Though the blue bushes bloomed—and bloom,
Still bloom in the agate eyes, red blue,
Red purple, never quite red itself.
The tongue, the fingers, and the nose
Are comic trash, the ears are dirt,
But the eyes are men in the palm of the hand.

This? A man must be very poor
With a single sense, though he smells clouds,
Or to see the sea on Sunday, or
To touch a woman cadaverous,
Of poorness as an earth, to taste
Dry seconds and insipid thirds,
To hear himself and not to speak.

The strawberries once in the Apennines . . .
They seem a little painted, now.
The mountains are scratched and used, clear fakes.

❀❀❀❀❀❀❀❀❀❀❀❀❀❀❀❀❀❀❀❀❀❀❀❀❀❀❀❀

OF HARTFORD IN A PURPLE LIGHT

A long time you have been making the trip
From Havre to Hartford, Master Soleil,
Bringing the lights of Norway and all that.

A long time the ocean has come with you,
Shaking the water off, like a poodle,
That splatters incessant thousands of drops,

Each drop a petty tricolor. For this,
The aunts in Pasadena, remembering,
Abhor the plaster of the western horses,

Souvenirs of museums. But, Master, there are
Lights masculine and lights feminine.
What is this purple, this parasol,

This stage-light of the Opera?
It is like a region full of intonings.
It is Hartford seen in a purple light.

A moment ago, light masculine,
Working, with big hands, on the town,
Arranged its heroic attitudes.

But now as in an amour of women
Purple sets purple round. Look, Master,
See the river, the railroad, the cathedral . . .

When male light fell on the naked back
Of the town, the river, the railroad were clear.
Now, every muscle slops away.

Hi! Whisk it, poodle, flick the spray
Of the ocean, ever-freshening,
On the irised hunks, the stone bouquet.

◇◇

CUISINE BOURGEOISE

These days of disinheritance, we feast
On human heads. True, birds rebuild
Old nests and there is blue in the woods.
The church bells clap one night in the week.
But that's all done. It is what used to be,
As they used to lie in the grass, in the heat,
Men on green beds and women half of sun.
The words are written, though not yet said.

It is like the season when, after summer,
It is summer and it is not, it is autumn
And it is not, it is day and it not,
As if last night's lamps continued to burn,
As if yesterday's people continued to watch
The sky, half porcelain, preferring that
To shaking out heavy bodies in the glares
Of this present, this science, this unrecognized,

This outpost, this douce, this dumb, this dead, in
    which
We feast on human heads, brought in on leaves,
Crowned with the first, cold buds. On these we live,
No longer on the ancient cake of seed,
The almond and deep fruit. This bitter meat
Sustains us . . . Who, then, are they, seated here?
Is the table a mirror in which they sit and look?
Are they men eating reflections of themselves?

FORCES, THE WILL & THE WEATHER

At the time of nougats, the peer yellow
Sighed in the evening that he lived
Without ideas in a land without ideas,
The pair yellow, the peer.

It was at the time, the place, of nougats.
There the dogwoods, the white ones and the pink
    ones,

228

Bloomed in sheets, as they bloom, and the girl,
A pink girl took a white dog walking.

The dog had to walk. He had to be taken.
The girl had to hold back and lean back to hold him,
At the time of the dogwoods, handfuls thrown up
To spread colors. There was not an idea

This side of Moscow. There were anti-ideas
And counter-ideas. There was nothing one had.
    There were
No horses to ride and no one to ride them
In the woods of the dogwoods,

No large white horses. But there was the fluffy dog.
There were the sheets high up on older trees,
Seeming to be liquid as leaves made of cloud,
Shells under water. These were nougats.

It had to be right: nougats. It was a shift
Of realities, that, in which it could be wrong.
The weather was like a waiter with a tray.
One had come early to a crisp café.

ON AN OLD HORN

I

The bird kept saying that birds had once been men,
Or were to be, animals with men's eyes,
Men fat as feathers, misers counting breaths,
Women of a melancholy one could sing.
Then the bird from his ruddy belly blew
A trumpet round the trees. Could one say that it was
A baby with the tail of a rat?

       The stones
Were violet, yellow, purple, pink. The grass
Of the iris bore white blooms. The bird then boomed.
Could one say that he sang the colors in the stones,
False as the mind, instead of the fragrance, warm
With sun?

   In the little of his voice, or the like,
Or less, he found a man, or more, against
Calamity, proclaimed himself, was proclaimed.

II

If the stars that move together as one, disband,
Flying like insects of fire in a cavern of night,
Pipperoo, pippera, pipperum . . . The rest is rot.

BOUQUET OF BELLE SCAVOIR

I

It is she alone that matters.
She made it. It is easy to say
The figures of speech, as why she chose
This dark, particular rose.

II

Everything in it is herself.
Yet the freshness of the leaves, the burn
Of the colors, are tinsel changes,
Out of the changes of both light and dew

III

How often had he walked
Beneath summer and the sky
To receive her shadow into his mind . . .
Miserable that it was not she.

IV

The sky is too blue, the earth too wide.
The thought of her takes her away.
The form of her in something else
Is not enough.

V

The reflection of her here, and then there,
Is another shadow, another evasion,
Another denial. If she is everywhere,
She is nowhere, to him.

231

But this she has made. If it is
Another image, it is one she has made.
It is she that he wants, to look at directly,
Someone before him to see and to know.

❖◇

VARIATIONS ON A SUMMER DAY

I

Say of the gulls that they are flying
In light blue air over dark blue sea.

II

A music more than a breath, but less
Than the wind, sub-music like sub-speech,
A repetition of unconscious things,
Letters of rock and water, words
Of the visible elements and of ours.

III

The rocks of the cliffs are the heads of dogs
That turn into fishes and leap
Into the sea.

IV

Star over Monhegan, Atlantic star,
Lantern without a bearer, you drift,
You, too, are drifting, in spite of your course;

Unless in the darkness, brightly-crowned,
You are the will, if there is a will,
Or the portent of a will that was,
One of the portents of the will that was.

V

The leaves of the sea are shaken and shaken.
There was a tree that was a father,
We sat beneath it and sang our songs.

VI

It is cold to be forever young,
To come to tragic shores and flow,
In sapphire, round the sun-bleached stones,
Being, for old men, time of their time.

VII

One sparrow is worth a thousand gulls,
When it sings. The gull sits on chimney-tops.
He mocks the guinea, challenges
The crow, inciting various modes.
The sparrow requites one, without intent.

VIII

An exercise in viewing the world.
On the motive! But one looks at the sea
As one improvises, on the piano.

IX

This cloudy world, by aid of land and sea,
Night and day, wind and quiet, produces
More nights, more days, more clouds, more
    worlds.

X

To change nature, not merely to change ideas,
To escape from the body, so to feel
Those feelings that the body balks,
The feelings of the natures round us here:
As a boat feels when it cuts blue water.

XI

Now, the timothy at Pemaquid
That rolled in heat is silver-tipped
And cold. The moon follows the sun like a
    French
Translation of a Russian poet.

XII

Everywhere the spruce trees bury soldiers:
Hugh March, a sergeant, a redcoat, killed,
With his men, beyond the barbican.
Everywhere spruce trees bury spruce trees.

XIII

Cover the sea with the sand rose. Fill
The sky with the radiantiana
Of spray. Let all the salt be gone.

XIV

Words add to the senses. The words for the
    dazzle
Of mica, the dithering of grass,
The Arachne integument of dead trees,
Are the eye grown larger, more intense.

234

XV

The last island and its inhabitant,
The two alike, distinguish blues,
Until the difference between air
And sea exists by grace alone,
In objects, as white this, white that.

XVI

Round and round goes the bell of the water
And round and round goes the water itself
And that which is the pitch of its motion,
The bell of its dome, the patron of sound.

XVII

Pass through the door and through the walls,
Those bearing balsam, its field fragrance,
Pine-figures bringing sleep to sleep.

XVIII

Low tide, flat water, sultry sun.
One observes profoundest shadows rolling.
Damariscotta da da doo.

XIX

One boy swims under a tub, one sits
On top. Hurroo, the man-boat comes,
In a man-makenesse, neater than Naples.

XX

You could almost see the brass on her gleaming,
Not quite. The mist was to light what red
Is to fire. And her mainmast tapered to nothing,

235

Without teetering a millimeter's measure.
The beads on her rails seemed to grasp at trans-
parence.
It was not yet the hour to be dauntlessly leaping.

❀❀❀❀❀❀❀❀❀❀❀❀❀❀❀❀❀❀❀❀❀❀❀❀❀❀❀❀❀❀❀❀❀❀

YELLOW AFTERNOON

It was in the earth only
That he was at the bottom of things
And of himself. There he could say
Of this I am, this is the patriarch,
This it is that answers when I ask,
This is the mute, the final sculpture
Around which silence lies on silence.
This reposes alike in springtime
And, arbored and bronzed, in autumn.

He said I had this that I could love,
As one loves visible and responsive peace,
As one loves one's own being,
As one loves that which is the end
And must be loved, as one loves that
Of which one is a part as in a unity,
A unity that is the life one loves,
So that one lives all the lives that comprise it
As the life of the fatal unity of war.

Everything comes to him
From the middle of his field. The odor
Of earth penetrates more deeply than any word.
There he touches his being. There as he is
He is. The thought that he had found all this
Among men, in a woman—she caught his breath—
But he came back as one comes back from the sun
To lie on one's bed in the dark, close to a face
Without eyes or mouth, that looks at one and
    speaks.

◇◇

MARTIAL CADENZA

I

Only this evening I saw again low in the sky
The evening star, at the beginning of winter, the star
That in spring will crown every western horizon,
Again . . . as if it came back, as if life came back,
Not in a later son, a different daughter, another place,
But as if evening found us young, still young,
Still walking in a present of our own.

II

It was like sudden time in a world without time,
This world, this place, the street in which I was,
Without time: as that which is not has no time,
Is not, or is of what there was, is full
Of the silence before the armies, armies without

Either trumpets or drums, the commanders mute, the
    arms
On the ground, fixed fast in a profound defeat.

III

What had this star to do with the world it lit,
With the blank skies over England, over France
And above the German camps? It looked apart.
Yet it is this that shall maintain—Itself
Is time, apart from any past, apart
From any future, the ever-living and being,
The ever-breathing and moving, the constant fire,

IV

The present close, the present realized,
Not the symbol but that for which the symbol stands,
The vivid thing in the air that never changes,
Though the air change. Only this evening I saw it
    again,
At the beginning of winter, and I walked and talked
Again, and lived and was again, and breathed again
And moved again and flashed again, time flashed again.

❀◇◇

MAN AND BOTTLE

The mind is the great poem of winter, the man,
Who, to find what will suffice,
Destroys romantic tenements
Of rose and ice

In the land of war. More than the man, it is
A man with the fury of a race of men,
A light at the centre of many lights,
A man at the centre of men.

It has to content the reason concerning war,
It has to persuade that war is part of itself,
A manner of thinking, a mode
Of destroying, as the mind destroys,

An aversion, as the world is averted
From an old delusion, an old affair with the sun,
An impossible aberration with the moon,
A grossness of peace.

It is not the snow that is the quill, the page.
The poem lashes more fiercely than the wind,
As the mind, to find what will suffice, destroys
Romantic tenements of rose and ice.

❖❖❖❖❖❖❖❖❖❖❖❖❖❖❖❖❖❖❖❖❖❖❖❖❖❖❖❖

OF MODERN POETRY

The poem of the mind in the act of finding
What will suffice. It has not always had
To find: the scene was set; it repeated what
Was in the script.
              Then the theatre was changed
To something else. Its past was a souvenir.

239

It has to be living, to learn the speech of the place.
It has to face the men of the time and to meet
The women of the time. It has to think about war
And it has to find what will suffice. It has
To construct a new stage. It has to be on that stage
And, like an insatiable actor, slowly and
With meditation, speak words that in the ear,
In the delicatest ear of the mind, repeat,
Exactly, that which it wants to hear, at the sound
Of which, an invisible audience listens,
Not to the play, but to itself, expressed
In an emotion as of two people, as of two
Emotions becoming one. The actor is
A metaphysician in the dark, twanging
An instrument, twanging a wiry string that gives
Sounds passing through sudden rightnesses, wholly
Containing the mind, below which it cannot descend,
Beyond which it has no will to rise.
                                    It must
Be the finding of a satisfaction, and may
Be of a man skating, a woman dancing, a woman
Combing. The poem of the act of the mind.

ARRIVAL AT THE WALDORF

Home from Guatemala, back at the Waldorf.
This arrival in the wild country of the soul,
All approaches gone, being completely there,

Where the wild poem is a substitute
For the woman one loves or ought to love,
One wild rhapsody a fake for another.

You touch the hotel the way you touch moonlight
Or sunlight and you hum and the orchestra
Hums and you say "The world in a verse,

A generation sealed, men remoter than mountains,
Women invisible in music and motion and color,"
After that alien, point-blank, green and actual Guate-
mala.

❖◆❖

LANDSCAPE WITH BOAT

An anti-master-man, floribund ascetic.

He brushed away the thunder, then the clouds,
Then the colossal illusion of heaven. Yet still
The sky was blue. He wanted imperceptible air.
He wanted to see. He wanted the eye to see
And not be touched by blue. He wanted to know,
A naked man who regarded himself in the glass
Of air, who looked for the world beneath the blue,
Without blue, without any turquoise tint or phase,
Any azure under-side or after-color. Nabob
Of bones, he rejected, he denied, to arrive

At the neutral centre, the ominous element,
The single-colored, colorless, primitive.
It was not as if the truth lay where he thought,
Like a phantom, in an uncreated night.
It was easier to think it lay there. If
It was nowhere else, it was there and because
It was nowhere else, its place had to be supposed,
Itself had to be supposed, a thing supposed
In a place supposed, a thing that he reached
In a place that he reached, by rejecting what he saw
And denying what he heard. He would arrive.
He had only not to live, to walk in the dark,
To be projected by one void into
Another.

       It was his nature to suppose,
To receive what others had supposed, without
Accepting. He received what he denied.
But as truth to be accepted, he supposed
A truth beyond all truths.

               He never supposed
That he might be truth, himself, or part of it,
That the things that he rejected might be part
And the irregular turquoise, part, the perceptible blue
Grown denser, part, the eye so touched, so played
Upon by clouds, the ear so magnified
By thunder, parts, and all these things together,
Parts, and more things, parts. He never supposed divine
Things might not look divine, nor that if nothing
Was divine then all things were, the world itself,
And that if nothing was the truth, then all
Things were the truth, the world itself was the truth.

Had he been better able to suppose:
He might sit on a sofa on a balcony
Above the Mediterranean, emerald
Becoming emeralds. He might watch the palms
Flap green ears in the heat. He might observe
A yellow wine and follow a steamer's track
And say, "The thing I hum appears to be
The rhythm of this celestial pantomime."

❁❁❁❁❁❁❁❁❁❁❁❁❁❁❁❁❁❁❁❁❁❁❁❁❁❁❁❁❁❁❁

ON THE ADEQUACY OF LANDSCAPE

The little owl flew through the night,
As if the people in the air
Were frightened and he frightened them,
By being there,

The people that turned off and came
To avoid the bright, discursive wings,
To avoid the hap-hallow hallow-ho
Of central things,

Nor in their empty hearts to feel
The blood-red redness of the sun,
To shrink to an insensible,
Small oblivion,

Beyond the keenest diamond day
Of people sensible to pain,
When cocks wake, clawing at their beds
To be again,

And who, for that, turn toward the cocks
And toward the start of day and trees
And light behind the body of night
And sun, as if these

Were what they are, the sharpest sun:
The sharpest self, the sensible range,
The extent of what they are, the strength
That they exchange,

So that he that suffers most desires
The red bird most and the strongest sky—
Not the people in the air that hear
The little owl fly.

<><><><><><><><><><><><><><><><><><><><><><><><><><><><><><><><><><><><><><><><><><>

LES PLUS BELLES PAGES

The milkman came in the moonlight and the moon-
    light
Was less than moonlight. Nothing exists by itself.
The moonlight seemed to.

Two people, three horses, an ox
And the sun, the waves together in the sea.

The moonlight and Aquinas seemed to. He spoke,
Kept speaking, of God. I changed the word to man.
The automaton, in logic self-contained,
Existed by itself. Or did the saint survive?
Did several spirits assume a single shape?

Theology after breakfast sticks to the eye.

❀◇

POEM WITH RHYTHMS

The hand between the candle and the wall
Grows large on the wall.

The mind between this light or that and space,
(This man in a room with an image of the world,
That woman waiting for the man she loves,)
Grows large against space:

There the man sees the image clearly at last.
There the woman receives her lover into her heart
And weeps on his breast, though he never comes.

It must be that the hand
Has a will to grow larger on the wall,

245

To grow larger and heavier and stronger than
The wall; and that the mind
Turns to its own figurations and declares,
"This image, this love, I compose myself
Of these. In these, I come forth outwardly.
In these, I wear a vital cleanliness,
Not as in air, bright-blue-resembling air,
But as in the powerful mirror of my wish and will."

❦❧❦❧❦❧❦❧❦❧❦❧❦❧❦❧❦❧❦❧❦❧❦❧❦❧❦❧❦❧❦❧

WOMAN LOOKING AT A VASE OF FLOWERS

It was as if thunder took form upon
The piano, that time: the time when the crude
And jealous grandeurs of sun and sky
Scattered themselves in the garden, like
The wind dissolving into birds,
The clouds becoming braided girls.
It was like the sea poured out again
In east wind beating the shutters at night.

Hoot, little owl within her, how
High blue became particular
In the leaf and bud and how the red,
Flicked into pieces, points of air,
Became—how the central, essential red
Escaped its large abstraction, became,
First, summer, then a lesser time,
Then the sides of peaches, of dusky pears.

246

Hoot how the inhuman colors fell
Into place beside her, where she was,
Like human conciliations, more like
A profounder reconciling, an act,
An affirmation free from doubt.
The crude and jealous formlessness
Became the form and the fragrance of things
Without clairvoyance, close to her.

◇◇◇

THE WELL DRESSED MAN WITH A BEARD

After the final no there comes a yes
And on that yes the future world depends.
No was the night. Yes is this present sun.
If the rejected things, the things denied,
Slid over the western cataract, yet one,
One only, one thing that was firm, even
No greater than a cricket's horn, no more
Than a thought to be rehearsed all day, a speech
Of the self that must sustain itself on speech,
One thing remaining, infallible, would be
Enough. Ah! douce campagna of that thing!
Ah! douce campagna, honey in the heart,
Green in the body, out of a petty phrase,
Out of a thing believed, a thing affirmed:
The form on the pillow humming while one sleeps,
The aureole above the humming house . . .

It can never be satisfied, the mind, never.

247

OF BRIGHT & BLUE BIRDS & THE GALA SUN

Some things, niño, some things are like this,
That instantly and in themselves they are gay
And you and I are such things, O most miserable . . .

For a moment they are gay and are a part
Of an element, the exactest element for us,
In which we pronounce joy like a word of our own.

It is there, being imperfect, and with these things
And erudite in happiness, with nothing learned,
That we are joyously ourselves and we think

Without the labor of thought, in that element,
And we feel, in a way apart, for a moment, as if
There was a bright *scienza* outside of ourselves,

A gaiety that is being, not merely knowing,
The will to be and to be total in belief,
Provoking a laughter, an agreement, by surprise.

MRS. ALFRED URUGUAY

So what said the others and the sun went down
And, in the brown blues of evening, the lady said,
In the donkey's ear, "I fear that elegance

Must struggle like the rest." She climbed until
The moonlight in her lap, mewing her velvet,
And her dress were one and she said, "I have said no
To everything, in order to get at myself.
I have wiped away moonlight like mud. Your innocent
    ear
And I, if I rode naked, are what remain."

The moonlight crumbled to degenerate forms,
While she approached the real, upon her mountain,
With lofty darkness. The donkey was there to ride,
To hold by the ear, even though it wished for a bell,
Wished faithfully for a falsifying bell.
Neither the moonlight could change it. And for her,
To be, regardless of velvet, could never be more
Than to be, she could never differently be,
Her no and no made yes impossible.

Who was it passed her there on a horse all will,
What figure of capable imagination?
Whose horse clattered on the road on which she rose,
As it descended, blind to her velvet and
The moonlight? Was it a rider intent on the sun,
A youth, a lover with phosphorescent hair,
Dressed poorly, arrogant of his streaming forces,
Lost in an integration of the martyrs' bones,
Rushing from what was real; and capable?

The villages slept as the capable man went down,
Time swished on the village clocks and dreams were
    alive,
The enormous gongs gave edges to their sounds,
As the rider, no chevalere and poorly dressed,

Impatient of the bells and midnight forms,
Rode over the picket rocks, rode down the road,
And, capable, created in his mind,
Eventual victor, out of the martyrs' bones,
The ultimate elegance: the imagined land.

◇◇◇

ASIDES ON THE OBOE

The prologues are over. It is a question, now,
Of final belief. So, say that final belief
Must be in a fiction. It is time to choose.

I

That obsolete fiction of the wide river in
An empty land; the gods that Boucher killed;
And the metal heroes that time granulates—
The philosophers' man alone still walks in dew,
Still by the sea-side mutters milky lines
Concerning an immaculate imagery.
If you say on the hautboy man is not enough,
Can never stand as god, is ever wrong
In the end, however naked, tall, there is still
The impossible possible philosophers' man,
The man who has had the time to think enough,
The central man, the human globe, responsive
As a mirror with a voice, the man of glass,
Who in a million diamonds sums us up.

II

He is the transparence of the place in which
He is and in his poems we find peace.
He sets this peddler's pie and cries in summer,
The glass man, cold and numbered, dewily cries,
"Thou art not August unless I make thee so."
Clandestine steps upon imagined stairs
Climb through the night, because his cuckoos call.

III

One year, death and war prevented the jasmine scent
And the jasmine islands were bloody martyrdoms.
How was it then with the central man? Did we
Find peace? We found the sum of men. We found,
If we found the central evil, the central good.
We buried the fallen without jasmine crowns.
There was nothing he did not suffer, no; nor we.

It was not as if the jasmine ever returned.
But we and the diamond globe at last were one.
We had always been partly one. It was as we came
To see him, that we were wholly one, as we heard
Him chanting for those buried in their blood,
In the jasmine haunted forests, that we knew
The glass man, without external reference.

EXTRACTS FROM ADDRESSES TO THE
ACADEMY OF FINE IDEAS

I

A crinkled paper makes a brilliant sound.
The wrinkled roses tinkle, the paper ones,
And the ear is glass, in which the noises pelt,
The false roses—Compare the silent rose of the sun
And rain, the blood-rose living in its smell,
With this paper, this dust. That states the point.

                              Messieurs,
It is an artificial world. The rose
Of paper is of the nature of its world.
The sea is so many written words; the sky
Is blue, clear, cloudy, high, dark, wide and round;
The mountains inscribe themselves upon the walls.
And, otherwise, the rainy rose belongs
To naked men, to women naked as rain.

Where is that summer warm enough to walk
Among the lascivious poisons, clean of them,
And in what covert may we, naked, be
Beyond the knowledge of nakedness, as part
Of reality, beyond the knowledge of what
Is real, part of a land beyond the mind?

Rain is an unbearable tyranny. Sun is
A monster-maker, an eye, only an eye,

A shapener of shapes for only the eye,
Of things no better than paper things, of days
That are paper days. The false and true are one.

II

The eye believes and its communion takes.
The spirit laughs to see the eye believe
And its communion take. And now of that.
Let the Secretary for Porcelain observe
That evil made magic, as in catastrophe,
If neatly glazed, becomes the same as the fruit
Of an emperor, the egg-plant of a prince.
The good is evil's last invention. Thus
The maker of catastrophe invents the eye
And through the eye equates ten thousand deaths
With a single well-tempered apricot, or, say,
An egg-plant of good air.

                My beards, attend
To the laughter of evil: the fierce ricanery
With the ferocious chu-chot-chu between, the sobs
For breath to laugh the louder, the deeper gasps
Uplifting the completest rhetoric
Of sneers, the fugues commencing at the toes
And ending at the finger-tips. . . . It is death
That is ten thousand deaths and evil death.
Be tranquil in your wounds. It is good death
That puts an end to evil death and dies.
Be tranquil in your wounds. The placating star
Shall be the gentler for the death you die
And the helpless philosophers say still helpful things.
Plato, the reddened flower, the erotic bird.

The lean cats of the arches of the churches,
That's the old world. In the new, all men are priests.

They preach and they are preaching in a land
To be described. They are preaching in a time
To be described. Evangelists of what?
If they could gather their theses into one,
Collect their thoughts together into one,
Into a single thought, thus: into a queen,
An intercessor by innate rapport,
Or into a dark-blue king, *un roi tonnerre*,
Whose merely being was his valiance,
Panjandrum and central heart and mind of minds—
If they could! Or is it the multitude of thoughts,
Like insects in the depths of the mind, that kill
The single thought? The multitudes of men
That kill the single man, starvation's head,
One man, their bread and their remembered wine?

The lean cats of the arches of the churches
Bask in the sun in which they feel transparent,
As if designed by X, the per-noble master.
They have a sense of their design and savor
The sunlight. They bear brightly the little beyond
Themselves, the slightly unjust drawing that is
Their genius: the exquisite errors of time.

IV

On an early Sunday in April, a feeble day,
He felt curious about the winter hills
And wondered about the water in the lake.

It had been cold since December. Snow fell, first,
At New Year and, from then until April, lay
On everything. Now it had melted, leaving
The gray grass like a pallet, closely pressed;
And dirt. The wind blew in the empty place.
The winter wind blew in an empty place—
There was that difference between the and an,
The difference between himself and no man,
No man that heard a wind in an empty place.
It was time to be himself again, to see
If the place, in spite of its witheredness, was still
Within the difference. He felt curious
Whether the water was black and lashed about
Or whether the ice still covered the lake. There was still
Snow under the trees and on the northern rocks,
The dead rocks not the green rocks, the live rocks. If,
When he looked, the water ran up the air or grew white
Against the edge of the ice, the abstraction would
Be broken and winter would be broken and done,
And being would be being himself again,
Being, becoming seeing and feeling and self,
Black water breaking into reality.

                              v
The law of chaos is the law of ideas,
Of improvisations and seasons of belief.

Ideas are men. The mass of meaning and
The mass of men are one. Chaos is not

The mass of meaning. It is three or four
Ideas or, say, five men or, possibly, six.

In the end, these philosophic assassins pull
Revolvers and shoot each other. One remains.

The mass of meaning becomes composed again.
He that remains plays on an instrument

A good agreement between himself and night,
A chord between the mass of men and himself,

Far, far beyond the putative canzones
Of love and summer. The assassin sings

In chaos and his song is a consolation.
It is the music of the mass of meaning.

And yet it is a singular romance,
This warmth in the blood-world for the pure idea,

This inability to find a sound,
That clings to the mind like that right sound, that song

Of the assassin that remains and sings
In the high imagination, triumphantly.

VI

Of systematic thinking . . . Ercole,
O, skin and spine and hair of you, Ercole,
Of what do you lie thinking in your cavern?
To think it is to think the way to death . . .

That other one wanted to think his way to life,
Sure that the ultimate poem was the mind,
Or of the mind, or of the mind in these

Elysia, these days, half earth, half mind;
Half sun, half thinking of the sun; half sky,
Half desire for indifference about the sky.

He, that one, wanted to think his way to life,
To be happy because people were thinking to be.
They had to think it to be. He wanted that,
To face the weather and be unable to tell
How much of it was light and how much thought,
In these Elysia, these origins,
This single place in which we are and stay,
Except for the images we make of it,
And for it, and by which we think the way,
And, being unhappy, talk of happiness
And, talking of happiness, know that it means
That the mind is the end and must be satisfied.

It cannot be half earth, half mind; half sun,
Half thinking; until the mind has been satisfied,
Until, for him, his mind is satisfied.
Time troubles to produce the redeeming thought.
Sometimes at sleepy mid-days it succeeds,
Too vaguely that it be written in character.

VII

To have satisfied the mind and turn to see,
(That being as much belief as we may have,)
And turn to look and say there is no more
Than this, in this alone I may believe,
Whatever it may be; then one's belief
Resists each past apocalypse, rejects
Ceylon, wants nothing from the sea, *la belle
Aux crinolines*, smears out mad mountains.

257

What
One believes is what matters. Ecstatic identities
Between one's self and the weather and the things
Of the weather are the belief in one's element,
The casual reunions, the long-pondered
Surrenders, the repeated sayings that
There is nothing more and that it is enough
To believe in the weather and in the things and men
Of the weather and in one's self, as part of that
And nothing more. So that if one went to the moon,
Or anywhere beyond, to a different element,
One would be drowned in the air of difference,
Incapable of belief, in the difference.
And then returning from the moon, if one breathed
The cold evening, without any scent or the shade
Of any woman, watched the thinnest light
And the most distant, single color, about to change,
And naked of any illusion, in poverty,
In the exactest poverty, if then
One breathed the cold evening, the deepest inhalation
Would come from that return to the subtle centre.

VIII

We live in a camp . . . Stanzas of final peace
Lie in the heart's residuum . . . Amen.
But would it be amen, in choirs, if once
In total war we died and after death
Returned, unable to die again, fated
To endure thereafter every mortal wound,
Beyond a second death, as evil's end?

258

It is only that we are able to die, to escape
The wounds. Yet to lie buried in evil earth,
If evil never ends, is to return
To evil after death, unable to die
Again and fated to endure beyond
Any mortal end. The chants of final peace
Lie in the heart's residuum.

                How can
We chant if we live in evil and afterward
Lie harshly buried there?

                  If earth dissolves
Its evil after death, it dissolves it while
We live. Thence come the final chants, the chants
Of the brooder seeking the acutest end
Of speech: to pierce the heart's residuum
And there to find music for a single line,
Equal to memory, one line in which
The vital music formulates the words.

Behold the men in helmets borne on steel,
Discolored, how they are going to defeat.

MONTRACHET–LE–JARDIN

What more is there to love than I have loved?
And if there be nothing more, O bright, O bright,
The chick, the chidder-barn and grassy chives

And great moon, cricket-impresario,
And, hoy, the impopulous purple-plated past,
Hoy, hoy, the blue bulls kneeling down to rest.

Chome! clicks the clock, if there be nothing more.
But if, but if there be something more to love,
Something in now a senseless syllable,

A shadow in the mind, a flourisher
Of sounds resembling sounds, efflorisant,
Approaching the feelings or come down from them,

These other shadows, not in the mind, players
Of aphonies, tuned in from zero and
Beyond, futura's fuddle-fiddling lumps,

But if there be something more to love, amen,
Amen to the feelings about familiar things,
The blessed regal dropped in daggers' dew,

Amen to thought, our singular skeleton,
Salt-flicker, amen to our accustomed cell,
The moonlight in the cell, words on the wall.

To-night, night's undeciphered murmuring
Comes close to the prisoner's ear, becomes a throat
The hand can touch, neither green bronze nor marble,

The hero's throat in which the words are spoken,
From which the chant comes close upon the ear,
Out of the hero's being, the deliverer

Delivering the prisoner by his words,
So that the skeleton in the moonlight sings,
Sings of an heroic world beyond the cell,

No, not believing, but to make the cell
A hero's world in which he is the hero.
Man must become the hero of his world.

The salty skeleton must dance because
He must, in the aroma of summer nights,
Licentious violet and lascive rose,

Midsummer love and softest silences,
Weather of night creatures, whistling all day, too,
And echoing rhetorics more than our own.

He hears the earliest poems of the world
In which man is the hero. He hears the words,
Before the speaker's youngest breath is taken!

Fear never the brute clouds nor winter-stop
And let the water-belly of ocean roar,
Nor feel the x malisons of other men,

Since in the hero-land to which we go,
A little nearer by each multitude,
To which we come as into bezeled plain,

The poison in the blood will have been purged,
An inner miracle and sun-sacrament,
One of the major miracles, that fall

As apples fall, without astronomy,
One of the sacraments between two breaths,
Magical only for the change they make.

The skeleton said it is a question of
The naked man, the naked man as last
And tallest hero and plus gaudiest vir.

Consider how the speechless, invisible gods
Ruled us before, from over Asia, by
Our merest apprehension of their will.

There must be mercy in Asia and divine
Shadows of scholars bent upon their books,
Divine orations from lean sacristans

Of the good, speaking of good in the voice of men.
All men can speak of it in the voice of gods.
But to speak simply of good is like to love,

To equate the root-man and the super-man,
The root-man swarming, tortured by his mass,
The super-man friseured, possessing and possessed.

A little while of Terra Paradise
I dreamed, of autumn rivers, silvas green,
Of sanctimonious mountains high in snow,

But in that dream a heavy difference
Kept waking and a mournful sense sought out,
In vain, life's season or death's element.

Bastard chateaux and smoky demoiselles,
No more. I can build towers of my own,
There to behold, there to proclaim, the grace

And free requiting of responsive fact,
To project the naked man in a state of fact,
As acutest virtue and ascetic trove.

Item: The cocks crow and the birds cry and
The sun expands, like a repetition on
One string, an absolute, not varying

Toward an inaccessible, pure sound.
Item: The wind is never rounding O
And, imageless, it is itself the most,

Mouthing its constant smatter throughout space.
Item: The green fish pensive in green reeds
Is an absolute. Item: The cataracts

As facts fall like rejuvenating rain,
Fall down through nakedness to nakedness,
To the auroral creature musing in the mind.

263

Item: Breathe, breathe upon the centre of
The breath life's latest, thousand senses.
But let this one sense be the single main.

And yet what good were yesterday's devotions?
I affirm and then at midnight the great cat
Leaps quickly from the fireside and is gone.

◇◇

THE NEWS AND THE WEATHER

I

The blue sun in his red cockade
Walked the United States today,

Taller than any eye could see,
Older than any man could be.

He caught the flags and the picket-lines
Of people, round the auto-works:

His manner slickened them. He milled
In the rowdy serpentines. He drilled.

His red cockade topped off a parade.
His manner took what it could find,

In the greenish greens he flung behind
And the sound of pianos in his mind.

Solange, the magnolia to whom I spoke,
A nigger tree and with a nigger name,

To which I spoke, near which I stood and spoke,
I am Solange, euphonious bane, she said.

I am a poison at the winter's end,
Taken with withered weather, crumpled clouds,

To smother the wry spirit's misery.
Inhale the purple fragrance. It becomes

Almost a nigger fragment, a *mystique*
For the spirit left helpless by the intelligence.

There's a moment in the year, Solange,
When the deep breath fetches another year of
    life.

❖◇

METAMORPHOSIS

Yillow, yillow, yillow,
Old worm, my pretty quirk,
How the wind spells out
Sep - tem - ber. . . .

Summer is in bones.
Cock-robin's at Caracas.

Make o, make o, make o,
Oto - otu - bre.

And the rude leaves fall.
The rain falls. The sky
Falls and lies with the worms.
The street lamps

Are those that have been hanged,
Dangling in an illogical
To and to and fro
Fro Niz - nil - imbo.

&)O)O)O)O)O)O)O)O)O)O)O)O)O)O)O)O)O)O)O)O)O)O)O)

CONTRARY THESES (I)

Now grapes are plush upon the vines.
A soldier walks before my door.

The hives are heavy with the combs.
Before, before, before my door.

And seraphs cluster on the domes,
And saints are brilliant in fresh cloaks.

Before, before, before my door.
The shadows lessen on the walls.

266

The bareness of the house returns.
An acid sunlight fills the halls.

Before, before. Blood smears the oaks.
A soldier stalks before my door.

◇◇◇

PHOSPHOR READING BY HIS OWN LIGHT

It is difficult to read. The page is dark.
Yet he knows what it is that he expects.

The page is blank or a frame without a glass
Or a glass that is empty when he looks.

The greenness of night lies on the page and goes
Down deeply in the empty glass . . .

Look, realist, not knowing what you expect.
The green falls on you as you look,

Falls on and makes and gives, even a speech.
And you think that that is what you expect,

That elemental parent, the green night,
Teaching a fusky alphabet.

267

THE SEARCH FOR SOUND FREE
FROM MOTION

All afternoon the gramophone
Parl-parled the West-Indian weather.
The zebra leaves, the sea
And it all spoke together.

The many-stanzaed sea, the leaves
And it spoke all together.
But you, you used the word,
Your self its honor.

All afternoon the gramaphoon,
All afternoon the gramaphoon,
The world as word,
Parl-parled the West-Indian hurricane.

The world lives as you live,
Speaks as you speak, a creature that
Repeats its vital words, yet balances
The syllable of a syllable.

268

JUMBO

The trees were plucked like iron bars
And jumbo, the loud general-large
Singsonged and singsonged, wildly free.

Who was the musician, fatly soft
And wildly free, whose clawing thumb
Clawed on the ear these consonants?

Who the transformer, himself transformed,
Whose single being, single form
Were their resemblances to ours?

The companion in nothingness,
Loud, general, large, fat, soft
And wild and free, the secondary man,

Cloud-clown, blue painter, sun as horn,
Hill-scholar, man that never is,
The bad-bespoken lacker,

Ancestor of Narcissus, prince
Of the secondary men. There are no rocks
And stones, only this imager.

269

CONTRARY THESES (II)

One chemical afternoon in mid-autumn,
When the grand mechanics of earth and sky were near,
Even the leaves of the locust were yellow then,

He walked with his year-old boy on his shoulder.
The sun shone and the dog barked and the baby slept.
The leaves, even of the locust, the green locust.

He wanted and looked for a final refuge,
From the bombastic intimations of winter
And the martyrs à la mode. He walked toward

An abstract, of which the sun, the dog, the boy
Were contours. Cold was chilling the wide-moving
    swans.
The leaves were falling like notes from a piano.

The abstract was suddenly there and gone again.
The negroes were playing football in the park.
The abstract that he saw, like the locust-leaves, plainly:

The premiss from which all things were conclusions,
The noble, Alexandrine verve. The flies
And the bees still sought the chrysanthemums' odor.

THE HAND AS A BEING

In the first canto of the final canticle,
Too conscious of too many things at once,
Our man beheld the naked, nameless dame,

Seized her and wondered: why beneath the tree
She held her hand before him in the air,
For him to see, wove round her glittering hair.

Too conscious of too many things at once,
In the first canto of the final canticle,
Her hand composed him and composed the tree.

The wind had seized the tree and ha, and ha,
It held the shivering, the shaken limbs,
Then bathed its body in the leaping lake.

Her hand composed him like a hand appeared,
Of an impersonal gesture, a stranger's hand.
He was too conscious of too many things

In the first canto of the final canticle.
Her hand took his and drew him near to her.
Her hair fell on him and the mi-bird flew

To the ruddier bushes at the garden's end.
Of her, of her alone, at last he knew
And lay beside her underneath the tree.

OAK LEAVES ARE HANDS

In Hydaspia, by Howzen,
Lived a lady, Lady Lowzen,
For whom what is was other things.

Flora she was once. She was florid
A bachelor of feen masquerie,
Evasive and metamorphorid.

Mac Mort she had been, ago,
Twelve-legged in her ancestral hells,
Weaving and weaving many arms.

Even now, the centre of something else,
Merely by putting hand to brow,
Brooding on centuries like shells.

As the acorn broods on former oaks
In memorials of Northern sound,
Skims the real for its unreal,

So she in Hydaspia created
Out of the movement of few words,
Flora Lowzen invigorated

Archaic and future happenings,
In glittering seven-colored changes,
By Howzen, the chromatic Lowzen.

272

EXAMINATION OF THE HERO
IN A TIME OF WAR

I

Force is my lot and not pink-clustered
Roma ni Avignon ni Leyden,
And cold, my element. Death is my
Master and, without light, I dwell. There
The snow hangs heavily on the rocks, brought
By a wind that seeks out shelter from snow. Thus
Each man spoke in winter. Yet each man spoke of
The brightness of arms, said Roma wasted
In its own dirt, said Avignon was
Peace in a time of peace, said Leyden
Was always the other mind. The brightness
Of arms, the will opposed to cold, fate
In its cavern, wings subtler than any mercy,
These were the psalter of their sybils.

II

The Got whome we serve is able to deliver
Us. Good chemistry, good common man, what
Of that angelic sword? Creature of
Ten times ten times dynamite, convulsive
Angel, convulsive shatterer, gun,
Click, click, the Got whom we serve is able,
Still, still to deliver us, still magic,
Still moving yet motionless in smoke, still
One with us, in the heaved-up noise, still

273

Captain, the man of skill, the expert
Leader, the creator of bursting color
And rainbow sortilege, the savage weapon
Against enemies, against the prester,
Presto, whose whispers prickle the spirit.

III

They are sick of each old romance, returning,
Of each old revolving dance, the music
Like a euphony in a museum
Of euphonies, a skin from Nubia,
A helio-horn. How strange the hero
To this accurate, exacting eye. Sight
Hangs heaven with flash drapery. Sight
Is a museum of things seen. Sight,
In war, observes each man profoundly.
Yes. But these sudden sublimations
Are to combat what his exaltations
Are to the unaccountable prophet or
What any fury to its noble centre.

IV

To grasp the hero, the eccentric
On a horse, in a plane, at the piano—
At the piano, scales, arpeggios
And chords, the morning exercises,
The afternoon's reading, the night's reflection,
That's how to produce a virtuoso.
The drill of a submarine. The voyage
Beyond the oyster-beds, indigo
Shadow, up the great sea and downward
And darkly beside the vulcanic

Sea-tower, sea-pinnacles, sea-mountain.
The signal . . . The sea-tower, shaken,
Sways slightly and the pinnacles frisson.
The mountain collapses. Chopiniana.

V

The common man is the common hero.
The common hero is the hero.
Imprimatur. But then there's common fortune,
Induced by what you will: the entrails
Of a cat, twelve dollars for the devil,
A kneeling woman, a moon's farewell;
And common fortune, induced by nothing,
Unwished for, chance, the merest riding
Of the wind, rain in a dry September,
The improvisations of the cuckoos
In a clock-shop. . . . Soldier, think, in the darkness,
Repeating your appointed paces
Between two neatly measured stations,
Of less neatly measured common-places.

VI

Unless we believe in the hero, what is there
To believe? Incisive what, the fellow
Of what good. Devise. Make him of mud,
For every day. In a civiler manner,
Devise, devise, and make him of winter's
Iciest core, a north star, central
In our oblivion, of summer's
Imagination, the golden rescue:
The bread and wine of the mind, permitted
In an ascetic room, its table

Red as a red table-cloth, its windows
West Indian, the extremest power
Living and being about us and being
Ours, like a familiar companion.

VII

Gazette Guerrière. A man might happen
To prefer *L'Observateur de la Paix*, since
The hero of the *Gazette* and the hero
Of *L'Observateur*, the classic hero
And the bourgeois, are different, much.
The classic changed. There have been many.
And there are many bourgeois heroes.
There are more heroes than marbles of them.
The marbles are pinchings of an idea,
Yet there is that idea behind the marbles,
The idea of things for public gardens,
Of men suited to public ferns . . . The hero
Glides to his meeting like a lover
Mumbling a secret, passionate message.

VIII

The hero is not a person. The marbles
Of Xenophon, his epitaphs, should
Exhibit Xenophon, what he was, since
Neither his head nor horse nor knife nor
Legend were part of what he was, forms
Of a still-life, symbols, brown things to think of
In brown books. The marbles of what he was stand
Like a white abstraction only, a feeling
In a feeling mass, a blank emotion,
An anti-pathos, until we call it

Xenophon, its implement and actor.
Obscure Satanas, make a model
Of this element, this force. Transfer it
Into a barbarism as its image.

IX

If the hero is not a person, the emblem
Of him, even if Xenophon, seems
To stand taller than a person stands, has
A wider brow, large and less human
Eyes and bruted ears: the man-like body
Of a primitive. He walks with a defter
And lither stride. His arms are heavy
And his breast is greatness. All his speeches
Are prodigies in longer phrases.
His thoughts begotten at clear sources,
Apparently in air, fall from him
Like chantering from an abundant
Poet, as if he thought gladly, being
Compelled thereto by an innate music.

X

And if the phenomenon, magnified, is
Further magnified, sua voluntate,
Beyond his circumstance, projected
High, low, far, wide, against the distance,
In parades like several equipages,
Painted by mad-men, seen as magic,
Leafed out in adjectives as private
And peculiar and appropriate glory,
Even enthroned on rainbows in the sight
Of the fishes of the sea, the colored

Birds and people of this too voluminous
Air-earth—Can we live on dry descriptions,
Feel everything starving except the belly
And nourish ourselves on crumbs of whimsy?

XI

But a profane parade, the basso
Preludes a-rub, a-rub-rub, for him that
Led the emperor astray, the tom trumpets
Curling round the steeple and the people,
The elephants of sound, the tigers
In trombones roaring for the children,
Young boys resembling pastry, hip-hip,
Young men as vegetables, hip-hip,
Home and the fields give praise, hurrah, hip,
Hip, hip, hurrah. Eternal morning . . .
Flesh on the bones. The skeleton throwing
His crust away eats of this meat, drinks
Of this tabernacle, this communion,
Sleeps in the sun no thing recalling.

XII

It is not an image. It is a feeling.
There is no image of the hero.
There is a feeling as definition.
How could there be an image, an outline,
A design, a marble soiled by pigeons?
The hero is a feeling, a man seen
As if the eye was an emotion,
As if in seeing we saw our feeling
In the object seen and saved that mystic
Against the sight, the penetrating,

Pure eye. Instead of allegory,
We have and are the man, capable
Of his brave quickenings, the human
Accelerations that seem inhuman.

XIII

These letters of him for the little,
The imaginative, ghosts that dally
With life's salt upon their lips and savor
The taste of it, secrete within them
Too many references. The hero
Acts in reality, adds nothing
To what he does. He is the heroic
Actor and act but not divided.
It is a part of his conception,
That he be not conceived, being real.
Say that the hero is his nation,
In him made one, and in that saying
Destroy all references. This actor
Is anonymous and cannot help it.

XIV

A thousand crystals' chiming voices,
Like the shiddow-shaddow of lights revolving
To momentary ones, are blended,
In hymns, through iridescent changes,
Of the apprehending of the hero.
These hymns are like a stubborn brightness
Approaching in the dark approaches
Of time and place, becoming certain,
The organic centre of responses,
Naked of hindrance, a thousand crystals.

To meditate the highest man, not
The highest supposed in him and over,
Creates, in the blissfuller perceptions,
What unisons create in music.

XV

The highest man with nothing higher
Than himself, his self, the self that embraces
The self of the hero, the solar single,
Man-sun, man-moon, man-earth, man-ocean,
Makes poems on the syllable *fa* or
Jumps from the clouds or, from his window,
Sees the petty gildings on February . . .
The man-sun being hero rejects that
False empire . . . These are the works and pastimes
Of the highest self: he studies the paper
On the wall, the lemons on the table.
This is his day. With nothing lost, he
Arrives at the man-man as he wanted.
This is his night and meditation.

XVI

Each false thing ends. The bouquet of summer
Turns blue and on its empty table
It is stale and the water is discolored.
True autumn stands then in the doorway.
After the hero, the familiar
Man makes the hero artificial.
But was the summer false? The hero?
How did we come to think that autumn
Was the veritable season, that familiar

Man was the veritable man? So
Summer, jangling the savagest diamonds and
Dressed in its azure-doubled crimsons,
May truly bear its heroic fortunes
For the large, the solitary figure.

TRANSPORT TO SUMMER

GOD IS GOOD. IT IS A BEAUTIFUL NIGHT

Look round, brown moon, brown bird, as you rise to
      fly,
Look round at the head and zither
On the ground.

Look round you as you start to rise, brown moon,
At the book and shoe, the rotted rose
At the door.

This was the place to which you came last night,
Flew close to, flew to without rising away.
Now, again,

In your light, the head is speaking. It reads the book.
It becomes the scholar again, seeking celestial
Rendezvous,

Picking thin music on the rustiest string,
Squeezing the reddest fragrance from the stump
Of summer.

The venerable song falls from your fiery wings.
The song of the great space of your age pierces
The fresh night.

CERTAIN PHENOMENA OF SOUND

I

The cricket in the telephone is still.
A geranium withers on the window-sill.

Cat's milk is dry in the saucer. Sunday song
Comes from the beating of the locust's wings,

That do not beat by pain, but calendar,
Nor meditate the world as it goes round.

Someone has left for a ride in a balloon
Or in a bubble examines the bubble of air.

The room is emptier than nothingness.
Yet a spider spins in the left shoe under the bed—

And old John Rocket dozes on his pillow.
It is safe to sleep to a sound that time brings back.

II

So you're home again, Redwood Roamer, and ready
To feast . . . Slice the mango, Naaman, and dress it

With white wine, sugar and lime juice. Then bring it,
After we've drunk the Moselle, to the thickest shade

Of the garden. We must prepare to hear the Roamer's
Story . . . The sound of that slick sonata,

286

Finding its way from the house, makes music seem
To be a nature, a place in which itself

Is that which produces everything else, in which
The Roamer is a voice taller than the redwoods,

Engaged in the most prolific narrative,
A sound producing the things that are spoken.

III

Eulalia, I lounged on the hospital porch,
On the east, sister and nun, and opened wide
A parasol, which I had found, against
The sun. The interior of a parasol,
It is a kind of blank in which one sees.
So seeing, I beheld you walking, white,
Gold-shined by sun, perceiving as I saw
That of that light Eulalia was the name.
Then I, Semiramide, dark-syllabled,
Contrasting our two names, considered speech.
You were created of your name, the word
Is that of which you were the personage.
There is no life except in the word of it.
I write *Semiramide* and in the script
I am and have a being and play a part.
You are that white Eulalia of the name.

THE MOTIVE FOR METAPHOR

You like it under the trees in autumn,
Because everything is half dead.
The wind moves like a cripple among the leaves
And repeats words without meaning.

In the same way, you were happy in spring,
With the half colors of quarter-things,
The slightly brighter sky, the melting clouds,
The single bird, the obscure moon—

The obscure moon lighting an obscure world
Of things that would never be quite expressed,
Where you yourself were never quite yourself
And did not want nor have to be,

Desiring the exhilarations of changes:
The motive for metaphor, shrinking from
The weight of primary noon,
The A B C of being,

The ruddy temper, the hammer
Of red and blue, the hard sound—
Steel against intimation—the sharp flash,
The vital, arrogant, fatal, dominant X.

GIGANTOMACHIA

They could not carry much, as soldiers.
There was no past in their forgetting,
No self in the mass: the braver being,
The body that could never be wounded,
The life that never would end, no matter
Who died, the being that was an abstraction,
A giant's heart in the veins, all courage.

But to strip off the complacent trifles,
To expel the ever-present seductions,
To reject the script for its lack-tragic,
To confront with plainest eye the changes,
That was to look on what war magnified.
It was increased, enlarged, made simple,
Made single, made one. This was not denial.

Each man himself became a giant,
Tipped out with largeness, bearing the heavy
And the high, receiving out of others,
As from an inhuman elevation
And origin, an inhuman person,
A mask, a spirit, an accoutrement.
For soldiers, the new moon stretches twenty feet.

DUTCH GRAVES IN BUCKS COUNTY

Angry men and furious machines
Swarm from the little blue of the horizon
To the great blue of the middle height.
Men scatter throughout clouds.
The wheels are too large for any noise.

And you, my semblables, in sooty residence
Tap skeleton drums inaudibly.

There are shouts and voices.
There are men shuffling on foot in air.
Men are moving and marching
And shuffling lightly, with the heavy lightness
Of those that are marching, many together.

And you, my semblables—the old flag of Holland
Flutters in tiny darkness.

There are circles of weapons in the sun.
The air attends the brightened guns,
As if sounds were forming
Out of themselves, a saying,
An expressive on-dit, a profession.

And you, my semblables, are doubly killed
To be buried in desert and deserted earth.

The flags are natures newly found.
Rifles grow sharper on the sight.
There is a rumble of autumnal marching,
From which no soft sleeve relieves us.
Fate is the present desperado.

And you, my semblables, are crusts that lie
In the shrivellings of your time and place.

There is a battering of the drums. The bugles
Cry loudly, cry out in the powerful heart.
A force gathers that will cry loudlier
Than the most metal music, loudlier,
Like an instinctive incantation.

And you, my semblables, in the total
Of remembrance share nothing of ourselves.

An end must come in a merciless triumph,
An end of evil in a profounder logic,
In a peace that is more than a refuge,
In the will of what is common to all men,
Spelled from spent living and spent dying.

And you, my semblables, in gaffer-green,
Know that the past is not part of the present.

There were other soldiers, other people,
Men came as the sun comes, early children
And late wanderers creeping under the barb of
    night,
Year, year and year, defeated at last and lost
In an ignorance of sleep with nothing won.

And you, my semblables, know that this time
Is not an early time that has grown late.

But these are not those rusted armies.
There are the lewdest and the lustiest,
The hullaballoo of health and have,
The much too many disinherited
In a storm of torn-up testaments.

And you, my semblables, know that your children
Are not your children, not your selves.

Who are the mossy cronies muttering,
Monsters antique and haggard with past thought?
What is this crackling of voices in the mind,
This pitter-patter of archaic freedom,
Of the thousands of freedoms except our own?

And you, my semblables, whose ecstasy
Was the glory of heaven in the wilderness—

Freedom is like a man who kills himself
Each night, an incessant butcher, whose knife
Grows sharp in blood. The armies kill themselves,
And in their blood an ancient evil dies—
The action of incorrigible tragedy.

And you, my semblables, behold in blindness
That a new glory of new men assembles.

This is the pit of torment that placid end
Should be illusion, that the mobs of birth

Avoid our stale perfections, seeking out
Their own, waiting until we go
To picnic in the ruins that we leave.

So that the stars, my semblables, chimeres,
Shine on the very living of those alive.

These violent marchers of the present,
Rumbling along the autumnal horizon,
Under the arches, over the arches, in arcs
Of a chaos composed in more than order,
March toward a generation's centre.

Time was not wasted in your subtle temples.
No: nor divergence made too steep to follow down.

<><><><><><><><><><><><><><><><><><><><><><><><><><><><><><><><><>

NO POSSUM, NO SOP, NO TATERS

He is not here, the old sun,
As absent as if we were asleep.

The field is frozen. The leaves are dry.
Bad is final in this light.

In this bleak air the broken stalks
Have arms without hands. They have trunks

Without legs or, for that, without heads.
They have heads in which a captive cry

Is merely the moving of a tongue.
Snow sparkles like eyesight falling to earth,

Like seeing fallen brightly away.
The leaves hop, scraping on the ground.

It is deep January. The sky is hard.
The stalks are firmly rooted in ice.

It is in this solitude, a syllable,
Out of these gawky flitterings,

Intones its single emptiness,
The savagest hollow of winter-sound.

It is here, in this bad, that we reach
The last purity of the knowledge of good.

The crow looks rusty as he rises up.
Bright is the malice in his eye . . .

One joins him there for company,
But at a distance, in another tree.

SO–AND–SO RECLINING ON HER COUCH

On her side, reclining on her elbow.
This mechanism, this apparition,
Suppose we call it Projection A.

She floats in air at the level of
The eye, completely anonymous,
Born, as she was, at twenty-one,

Without lineage or language, only
The curving of her hip, as motionless gesture,
Eyes dripping blue, so much to learn.

If just above her head there hung,
Suspended in air, the slightest crown
Of Gothic prong and practick bright,

The suspension, as in solid space,
The suspending hand withdrawn, would be
An invisible gesture. Let this be called

Projection B. To get at the thing
Without gestures is to get at it as
Idea. She floats in the contention, the flux

Between the thing as idea and
The idea as thing. She is half who made her.
This is the final Projection, C.

The arrangement contains the desire of
The artist. But one confides in what has no
Concealed creator. One walks easily

The unpainted shore, accepts the world
As anything but sculpture. Good-bye,
Mrs. Pappadopoulos, and thanks.

CHOCORUA TO ITS NEIGHBOR

I

To speak quietly at such a distance, to speak
And to be heard is to be large in space,
That, like your own, is large, hence, to be part
Of sky, of sea, large earth, large air. It is
To perceive men without reference to their form.

II

The armies are forms in number, as cities are.
The armies are cities in movement. But a war
Between cities is a gesticulation of forms,
A swarming of number over number, not
One foot approaching, one uplifted arm.

III

At the end of night last night a crystal star,
The crystal-pointed star of morning, rose

And lit the snow to a light congenial
To this prodigious shadow, who then came
In an elemental freedom, sharp and cold.

IV

The feeling of him was the feel of day,
And of a day as yet unseen, in which
To see was to be. He was the figure in
A poem for Liadoff, the self of selves:
To think of him destroyed the body's form.

V

He was a shell of dark blue glass, or ice,
Or air collected in a deep essay,
Or light embodied, or almost, a flash
On more than muscular shoulders, arms and chest,
Blue's last transparence as it turned to black,

VI

The glitter of a being, which the eye
Accepted yet which nothing understood,
A fusion of night, its blue of the pole of blue
And of the brooding mind, fixed but for a slight
Illumination of movement as he breathed.

VII

He was as tall as a tree in the middle of
The night. The substance of his body seemed
Both substance and non-substance, luminous flesh
Or shapely fire: fire from an underworld,
Of less degree than flame and lesser shine.

VIII

Upon my top he breathed the pointed dark.
He was not man yet he was nothing else.
If in the mind, he vanished, taking there
The mind's own limits, like a tragic thing
Without existence, existing everywhere.

IX

He breathed in crystal-pointed change the whole
Experience of night, as if he breathed
A consciousness from solitude, inhaled
A freedom out of silver-shaping size,
Against the whole experience of day.

X

The silver-shapeless, gold-encrusted size
Of daylight came while he sat thinking. He said,
"The moments of enlargement overlook
The enlarging of the simplest soldier's cry
In what I am, as he falls. Of what I am,

XI

The cry is part. My solitaria
Are the meditations of a central mind.
I hear the motions of the spirit and the sound
Of what is secret becomes, for me, a voice
That is my own voice speaking in my ear.

XII

There lies the misery, the coldest coil
That grips the centre, the actual bite, that life

Itself is like a poverty in the space of life,
So that the flapping of wind around me here
Is something in tatters that I cannot hold."

XIII

In spite of this, the gigantic bulk of him
Grew strong, as if doubt never touched his heart.
Of what was this the force? From what desire
And from what thinking did his radiance come?
In what new spirit had his body birth?

XIV

He was more than an external majesty,
Beyond the sleep of those that did not know,
More than a spokesman of the night to say
Now, time stands still. He came from out of sleep.
He rose because men wanted him to be.

XV

They wanted him by day to be, image,
But not the person, of their power, thought,
But not the thinker, large in their largeness, beyond
Their form, beyond their life, yet of themselves,
Excluding by his largeness their defaults.

XVI

Last night at the end of night his starry head,
Like the head of fate, looked out in darkness, part
Thereof and part desire and part the sense
Of what men are. The collective being knew
There were others like him safely under roof:

299

XVII

The captain squalid on his pillow, the great
Cardinal, saying the prayers of earliest day;
The stone, the categorical effigy;
And the mother, the music, the name; the scholar,
Whose green mind bulges with complicated hues:

XVIII

True transfigurers fetched out of the human moun-
    tain,
True genii for the diminished, spheres,
Gigantic embryos of populations,
Blue friends in shadows, rich conspirators,
Confiders and comforters and lofty kin.

XIX

To say more than human things with human voice,
That cannot be; to say human things with more
Than human voice, that, also, cannot be;
To speak humanly from the height or from the
    depth
Of human things, that is acutest speech.

XX

Now, I, Chocorua, speak of this shadow as
A human thing. It is an eminence,
But of nothing, trash of sleep that will disappear
With the special things of night, little by little,
In day's constellation, and yet remain, yet be,

XXI

Not father, but bare brother, megalfrere,
Or by whatever boorish name a man

Might call the common self, interior fons.
And fond, the total man of glubbal glub,
Political tramp with an heraldic air,

XXII

Cloud-casual, metaphysical metaphor,
But resting on me, thinking in my snow,
Physical if the eye is quick enough,
So that, where he was, there is an enkindling, where
He is, the air changes and grows fresh to breathe.

XXIII

The air changes, creates and re-creates, like strength,
And to breathe is a fulfilling of desire,
A clearing, a detecting, a completing,
A largeness lived and not conceived, a space
That is an instant nature, brilliantly.

XXIV

Integration for integration, the great arms
Of the armies, the solid men, make big the fable.
This is their captain and philosopher,
He that is fortelleze, though he be
Hard to perceive and harder still to touch.

XXV

Last night at the end of night and in the sky,
The lesser night, the less than morning light,
Fell on him, high and cold, searching for what
Was native to him in that height, searching
The pleasure of his spirit in the cold.

301

XXVI

How singular he was as man, how large,
If nothing more than that, for the moment, large
In my presence, the companion of presences
Greater than mine, of his demanding, head
And, of human realizings, rugged roy . . .

◇◇◇

POESIE ABRUTIE

The brooks are bristling in the field,
Now, brooks are bristling in the fields
And gelid Januar has gone to hell.

II

The water puddles puddles are
And ice is still in Februar.
It still is ice in Februar.

III

The figures of the past go cloaked.
They walk in mist and rain and snow
And go, go slowly, but they go.

IV

The greenhouse on the village green
Is brighter than the sun itself.
Cinerarias have a speaking sheen.

302

THE LACK OF REPOSE

A young man seated at his table
Holds in his hand a book you have never written
Staring at the secretions of the words as
They reveal themselves.

It is not midnight. It is mid-day,
The young man is well-disclosed, one of the gang,
Andrew Jackson Something. But this book
Is a cloud in which a voice mumbles.

It is a ghost that inhabits a cloud,
But a ghost for Andrew, not lean, catarrhal
And pallid. It is the grandfather he liked,
With an understanding compounded by death

And the associations beyond death, even if only
Time. What a thing it is to believe that
One understands, in the intense disclosures
Of a parent in the French sense.

And not yet to have written a book in which
One is already a grandfather and to have put there
A few sounds of meaning, a momentary end
To the complication, is good, is a good.

303

SOMNAMBULISMA

On an old shore, the vulgar ocean rolls
Noiselessly, noiselessly, resembling a thin bird,
That thinks of settling, yet never settles, on a nest.

The wings keep spreading and yet are never wings.
The claws keep scratching on the shale, the shallow
    shale,
The sounding shallow, until by water washed away.

The generations of the bird are all
By water washed away. They follow after.
They follow, follow, follow, in water washed away.

Without this bird that never settles, without
Its generations that follow in their universe,
The ocean, falling and falling on the hollow shore,

Would be a geography of the dead: not of that land
To which they may have gone, but of the place in
    which
They lived, in which they lacked a pervasive being,

In which no scholar, separately dwelling,
Poured forth the fine fins, the gawky beaks, the per-
    sonalia,
Which, as a man feeling everything, were his.

CRUDE FOYER

Thought is false happiness: the idea
That merely by thinking one can,
Or may, penetrate, not may,
But can, that one is sure to be able—

That there lies at the end of thought
A foyer of the spirit in a landscape
Of the mind, in which we sit
And wear humanity's bleak crown;

In which we read the critique of paradise
And say it is the work
Of a comedian, this critique;
In which we sit and breathe

An innocence of an absolute,
False happiness, since we know that we use
Only the eye as faculty, that the mind
Is the eye, and that this landscape of the mind

Is a landscape only of the eye; and that
We are ignorant men incapable
Of the least, minor, vital metaphor, content,
At last, there, when it turns out to be here.

REPETITIONS OF A YOUNG CAPTAIN

I

A tempest cracked on the theatre. Quickly,
The wind beat in the roof and half the walls.
The ruin stood still in an external world.

It had been real. It was something overseas
That I remembered, something that I remembered
Overseas, that stood in an external world.

It had been real. It was not now. The rip
Of the wind and the glittering were real now,
In the spectacle of a new reality.

II

The people sat in the theatre, in the ruin,
As if nothing had happened. The dim actor spoke.
His hands became his feelings. His thick shape

Issued thin seconds glibly gapering.
Then faintly encrusted, a tissue of the moon
Walked toward him on the stage and they embraced.

They polished the embracings of a pair
Born old, familiar with the depths of the heart,
Like a machine left running, and running down.

It was a blue scene washing white in the rain,
Like something I remembered overseas.
It was something overseas that I remembered.

306

III

Millions of major men against their like
Make more than thunder's rural rumbling. They make
The giants that each one of them becomes

In a calculated chaos: he that takes form
From the others, being larger than he was,
Accoutred in a little of the strength

That sweats the sun up on its morning way
To giant red, sweats up a giant sense
To the make-matter, matter-nothing mind,

Until this matter-makes in years of war.
This being in a reality beyond
The finikin spectres in the memory,

This elevation, in which he seems to be tall,
Makes him rise above the houses, looking down.
His route lies through an image in his mind:

My route lies through an image in my mind,
It is the route that milky millions find,
An image that leaves nothing much behind.

IV

If these were only words that I am speaking
Indifferent sounds and not the heraldic-ho
Of the clear sovereign that is reality,

Of the clearest reality that is sovereign,
How should I repeat them, keep repeating them,
As if they were desperate with a know-and-know,

Central responses to a central fear,
The adobe of the angels? Constantly,
At the railway station, a soldier steps away,

Sees a familiar building drenched in cloud
And goes to an external world, having
Nothing of place. There is no change of place

Nor of time. The departing soldier is as he is,
Yet in that form will not return. But does
He find another? The giant of sense remains

A giant without a body. If, as giant,
He shares a gigantic life, it is because
The gigantic has a reality of its own.

v

On a few words of what is real in the world
I nourish myself. I defend myself against
Whatever remains. Of what is real I say,

Is it the old, the roseate parent or
The bride come jingling, kissed and cupped, or else
The spirit and all ensigns of the self?

A few words, a memorandum voluble
Of the giant sense, the enormous harnesses
And writhing wheels of this world's business,

The drivers in the wind-blows cracking whips,
The pulling into the sky and the setting there
Of the expanses that are mountainous rock and sea;

And beyond the days, beyond the slow-foot litters
Of the nights, the actual, universal strength,
Without a word of rhetoric—there it is.

A memorandum of the people sprung
From that strength, whose armies set their own ex-
    panses.
A few words of what is real or may be

Or of glistening reference to what is real,
The universe that supplements the manqué,
The soldier seeking his point between the two,

The organic consolation, the complete
Society of the spirit when it is
Alone, the half-arc hanging in mid-air

Composed, appropriate to the incomplete,
Supported by a half-arc in mid-earth.
Millions of instances of which I am one.

VI

And if it be theatre for theatre,
The powdered personals against the giants' rage,
Blue and its deep inversions in the moon

Against gold whipped reddened in big-shadowed
    black,
Her vague "Secrete me from reality,"
His "That reality secrete itself,"

The choice is made. Green is the orator
Of our passionate height. He wears a tufted green,
And tosses green for those for whom green speaks.

Secrete us in reality. It is there
My orator. Let this giantness fall down
And come to nothing. Let the rainy arcs

And pathetic magnificences dry in the sky.
Secrete us in reality. Discover
A civil nakedness in which to be,

In which to bear with the exactest force
The precisions of fate, nothing fobbed off, nor
    changed
In a beau language without a drop of blood.

＊＊＊＊＊＊＊＊＊＊＊＊＊＊＊＊＊＊＊＊＊＊＊＊＊＊＊

THE CREATIONS OF SOUND

If the poetry of X was music,
So that it came to him of its own,
Without understanding, out of the wall

Or in the ceiling, in sounds not chosen,
Or chosen quickly, in a freedom
That was their element, we should not know

That X is an obstruction, a man
Too exactly himself, and that there are words
Better without an author, without a poet,

Or having a separate author, a different poet,
An accretion from ourselves, intelligent
Beyond intelligence, an artificial man

At a distance, a secondary expositor,
A being of sound, whom one does not approach
Through any exaggeration. From him, we collect.

Tell X that speech is not dirty silence
Clarified. It is silence made still dirtier.
It is more than an imitation for the ear.

He lacks this venerable complication.
His poems are not of the second part of life.
They do not make the visible a little hard

To see nor, reverberating, eke out the mind
On peculiar horns, themselves eked out
By the spontaneous particulars of sound.

We do not say ourselves like that in poems.
We say ourselves in syllables that rise
From the floor, rising in speech we do not speak.

HOLIDAY IN REALITY

I

It was something to see that their white was different,
Sharp as white paint in the January sun;

Something to feel that they needed another yellow,
Less Aix than Stockholm, hardly a yellow at all,

A vibrancy not to be taken for granted, from
A sun in an almost colorless, cold heaven.

They had known that there was not even a common
     speech,
Palabra of a common man who did not exist.

Why should they not know they had everything of
     their own
As each had a particular woman and her touch?

After all, they knew that to be real each had
To find for himself his earth, his sky, his sea.

And the words for them and the colors that they pos-
     sessed.
It was impossible to breathe at Durand-Ruel's.

II

The flowering Judas grows from the belly or not at all.
The breast is covered with violets. It is a green leaf.

312

Spring is umbilical or else it is not spring.
Spring is the truth of spring or nothing, a waste, a fake.

These trees and their argentines, their dark-spiced
        branches,
Grow out of the spirit or they are fantastic dust.

The bud of the apple is desire, the down-falling gold,
The catbird's gobble in the morning half-awake—

These are real only if I make them so. Whistle
For me, grow green for me and, as you whistle and grow
        green,

Intangible arrows quiver and stick in the skin
And I taste at the root of the tongue the unreal of what
        is real.

❖◇

ESTHÉTIQUE DU MAL

I

He was at Naples writing letters home
And, between his letters, reading paragraphs
On the sublime. Vesuvius had groaned
For a month. It was pleasant to be sitting there,
While the sultriest fulgurations, flickering,

Cast corners in the glass. He could describe
The terror of the sound because the sound
Was ancient. He tried to remember the phrases: pain
Audible at noon, pain torturing itself,
Pain killing pain on the very point of pain.
The volcano trembled in another ether,
As the body trembles at the end of life.

It was almost time for lunch. Pain is human.
There were roses in the cool café. His book
Made sure of the most correct catastrophe.
Except for us, Vesuvius might consume
In solid fire the utmost earth and know
No pain (ignoring the cocks that crow us up
To die). This is a part of the sublime
From which we shrink. And yet, except for us,
The total past felt nothing when destroyed.

II

At a town in which acacias grew, he lay
On his balcony at night. Warblings became
Too dark, too far, too much the accents of
Afflicted sleep, too much the syllables
That would form themselves, in time, and communi-
cate
The intelligence of his despair, express
What meditation never quite achieved.

The moon rose up as if it had escaped
His meditation. It evaded his mind.
It was part of a supremacy always
Above him. The moon was always free from him,

314

As night was free from him. The shadow touched
Or merely seemed to touch him as he spoke
A kind of elegy he found in space:

It is pain that is indifferent to the sky
In spite of the yellow of the acacias, the scent
Of them in the air still hanging heavily
In the hoary-hanging night. It does not regard
This freedom, this supremacy, and in
Its own hallucination never sees
How that which rejects it saves it in the end.

III

His firm stanzas hang like hives in hell
Or what hell was, since now both heaven and hell
Are one, and here, O terra infidel.

The fault lies with an over-human god,
Who by sympathy has made himself a man
And is not to be distinguished, when we cry

Because we suffer, our oldest parent, peer
Of the populace of the heart, the reddest lord,
Who has gone before us in experience.

If only he would not pity us so much,
Weaken our fate, relieve us of woe both great
And small, a constant fellow of destiny,

A too, too human god, self-pity's kin
And uncourageous genesis . . . It seems
As if the health of the world might be enough.

315

It seems as if the honey of common summer
Might be enough, as if the golden combs
Were part of a sustenance itself enough,

As if hell, so modified, had disappeared,
As if pain, no longer satanic mimicry,
Could be borne, as if we were sure to find our way.

IV

Livre de Toutes Sortes de Fleurs d'après Nature.
All sorts of flowers. That's the sentimentalist.
When B. sat down at the piano and made
A transparence in which we heard music, made
    music,
In which we heard transparent sounds, did he play
All sorts of notes? Or did he play only one
In an ecstasy of its associates,
Variations in the tones of a single sound,
The last, or sounds so single they seemed one?

And then that Spaniard of the rose, itself
Hot-hooded and dark-blooded, rescued the rose
From nature, each time he saw it, making it,
As he saw it, exist in his own especial eye.
Can we conceive of him as rescuing less,
As muffing the mistress for her several maids,
As foregoing the nakedest passion for barefoot
Philandering? . . . The genius of misfortune
Is not a sentimentalist. He is
That evil, that evil in the self, from which
In desperate hallow, rugged gesture, fault
Falls out on everything: the genius of

The mind, which is our being, wrong and wrong,
The genius of the body, which is our world,
Spent in the false engagements of the mind.

v

Softly let all true sympathizers come,
Without the inventions of sorrow or the sob
Beyond invention. Within what we permit,
Within the actual, the warm, the near,
So great a unity, that it is bliss,
Ties us to those we love. For this familiar,
This brother even in the father's eye,
This brother half-spoken in the mother's throat
And these regalia, these things disclosed,
These nebulous brilliancies in the smallest look
Of the being's deepest darling, we forego
Lament, willingly forfeit the ai-ai

Of parades in the obscurer selvages.
Be near me, come closer, touch my hand, phrases
Compounded of dear relation, spoken twice,
Once by the lips, once by the services
Of central sense, these minutiae mean more
Than clouds, benevolences, distant heads.
These are within what we permit, in-bar
Exquisite in poverty against the suns
Of ex-bar, in-bar retaining attributes
With which we vested, once, the golden forms
And the damasked memory of the golden forms
And ex-bar's flower and fire of the festivals
Of the damasked memory of the golden forms,
Before we were wholly human and knew ourselves.

317

The sun, in clownish yellow, but not a clown,
Brings the day to perfection and then fails. He dwells
In a consummate prime, yet still desires
A further consummation. For the lunar month
He makes the tenderest research, intent
On a transmutation which, when seen, appears
To be askew. And space is filled with his
Rejected years. A big bird pecks at him
For food. The big bird's bony appetite
Is as insatiable as the sun's. The bird
Rose from an imperfection of its own
To feed on the yellow bloom of the yellow fruit
Dropped down from turquoise leaves. In the land-
    scape of
The sun, its grossest appetite becomes less gross,
Yet, when corrected, has its curious lapses,
Its glitters, its divinations of serene
Indulgence out of all celestial sight.

The sun is the country wherever he is. The bird
In the brightest landscape downwardly revolves
Disdaining each astringent ripening,
Evading the point of redness, not content
To repose in an hour or season or long era
Of the country colors crowding against it, since
The yellow grassman's mind is still immense,
Still promises perfections cast away.

VII

How red the rose that is the soldier's wound,
The wounds of many soldiers, the wounds of all

The soldiers that have fallen, red in blood,
The soldier of time grown deathless in great size.

A mountain in which no ease is ever found,
Unless indifference to deeper death
Is ease, stands in the dark, a shadows' hill,
And there the soldier of time has deathless rest.

Concentric circles of shadows, motionless
Of their own part, yet moving on the wind,
Form mystical convolutions in the sleep
Of time's red soldier deathless on his bed.

The shadows of his fellows ring him round
In the high night, the summer breathes for them
Its fragrance, a heavy somnolence, and for him,
For the soldier of time, it breathes a summer sleep,

In which his wound is good because life was.
No part of him was ever part of death.
A woman smoothes her forehead with her hand
And the soldier of time lies calm beneath that stroke.

VIII

The death of Satan was a tragedy
For the imagination. A capital
Negation destroyed him in his tenement
And, with him, many blue phenomena.
It was not the end he had foreseen. He knew
That his revenge created filial
Revenges. And negation was eccentric.
It had nothing of the Julian thunder-cloud:

The assassin flash and rumble . . . He was denied.
Phantoms, what have you left? What underground?
What place in which to be is not enough
To be? You go, poor phantoms, without place
Like silver in the sheathing of the sight,
As the eye closes . . . How cold the vacancy
When the phantoms are gone and the shaken realist
First sees reality. The mortal no
Has its emptiness and tragic expirations.
The tragedy, however, may have begun,
Again, in the imagination's new beginning,
In the yes of the realist spoken because he must
Say yes, spoken because under every no
Lay a passion for yes that had never been broken.

IX

Panic in the face of the moon—round effendi
Or the phosphored sleep in which he walks abroad
Or the majolica dish heaped up with phosphored
    fruit
That he sends ahead, out of the goodness of his
    heart,
To anyone that comes—panic, because
The moon is no longer these nor anything
And nothing is left but comic ugliness
Or a lustred nothingness. Effendi, he
That has lost the folly of the moon becomes
The prince of the proverbs of pure poverty.
To lose sensibility, to see what one sees,
As if sight had not its own miraculous thrift,
To hear only what one hears, one meaning alone,
As if the paradise of meaning ceased

320

To be paradise, it is this to be destitute.
This is the sky divested of its fountains.
Here in the west indifferent crickets chant
Through our indifferent crises. Yet we require
Another chant, an incantation, as in
Another and later genesis, music
That buffets the shapes of its possible halcyon
Against the haggardie . . . A loud, large water
Bubbles up in the night and drowns the crickets'
    sound.
It is a declaration, a primitive ecstasy,
Truth's favors sonorously exhibited.

x

He had studied the nostalgias. In these
He sought the most grossly maternal, the creature
Who most fecundly assuaged him, the softest
Woman with a vague moustache and not the mauve
Maman. His anima liked its animal
And liked it unsubjugated, so that home
Was a return to birth, a being born
Again in the savagest severity,
Desiring fiercely, the child of a mother fierce
In his body, fiercer in his mind, merciless
To accomplish the truth in his intelligence.
It is true there were other mothers, singular
In form, lovers of heaven and earth, she-wolves
And forest tigresses and women mixed
With the sea. These were fantastic. There were
    homes
Like things submerged with their englutted sounds,
That were never wholly still. The softest woman,

Because she is as she was, reality,
The gross, the fecund, proved him against the touch
Of impersonal pain. Reality explained.
It was the last nostalgia: that he
Should understand. That he might suffer or that
He might die was the innocence of living, if life
Itself was innocent. To say that it was
Disentangled him from sleek ensolacings.

XI

Life is a bitter aspic. We are not
At the centre of a diamond. At dawn,
The paratroopers fall and as they fall
They mow the lawn. A vessel sinks in waves
Of people, as big bell-billows from its bell
Bell-bellow in the village steeple. Violets,
Great tufts, spring up from buried houses
Of poor, dishonest people, for whom the steeple,
Long since, rang out farewell, farewell, farewell.

Natives of poverty, children of malheur,
The gaiety of language is our seigneur.

A man of bitter appetite despises
A well-made scene in which paratroopers
Select adieux; and he despises this:
A ship that rolls on a confected ocean,
The weather pink, the wind in motion; and this:
A steeple that tip-tops the classic sun's
Arrangements; and the violets' exhumo.

322

The tongue caresses these exacerbations.
They press it as epicure, distinguishing
Themselves from its essential savor,
Like hunger that feeds on its own hungriness.

XII

He disposes the world in categories, thus:
The peopled and the unpeopled. In both, he is
Alone. But in the peopled world, there is,
Besides the people, his knowledge of them. In
The unpeopled, there is his knowledge of himself.
Which is more desperate in the moments when
The will demands that what he thinks be true?

Is it himself in them that he knows or they
In him? If it is himself in them, they have
No secret from him. If it is they in him,
He has no secret from them. This knowledge
Of them and of himself destroys both worlds,
Except when he escapes from it. To be
Alone is not to know them or himself.

This creates a third world without knowledge,
In which no one peers, in which the will makes no
Demands. It accepts whatever is as true,
Including pain, which, otherwise, is false.
In the third world, then, there is no pain. Yes, but
What lover has one in such rocks, what woman,
However known, at the centre of the heart?

XIII

It may be that one life is a punishment
For another, as the son's life for the father's.

But that concerns the secondary characters.
It is a fragmentary tragedy
Within the universal whole. The son
And the father alike and equally are spent,
Each one, by the necessity of being
Himself, the unalterable necessity
Of being this unalterable animal.
This force of nature in action is the major
Tragedy. This is destiny unperplexed,
The happiest enemy. And it may be
That in his Mediterranean cloister a man,
Reclining, eased of desire, establishes
The visible, a zone of blue and orange
Versicolorings, establishes a time
To watch the fire-feinting sea and calls it good,
The ultimate good, sure of a reality
Of the longest meditation, the maximum,
The assassin's scene. Evil in evil is
Comparative. The assassin discloses himself,
The force that destroys us is disclosed, within
This maximum, an adventure to be endured
With the politest helplessness. Ay-mi!
One feels its action moving in the blood.

XIV

Victor Serge said, "I followed his argument
With the blank uneasiness which one might feel
In the presence of a logical lunatic."
He said it of Konstantinov. Revolution
Is the affair of logical lunatics.
The politics of emotion must appear
To be an intellectual structure. The cause

Creates a logic not to be distinguished
From lunacy . . . One wants to be able to walk
By the lake at Geneva and consider logic:
To think of the logicians in their graves
And of the worlds of logic in their great tombs.
Lakes are more reasonable than oceans. Hence,
A promenade amid the grandeurs of the mind,
By a lake, with clouds like lights among great tombs,
Gives one a blank uneasiness, as if
One might meet Konstantinov, who would interrupt
With his lunacy. He would not be aware of the lake.
He would be the lunatic of one idea
In a world of ideas, who would have all the people
Live, work, suffer and die in that idea
In a world of ideas. He would not be aware of the
        clouds,
Lighting the martyrs of logic with white fire.
His extreme of logic would be illogical.

xv

The greatest poverty is not to live
In a physical world, to feel that one's desire
Is too difficult to tell from despair. Perhaps,
After death, the non-physical people, in paradise,
Itself non-physical, may, by chance, observe
The green corn gleaming and experience
The minor of what we feel. The adventurer
In humanity has not conceived of a race
Completely physical in a physical world.
The green corn gleams and the metaphysicals
Lie sprawling in majors of the August heat,
The rotund emotions, paradise unknown.

325

This is the thesis scrivened in delight,
The reverberating psalm, the right chorale.

One might have thought of sight, but who could
     think
Of what it sees, for all the ill it sees?
Speech found the ear, for all the evil sound,
But the dark italics it could not propound.
And out of what one sees and hears and out
Of what one feels, who could have thought to make
So many selves, so many sensuous worlds,
As if the air, the mid-day air, was swarming
With the metaphysical changes that occur,
Merely in living as and where we live.

THE BED OF OLD JOHN ZELLER

This structure of ideas, these ghostly sequences
Of the mind, result only in disaster. It follows,
Casual poet, that to add your own disorder to disaster

Makes more of it. It is easy to wish for another structure
Of ideas and to say as usual that there must be
Other ghostly sequences and, it would be, luminous

Sequences, thought of among spheres in the old peak of
     night:

This is the habit of wishing, as if one's grandfather lay
In one's heart and wished as he had always wished, unable

To sleep in that bed for its disorder, talking of ghostly
Sequences that would be sleep and ting-tang tossing, so
    that
He might slowly forget. It is more difficult to evade

That habit of wishing and to accept the structure
Of things as the structure of ideas. It was the structure
Of things at least that was thought of in the old peak of
    night.

◇◇

LESS AND LESS HUMAN, O SAVAGE SPIRIT

If there must be a god in the house, must be,
Saying things in the rooms and on the stair,

Let him move as the sunlight moves on the floor,
Or moonlight, silently, as Plato's ghost

Or Aristotle's skeleton. Let him hang out
His stars on the wall. He must dwell quietly.

He must be incapable of speaking, closed,
As those are: as light, for all its motion, is;

327

As color, even the closest to us, is;
As shapes, though they portend us, are.

It is the human that is the alien,
The human that has no cousin in the moon.

It is the human that demands his speech
From beasts or from the incommunicable mass.

If there must be a god in the house, let him be one
That will not hear us when we speak: a coolness,

A vermilioned nothingness, any stick of the mass
Of which we are too distantly a part.

❀◇

WILD DUCKS, PEOPLE AND DISTANCES

The life of the world depends on that he is
Alive, on that people are alive, on that
There is village and village of them, without regard
To that be-misted one and apart from her.

Did we expect to live in other lives?
We grew used so soon, too soon, to earth itself,
As an element; to the sky, as an element.
People might share but were never an element,

Like earth and sky. Then he became nothing else
And they were nothing else. It was late in the year.
The wild ducks were enveloped. The weather was cold.
Yet, under the migrations to solitude,

There remained the smoke of the villages. Their fire
Was central in distances the wild ducks could
Not span, without any weather at all, except
The weather of other lives, from which there could

Be no migrating. It was that they were there
That held the distances off: the villages
Held off the final, fatal distances,
Between us and the place in which we stood.

❖❖❖❖❖❖❖❖❖❖❖❖❖❖❖❖❖❖❖❖❖❖❖❖❖❖❖❖❖❖❖

THE PURE GOOD OF THEORY

I

All the Preludes to Felicity

It is time that beats in the breast and it is time
That batters against the mind, silent and proud,
The mind that knows it is destroyed by time.

Time is a horse that runs in the heart, a horse
Without a rider on a road at night.
The mind sits listening and hears it pass.

329

It is someone walking rapidly in the street.
The reader by the window has finished his book
And tells the hour by the lateness of the sounds.

Even breathing is the beating of time, in kind:
A retardation of its battering,
A horse grotesquely taut, a walker like

A shadow in mid-earth . . . If we propose
A large-sculptured, platonic person, free from time,
And imagine for him the speech he cannot speak,

A form, then, protected from the battering, may
Mature: A capable being may replace
Dark horse and walker walking rapidly.

Felicity, ah! Time is the hooded enemy,
The inimical music, the enchantered space
In which the enchanted preludes have their place.

II

Description of a Platonic Person

Then came Brazil to nourish the emaciated
Romantic with dreams of her avoirdupois, green
    glade
Of serpents like z rivers simmering,

Green glade and holiday hotel and world
Of the future, in which the memory had gone
From everything, flying the flag of the nude,

330

The flag of the nude above the holiday hotel.
But there was one invalid in that green glade
And beneath that handkerchief drapeau, severe,

Signal, a character out of solitude,
Who was what people had been and still were,
Who lay in bed on the west wall of the sea,

Ill of a question like a malady,
Ill of a constant question in his thought,
Unhappy about the sense of happiness.

Was it that—a sense and beyond intelligence?
Could the future rest on a sense and be beyond
Intelligence? On what does the present rest?

This platonic person discovered a soul in the world
And studied it in his holiday hotel.
He was a Jew from Europe or might have been.

III
Fire-monsters in the Milky Brain

Man, that is not born of woman but of air,
That comes here in the solar chariot,
Like rhetoric in a narration of the eye—

We knew one parent must have been divine,
Adam of beau regard, from fat Elysia,
Whose mind malformed this morning metaphor,

While all the leaves leaked gold. His mind made
    morning,
As he slept. He woke in a metaphor: this was
A metamorphosis of paradise,

Malformed, the world was paradise malformed . . .
Now, closely the ear attends the varying
Of this precarious music, the change of key

Not quite detected at the moment of change
And, now, it attends the difficult difference.
To say the solar chariot is junk

Is not a variation but an end.
Yet to speak of the whole world as metaphor
Is still to stick to the contents of the mind

And the desire to believe in a metaphor.
It is to stick to the nicer knowledge of
Belief, that what it believes in is not true.

IV

Dry Birds Are Fluttering in Blue Leaves

It is never the thing but the version of the thing:
The fragrance of the woman not her self,
Her self in her manner not the solid block,

The day in its color not perpending time,
Time in its weather, our most sovereign lord,
The weather in words and words in sounds of sound.

These devastations are the divertissements
Of a destroying spiritual that digs-a-dog,
Whines in its hole for puppies to come see,

Springs outward, being large, and, in the dust,
Being small, inscribes ferocious alphabets,
Flies like a bat expanding as it flies,

332

Until its wings bear off night's middle witch;
And yet remains the same, the beast of light,
Groaning in half-exploited gutturals

The need of its element, the final need
Of final access to its element—
Of access like the page of a wiggy book,

Touched suddenly by the universal flare
For a moment, a moment in which we read and re-
     peat
The eloquences of light's faculties.

A WORD WITH JOSÉ RODRÍGUEZ–FEO

As one of the secretaries of the moon,
The queen of ignorance, you have deplored
How she presides over imbeciles. The night
Makes everything grotesque. Is it because
Night is the nature of man's interior world?
Is lunar Habana the Cuba of the self?

We must enter boldly that interior world
To pick up relaxations of the known.
For example, this old man selling oranges
Sleeps by his basket. He snores. His bloated breath
Bursts back. What not quite realized transit
Of ideas moves wrinkled in a motion like

The cry of an embryo? The spirit tires,
It has, long since, grown tired, of such ideas.
It says there is an absolute grotesque.
There is a nature that is grotesque within
The boulevards of the generals. Why should
We say that it is man's interior world

Or seeing the spent, unconscious shapes of night,
Pretend they are shapes of another consciousness?
The grotesque is not a visitation. It is
Not apparition but appearance, part
Of that simplified geography, in which
The sun comes up like news from Africa.

❁◆

PAISANT CHRONICLE

What are the major men? All men are brave.
All men endure. The great captain is the choice
Of chance. Finally, the most solemn burial
Is a paisant chronicle.

           Men live to be
Admired by men and all men, therefore, live
To be admired by all men. Nations live
To be admired by nations. The race is brave.
The race endures. The funeral pomps of the race
Are a multitude of individual pomps

334

And the chronicle of humanity is the sum
Of paisant chronicles.

              The major men—
That is different. They are characters beyond
Reality, composed thereof. They are
The fictive man created out of men.
They are men but artificial men. They are
Nothing in which it is not possible
To believe, more than the casual hero, more
Than Tartuffe as myth, the most Molière,
The easy projection long prohibited.

The baroque poet may see him as still a man
As Virgil, abstract. But see him for yourself,
The fictive man. He may be seated in
A café. There may be a dish of country cheese
And a pineapple on the table. It must be so.

❁❁❁❁❁❁❁❁❁❁❁❁❁❁❁❁❁❁❁❁❁❁❁❁❁❁❁❁❁

SKETCH OF THE ULTIMATE POLITICIAN

He is the final builder of the total building,
The final dreamer of the total dream,
Or will be. Building and dream are one.

There is a total building and there is
A total dream. There are words of this,
Words, in a storm, that beat around the shapes.

There is a storm much like the crying of the wind,
Words that come out of us like words within,
That have rankled for many lives and made no
      sound.

He can hear them, like people on the walls,
Running in the rises of common speech,
Crying as that speech falls as if to fail.

There is a building stands in a ruinous storm,
A dream interrupted out of the past,
From beside us, from where we have yet to live.

❖❖❖

FLYER'S FALL

This man escaped the dirty fates,
Knowing that he died nobly, as he died.

Darkness, nothingness of human after-death,
Receive and keep him in the deepnesses of space—

Profundum, physical thunder, dimension in which
We believe without belief, beyond belief.

JOUGA

The physical world is meaningless tonight
And there is no other. There is Ha-eé-me, who sits
And plays his guitar. Ha-eé-me is a beast.

Or perhaps his guitar is a beast or perhaps they are
Two beasts. But of the same kind—two conjugal beasts.
Ha-eé-me is the male beast . . . an imbecile,

Who knocks out a noise. The guitar is another beast
Beneath his tip-tap-tap. It is she that responds.
Two beasts but two of a kind and then not beasts.

Yet two not quite of a kind. It is like that here.
There are many of these beasts that one never sees,
Moving so that the foot-falls are slight and almost
          nothing.

This afternoon the wind and the sea were like that—
And after a while, when Ha-eé-me has gone to sleep,
A great jaguar running will make a little sound.

DEBRIS OF LIFE AND MIND

There is so little that is close and warm.
It is as if we were never children.

Sit in the room. It is true in the moonlight
That it is as if we had never been young.

We ought not to be awake. It is from this
That a bright red woman will be rising

And, standing in violent golds, will brush her hair.
Shc will speak thoughtfully the words of a line.

She will think about them not quite able to sing.
Besides, when the sky is so blue, things sing themselves,

Even for her, already for her. She will listen
And feel that her color is a meditation,

The most gay and yet not so gay as it was.
Stay here. Speak of familiar things a while.

338

DESCRIPTION WITHOUT PLACE

I

It is possible that to seem—it is to be,
As the sun is something seeming and it is.

The sun is an example. What it seems
It is and in such seeming all things are.

Thus things are like a seeming of the sun
Or like a seeming of the moon or night

Or sleep. It was a queen that made it seem
By the illustrious nothing of her name.

Her green mind made the world around her green.
The queen is an example . . . This green queen

In the seeming of the summer of her sun
By her own seeming made the summer change.

In the golden vacancy she came, and comes,
And seems to be on the saying of her name.

Her time becomes again, as it became,
The crown and week-day coronal of her fame.

II

Such seemings are the actual ones: the way
Things look each day, each morning, or the style

Peculiar to the queen, this queen or that,
The lesser seeming original in the blind

Forward of the eye that, in its backward, sees
The greater seeming of the major mind.

An age is a manner collected from a queen.
An age is green or red. An age believes

Or it denies. An age is solitude
Or a barricade against the singular man

By the incalculably plural. Hence
Its identity is merely a thing that seems,

In the seeming of an original in the eye,
In the major manner of a queen, the green

The red, the blue, the argent queen. If not,
What subtlety would apparition have?

In flat appearance we should be and be,
Except for delicate clinkings not explained.

These are the actual seemings that we see,
Hear, feel and know. We feel and know them so.

III
There are potential seemings, arrogant
To be, as on the youngest poet's page,

Or in the dark musician, listening
To hear more brightly the contriving chords.

340

There are potential seemings turbulent
In the death of a soldier, like the utmost will,

The more than human commonplace of blood,
The breath that gushes upward and is gone,

And another breath emerging out of death,
That speaks for him such seemings as death gives.

There might be, too, a change immenser than
A poet's metaphors in which being would

Come true, a point in the fire of music where
Dazzle yields to a clarity and we observe,

And observing is completing and we are content,
In a world that shrinks to an immediate whole,

That we do not need to understand, complete
Without secret arrangements of it in the mind.

There might be in the curling-out of spring
A purple-leaping element that forth

Would froth the whole heaven with its seeming-so,
The intentions of a mind as yet unknown,

The spirit of one dwelling in a seed,
Itself that seed's ripe, unpredictable fruit.

Things are as they seemed to Calvin or to Anne
Of England, to Pablo Neruda in Ceylon,

341

To Nietzsche in Basel, to Lenin by a lake.
But the integrations of the past are like

A *Museo Olimpico,* so much
So little, our affair, which is the affair

Of the possible: seemings that are to be,
Seemings that it is possible may be.

IV

Nietzsche in Basel studied the deep pool
Of these discolorations, mastering

The moving and the moving of their forms
In the much-mottled motion of blank time.

His revery was the deepness of the pool,
The very pool, his thoughts the colored forms,

The eccentric souvenirs of human shapes,
Wrapped in their seemings, crowd on curious crowd,

In a kind of total affluence, all first,
All final, colors subjected in revery

To an innate grandiose, an innate light,
The sun of Nietzsche gildering the pool,

Yes: gildering the swarm-like manias
In perpetual revolution, round and round . . .

Lenin on a bench beside a lake disturbed
The swans. He was not the man for swans.

The slouch of his body and his look were not
In suavest keeping. The shoes, the clothes, the hat

Suited the decadence of those silences,
In which he sat. All chariots were drowned. The
    swans

Moved on the buried water where they lay.
Lenin took bread from his pocket, scattered it—

The swans fled outward to remoter reaches,
As if they knew of distant beaches; and were

Dissolved. The distances of space and time
Were one and swans far off were swans to come.

The eye of Lenin kept the far-off shapes.
His mind raised up, down-drowned, the chariots.

And reaches, beaches, tomorrow's regions became
One thinking of apocalyptic legions.

v

If seeming is description without place,
The spirit's universe, then a summer's day,

Even the seeming of a summer's day,
Is description without place. It is a sense

To which we refer experience, a knowledge
Incognito, the column in the desert,

On which the dove alights. Description is
Composed of a sight indifferent to the eye.

343

It is an expectation, a desire,
A palm that rises up beyond the sea,

A little different from reality:
The difference that we make in what we see

And our memorials of that difference,
Sprinklings of bright particulars from the sky.

The future is description without place,
The categorical predicate, the arc.

It is a wizened starlight growing young,
In which old stars are planets of morning, fresh

In the brilliantest descriptions of new day,
Before it comes, the just anticipation

Of the appropriate creatures, jubilant,
The forms that are attentive in thin air.

VI

Description is revelation. It is not
The thing described, nor false facsimile.

It is an artificial thing that exists,
In its own seeming, plainly visible,

Yet not too closely the double of our lives,
Intenser than any actual life could be,

A text we should be born that we might read,
More explicit than the experience of sun

344

And moon, the book of reconciliation,
Book of a concept only possible

In description, canon central in itself,
The thesis of the plentifullest John.

VII

Thus the theory of description matters most.
It is the theory of the word for those

For whom the word is the making of the world,
The buzzing world and lisping firmament.

It is a world of words to the end of it,
In which nothing solid is its solid self.

As, men make themselves their speech: the hard
　　hidalgo
Lives in the mountainous character of his speech;

And in that mountainous mirror Spain acquires
The knowledge of Spain and of the hidalgo's hat—

A seeming of the Spaniard, a style of life,
The invention of a nation in a phrase,

In a description hollowed out of hollow-bright,
The artificer of subjects still half night.

It matters, because everything we say
Of the past is description without place, a cast

Of the imagination, made in sound;
And because what we say of the future must portend,

Be alive with its own seemings, seeming to be
Like rubies reddened by rubies reddening.

❀◇

TWO TALES OF LIADOFF

I

Do you remember how the rocket went on
And on, at night, exploding finally
In an ovation of resplendent forms—

Ovation on ovation of large blue men
In pantaloons of fire and of women hatched,
Like molten citizens of the vacuum?

Do you remember the children there like wicks,
That constantly sparkled their small gold? The town
Had crowded into the rocket and touched the fuse.

That night, Liadoff, a long time after his death,
At a piano in a cloud sat practicing,
On a black piano practiced epi-tones.

Do you remember what the townsmen said,
As they fell down, as they heard Liadoff's cloud
And its tragical, its haunted arpeggios?

346

And is it true that what they said, as they fell,
Was repeated by Liadoff in a narration
Of incredible colors ex, ex and ex and out?

II

The feeling of Liadoff was changed. It is
The instant of the change that was the poem,
When the cloud pressed suddenly the whole return

From thought, like a violent pulse in the cloud itself,
As if Liadoff no longer remained a ghost
And, being straw, turned green, lived backward,
        shared

The fantastic fortune of fantastic blood,
Until his body smothered him, until
His being felt the need of soaring, the need

Of air . . . But then that cloud, that piano placed
Just where it was, oh beau caboose . . . It was part
Of the instant to perceive, after the shock,

That the rocket was only an inferior cloud.
There was no difference between the town
And him. Both wanted the same thing. Both sought

His epi-tones, the colors of the ear,
The sounds that soon become a voluble speech—
Voluble but archaic and hard to hear.

ANALYSIS OF A THEME

THEME

How happy I was the day I told the young Blandina of three-
legged giraffes . . .

ANALYSIS

In the conscious world, the great clouds
Potter in the summer sky.
It is a province—

Of ugly, subconscious time, in which
There is no beautiful eye
And no true tree,

There being no subconscious place,
Only Indyterranean
Resemblances

Of place: time's haggard mongrels.
Yet in time's middle deep,
In its abstract motion,

Its immaterial monsters move,
Without physical pedantry
Or any name.

Invisible, they move and are,
Not speaking worms, nor birds
Of mutable plume,

348

Pure coruscations, that lie beyond
The imagination, intact
And unattained,

Even in Paris, in the Gardens
Of Acclimatization,
On a holiday.

The knowledge of bright-ethered things
Bears us toward time, on its
Perfective wings.

We enjoy the ithy oonts and long-haired
Plomets, as the Herr Gott
Enjoys his comets.

◇◆◇

LATE HYMN FROM THE MYRRH–MOUNTAIN

Unsnack your snood, madanna, for the stars
Are shining on all brows of Neversink.

Already the green bird of summer has flown
Away. The night-flies acknowledge these planets,

Predestined to this night, this noise and the place
Of summer. Tomorrow will look like today,

Will appear like it. But it will be an appearance,
A shape left behind, with like wings spreading out,

Brightly empowered with like colors, swarmingly,
But not quite molten, not quite the fluid thing,

A little changed by tips of artifice, changed
By the glints of sound from the grass. These are not

The early constellations, from which came the first
Illustrious intimations—uncertain love,

The knowledge of being, sense without sense of time.
Take the diamonds from your hair and lay them down.

The deer-grass is thin. The timothy is brown.
The shadow of an external world comes near.

❁◇

MAN CARRYING THING

The poem must resist the intelligence
Almost successfully. Illustration:

A brune figure in winter evening resists
Identity. The thing he carries resists

The most necessitous sense. Accept them, then,
As secondary (parts not quite perceived

Of the obvious whole, uncertain particles
Of the certain solid, the primary free from doubt,

Things floating like the first hundred flakes of snow
Out of a storm we must endure all night,

Out of a storm of secondary things),
A horror of thoughts that suddenly are real.

We must endure our thoughts all night, until
The bright obvious stands motionless in cold.

PIECES

Tinsel in February, tinsel in August.
There are things in a man besides his reason.
Come home, wind, he kept crying and crying.

Snow glistens in its instant in the air,
Instant of millefiori bluely magnified—
Come home, wind, he said as he climbed the
    stair—

Crystal on crystal until crystal clouds
Become an over-crystal out of ice,
Exhaling these creations of itself.

There is a sense in sounds beyond their meaning.
The tinsel of August falling was like a flame
That breathed on ground, more blue than red,
    more red

Than green, fidgets of all-related fire.
The wind is like a dog that runs away.
But it is like a horse. It is like motion

That lives in space. It is a person at night,
A member of the family, a tie,
An ethereal cousin, another milleman.

◇◇

A COMPLETELY NEW SET OF OBJECTS

From a Schuylkill in mid-earth there came emerging
Flotillas, willed and wanted, bearing in them

Shadows of friends, of those he knew, each bringing
From the water in which he believed and out of desire

Things made by mid-terrestrial, mid-human
Makers without knowing, or intending, uses.

These figures verdant with time's buried verdure
Came paddling their canoes, a thousand thousand,

Carrying such shapes, of such alleviation,
That the beholder knew their subtle purpose,

Knew well the shapes were the exactest shaping
Of a vast people old in meditation . . .

Under Tinicum or small Cohansey,
The fathers of the makers may lie and weather.

❖◇

ADULT EPIGRAM

The romance of the precise is not the elision
Of the tired romance of imprecision.
It is the ever-never-changing same,
An appearance of Again, the diva-dame.

◇⁊

TWO VERSIONS OF THE SAME POEM

That Which Cannot Be Fixed

I

Once more he turned to that which could not be
    fixed.
By the sea, insolid rock, stentor, and said:

353

Lascar, is there a body, turbulent
With time, in wavering water lies, swollen

With thought, through which it cannot see? Does it
Lie lengthwise like the cloud of sleep, not quite

Reposed? And does it have a puissant heart
To toll its pulses, vigors of its self?

Lascar, and water-carcass never-named,
These vigors make, thrice-triple-syllabled,

The difficult images of possible shapes,
That cannot now be fixed. Only there is

A beating and a beating in the centre of
The sea, a strength that tumbles everywhere,

Like more and more becoming less and less,
Like space dividing its blue and by division

Being changed from space to the sailor's metier,
Or say from that which was conceived to that

Which was realized, like reason's constant ruin.
Sleep deep, good eel, in your perverse marine.

II

The human ocean beats against this rock
Of earth, rises against it, tide by tide,

Continually. And old John Zeller stands
On his hill, watching the rising and falling, and
    says:

354

Of what are these the creatures, what element
Or—yes: what elements, unreconciled

Because there is no golden solvent here?
If they were creatures of the sea alone,

But singular, they would, like water, scale
The uptopping top and tip of things, borne up

By the cadaver of these caverns, half-asleep.
But if they are of sea, earth, sky—water

And fire and air and things not discomposed
From ignorance, not an undivided whole,

It is an ocean of watery images
And shapes of fire, and wind that bears them
          down.

Perhaps these forms are seeking to escape
Cadaverous undulations. Rest, old mould . . .

◇◇

MEN MADE OUT OF WORDS

What should we be without the sexual myth,
The human revery or poem of death?

Castratos of moon-mash—Life consists
Of propositions about life. The human

Revery is a solitude in which
We compose these propositions, torn by dreams,

By the terrible incantations of defeats
And by the fear that defeats and dreams are one.

The whole race is a poet that writes down
The eccentric propositions of its fate.

❀◇

THINKING OF A RELATION BETWEEN
THE IMAGES OF METAPHORS

The wood-doves are singing along the Perkiomen.
The bass lie deep, still afraid of the Indians.

In the one ear of the fisherman, who is all
One ear, the wood-doves are singing a single song.

The bass keep looking ahead, upstream, in one
Direction, shrinking from the spit and splash

Of waterish spears. The fisherman is all
One eye, in which the dove resembles the dove.

There is one dove, one bass, one fisherman.
Yet coo becomes rou-coo, rou-coo. How close

To the unstated theme each variation comes . . .
In that one ear it might strike perfectly:

State the disclosure. In that one eye the dove
Might spring to sight and yet remain a dove.

The fisherman might be the single man
In whose breast, the dove, alighting, would grow still.

❉❉❉❉❉❉❉❉❉❉❉❉❉❉❉❉❉❉❉❉❉❉❉❉❉❉❉❉❉

CHAOS IN MOTION AND NOT IN MOTION

Oh, that this lashing wind was something more
Than the spirit of Ludwig Richter . . .

The rain is pouring down. It is July.
There is lightning and the thickest thunder.

It is a spectacle. Scene 10 becomes 11,
In Series X, Act IV, et cetera.

People fall out of windows, trees tumble down,
Summer is changed to winter, the young grow old,

The air is full of children, statues, roofs
And snow. The theatre is spinning round,

Colliding with deaf-mute churches and optical trains.
The most massive sopranos are singing songs of scales.

And Ludwig Richter, turbulent Schlemihl,
Has lost the whole in which he was contained,

Knows desire without an object of desire,
All mind and violence and nothing felt.

He knows he has nothing more to think about.
Like the wind that lashes everything at once.

◇◇◇

THE HOUSE WAS QUIET AND
THE WORLD WAS CALM

The house was quiet and the world was calm.
The reader became the book; and summer night

Was like the conscious being of the book.
The house was quiet and the world was calm.

The words were spoken as if there was no book,
Except that the reader leaned above the page,

Wanted to lean, wanted much most to be
The scholar to whom his book is true, to whom

The summer night is like a perfection of thought.
The house was quiet because it had to be.

The quiet was part of the meaning, part of the mind:
The access of perfection to the page.

358

And the world was calm. The truth in a calm world,
In which there is no other meaning, itself

Is calm, itself is summer and night, itself
Is the reader leaning late and reading there.

❖◇

CONTINUAL CONVERSATION WITH
A SILENT MAN

The old brown hen and the old blue sky,
Between the two we live and die—
The broken cartwheel on the hill.

As if, in the presence of the sea,
We dried our nets and mended sail
And talked of never-ending things,

Of the never-ending storm of will,
One will and many wills, and the wind,
Of many meanings in the leaves,

Brought down to one below the eaves,
Link, of that tempest, to the farm,
The chain of the turquoise hen and sky

And the wheel that broke as the cart went by.
It is not a voice that is under the eaves.
It is not speech, the sound we hear

359

In this conversation, but the sound
Of things and their motion: the other man,
A turquoise monster moving round.

❋❋

A WOMAN SINGS A SONG FOR
A SOLDIER COME HOME

The wound kills that does not bleed.
It has no nurse nor kin to know
Nor kin to care.

And the man dies that does not fall.
He walks and dies. Nothing survives
Except what was,

Under the white clouds piled and piled
Like gathered-up forgetfulness,
In sleeping air.

The clouds are over the village, the town,
To which the walker speaks
And tells of his wound,

Without a word to the people, unless
One person should come by chance,
This man or that,

360

So much a part of the place, so little
A person he knows, with whom he might
Talk of the weather—

And let it go, with nothing lost,
Just out of the village, at its edge,
In the quiet there.

◇◇

THE PEDIMENT OF APPEARANCE

Young men go walking in the woods,
Hunting for the great ornament,
The pediment of appearance.

They hunt for a form which by its form alone,
Without diamond—blazons or flashing or
Chains of circumstance,

By its form alone, by being right,
By being high, is the stone
For which they are looking:

The savage transparence. They go crying
The world is myself, life is myself,
Breathing as if they breathed themselves,

Full of their ugly lord,
Speaking the phrases that follow the sight
Of this essential ornament

In the woods, in this full-blown May,
The months of understanding. The pediment
Lifts up its heavy scowl before them.

❖❖❖❖❖❖❖❖❖❖❖❖❖❖❖❖❖❖❖❖❖❖❖❖❖❖❖❖❖❖❖❖❖❖❖

BURGHERS OF PETTY DEATH

These two by the stone wall
Are a slight part of death.
The grass is still green.

But there is a total death,
A devastation, a death of great height
And depth, covering all surfaces,
Filling the mind.

These are the small townsmen of death,
A man and a woman, like two leaves
That keep clinging to a tree,
Before winter freezes and grows black—

Of great height and depth
Without any feeling, an imperium of quiet,
In which a wasted figure, with an instrument,
Propounds blank final music.

HUMAN ARRANGEMENT

Place-bound and time-bound in evening rain
And bound by a sound which does not change,

Except that it begins and ends,
Begins again and ends again—

Rain without change within or from
Without. In this place and in this time

And in this sound, which do not change,
In which the rain is all one thing,

In the sky, an imagined, wooden chair
Is the clear-point of an edifice,

Forced up from nothing, evening's chair,
Blue-strutted curule, true—unreal,

The centre of transformations that
Transform for transformation's self,

In a glitter that is a life, a gold
That is a being, a will, a fate.

THE GOOD MAN HAS NO SHAPE

Through centuries he lived in poverty.
God only was his only elegance.

Then generation by generation he grew
Stronger and freer, a little better off.

He lived each life because, if it was bad,
He said a good life would be possible.

At last the good life came, good sleep, bright fruit,
And Lazarus betrayed him to the rest,

Who killed him, sticking feathers in his flesh
To mock him. They placed with him in his grave

Sour wine to warn him, an empty book to read;
And over it they set a jagged sign,

Epitaphium to his death, which read,
The Good Man Has No Shape, as if they knew.

THE RED FERN

The large-leaved day grows rapidly,
And opens in this familiar spot
Its unfamiliar, difficult fern,
Pushing and pushing red after red.

There are doubles of this fern in clouds,
Less firm than the paternal flame,
Yet drenched with its identity,
Reflections and off-shoots, mimic-motes

And mist-mites, dangling seconds, grown
Beyond relation to the parent trunk:
The dazzling, bulging, brightest core,
The furiously burning father-fire . . .

Infant, it is enough in life
To speak of what you see. But wait
Until sight wakens the sleepy eye
And pierces the physical fix of things.

FROM THE PACKET OF ANACHARSIS

In his packet Anacharsis found the lines:
"The farm was fat and the land in which it lay
Seemed in the morning like a holiday."

365

He had written them near Athens. The farm was
    white.
The buildings were of marble and stood in marble
    light.
It was his clarity that made the vista bright.

A subject for Puvis. He would compose
The scene in his gray-rose with violet rocks.
And Bloom would see what Puvis did, protest

And speak of the floridest reality . . .
In the punctual centre of all circles white
Stands truly. The circles nearest to it share

Its color, but less as they recede, impinged
By difference and then by definition
As a tone defines itself and separates

And the circles quicken and crystal colors come
And flare and Bloom with his vast accumulation
Stands and regards and repeats the primitive lines.

◇◇◇

THE DOVE IN THE BELLY

The whole of appearance is a toy. For this,
The dove in the belly builds his nest and coos,

Selah, tempestuous bird. How is it that
The rivers shine and hold their mirrors up,

Like excellence collecting excellence?
How is it that the wooden trees stand up

And live and heap their panniers of green
And hold them round the sultry day? Why should

These mountains being high be, also, bright,
Fetched up with snow that never falls to earth?

And this great esplanade of corn, miles wide,
Is something wished for made effectual

And something more. And the people in costumes,
Though poor, though raggeder than ruin, have that

Within them right for terraces—oh, brave salut!
Deep dove, placate you in your hiddenness.

✿◇

MOUNTAINS COVERED WITH CATS

The sea full of fishes in shoals, the woods that let
One seed alone grow wild, the railway-stops
In Russia at which the same statue of Stalin greets
The same railway passenger, the ancient tree
In the centre of its cones, the resplendent flights
Of red facsimiles through related trees,
White houses in villages, black communicants—
The catalogue is too commodious.

367

Regard the invalid personality
Instead, outcast, without the will to power
And impotent, like the imagination seeking
To propagate the imagination or like
War's miracle begetting that of peace.

Freud's eye was the microscope of potency.
By fortune, his gray ghost may meditate
The spirits of all the impotent dead, seen clear,
And quickly understand, without their flesh,
How truly they had not been what they were.

THE PREJUDICE AGAINST THE PAST

Day is the children's friend.
It is Marianna's Swedish cart.
It is that and a very big hat.

Confined by what they see,
Aquiline pedants treat the cart,
As one of the relics of the heart.

They treat the philosopher's hat,
Left thoughtlessly behind,
As one of the relics of the mind . . .

Of day, then, children make
What aquiline pedants take
For souvenirs of time, lost time,

Adieux, shapes, images—
No, not of day, but of themselves,
Not of perpetual time.

And, therefore, aquiline pedants find
The philosopher's hat to be part of the mind,
The Swedish cart to be part of the heart.

◇◇◇

EXTRAORDINARY REFERENCES

The mother ties the hair-ribbons of the child
And she has peace. *My Jacomyntje!*
Your great-grandfather was an Indian fighter.

The cool sun of the Tulpehocken refers
To its barbed, barbarous rising and has peace.
These earlier dissipations of the blood

And brain, as the extraordinary references
Of ordinary people, places, things,
Compose us in a kind of eulogy.

My Jacomyntje! This first spring after the war,
In which your father died, still breathes for him
And breathes again for us a fragile breath.

In the inherited garden, a second-hand
Vertumnus creates an equilibrium.
The child's three ribbons are in her plaited hair.

369

ATTEMPT TO DISCOVER LIFE

At San Miguel de los Baños,
The waitress heaped up black Hermosas
In the magnificence of a volcano.
Round them she spilled the roses
Of the place, blue and green, both streaked.
And white roses shaded emerald on petals
Out of the deadliest heat.

There entered a cadaverous person,
Who bowed and, bowing, brought, in her mantilla,
A woman brilliant and pallid-skinned,
Of fiery eyes and long thin arms.
She stood with him at the table,
Smiling and wetting her lips
In the heavy air.

The green roses drifted up from the table
In smoke. The blue petals became
The yellowing fomentations of effulgence,
Among fomentations of black bloom and of white
    bloom.
The cadaverous persons were dispelled.
On the table near which they stood
Two coins were lying—dos centavos.

A LOT OF PEOPLE BATHING IN A STREAM

It was like passing a boundary to dive
Into the sun-filled water, brightly leafed
And limbed and lighted out from bank to bank.

That's how the stars shine during the day. There,
    then,
The yellow that was yesterday, refreshed,
Became to-day, among our children and

Ourselves, in the clearest green—well, call it green.
We bathed in yellow green and yellow blue
And in these comic colors dangled down,

Like their particular characters, addicts
To blotches, angular anonymids
Gulping for shape among the reeds. No doubt,

We were the appropriate conceptions, less
Than creatures, of the sky between the banks,
The water flowing in the flow of space.

It was passing a boundary, floating without a head
And naked, or almost so, into the grotesque
Of being naked, or almost so, in a world

Of nakedness, in the company of the sun,
Good-fortuner of the grotesque, patroon,
A funny foreigner of meek address.

How good it was at home again at night
To prepare for bed, in the frame of the house, and
    move
Round the rooms, which do not ever seem to
    change . . .

◇◇

CREDENCES OF SUMMER

I

Now in midsummer come and all fools slaughtered
And spring's infuriations over and a long way
To the first autumnal inhalations, young broods
Are in the grass, the roses are heavy with a weight
Of fragrance and the mind lays by its trouble.

Now the mind lays by its trouble and considers.
The fidgets of remembrance come to this.
This is the last day of a certain year
Beyond which there is nothing left of time.
It comes to this and the imagination's life.

There is nothing more inscribed nor thought nor felt
And this must comfort the heart's core against
Its false disasters—these fathers standing round,
These mothers touching, speaking, being near,
These lovers waiting in the soft dry grass.

372

II

Postpone the anatomy of summer, as
The physical pine, the metaphysical pine.
Let's see the very thing and nothing else.
Let's see it with the hottest fire of sight.
Burn everything not part of it to ash.

Trace the gold sun about the whitened sky
Without evasion by a single metaphor.
Look at it in its essential barrenness
And say this, this is the centre that I seek.
Fix it in an eternal foliage

And fill the foliage with arrested peace,
Joy of such permanence, right ignorance
Of change still possible. Exile desire
For what is not. This is the barrenness
Of the fertile thing that can attain no more.

III

It is the natural tower of all the world,
The point of survey, green's green apogee,
But a tower more precious than the view beyond,
A point of survey squatting like a throne,
Axis of everything, green's apogee

And happiest folk-land, mostly marriage-hymns.
It is the mountain on which the tower stands,
It is the final mountain. Here the sun,
Sleepless, inhales his proper air, and rests.
This is the refuge that the end creates.

It is the old man standing on the tower,
Who reads no book. His ruddy ancientness
Absorbs the ruddy summer and is appeased,
By an understanding that fulfils his age,
By a feeling capable of nothing more.

IV

One of the limits of reality
Presents itself in Oley when the hay,
Baked through long days, is piled in mows. It is
A land too ripe for enigmas, too serene.
There the distant fails the clairvoyant eye

And the secondary senses of the ear
Swarm, not with secondary sounds, but choirs,
Not evocations but last choirs, last sounds
With nothing else compounded, carried full,
Pure rhetoric of a language without words.

Things stop in that direction and since they stop
The direction stops and we accept what is
As good. The utmost must be good and is
And is our fortune and honey hived in the trees
And mingling of colors at a festival.

V

One day enriches a year. One woman makes
The rest look down. One man becomes a race,
Lofty like him, like him perpetual.
Or do the other days enrich the one?
And is the queen humble as she seems to be,

374

The charitable majesty of her whole kin?
The bristling soldier, weather-foxed, who looms
In the sunshine is a filial form and one
Of the land's children, easily born, its flesh,
Not fustian. The more than casual blue

Contains the year and other years and hymns
And people, without souvenir. The day
Enriches the year, not as embellishment.
Stripped of remembrance, it displays its strength—
The youth, the vital son, the heroic power.

VI

The rock cannot be broken. It is the truth.
It rises from land and sea and covers them.
It is a mountain half way green and then,
The other immeasurable half, such rock
As placid air becomes. But it is not

A hermit's truth nor symbol in hermitage.
It is the visible rock, the audible,
The brilliant mercy of a sure repose,
On this present ground, the vividest repose,
Things certain sustaining us in certainty.

It is the rock of summer, the extreme,
A mountain luminous half way in bloom
And then half way in the extremest light
Of sapphires flashing from the central sky,
As if twelve princes sat before a king.

375

Far in the woods they sang their unreal songs,
Secure. It was difficult to sing in face
Of the object. The singers had to avert themselves
Or else avert the object. Deep in the woods
They sang of summer in the common fields.

They sang desiring an object that was near,
In face of which desire no longer moved,
Nor made of itself that which it could not find . . .
Three times the concentred self takes hold, three
    times
The thrice concentred self, having possessed

The object, grips it in savage scrutiny,
Once to make captive, once to subjugate
Or yield to subjugation, once to proclaim
The meaning of the capture, this hard prize,
Fully made, fully apparent, fully found.

VIII

The trumpet of morning blows in the clouds and
    through
The sky. It is the visible announced,
It is the more than visible, the more
Than sharp, illustrious scene. The trumpet cries
This is the successor of the invisible.

This is its substitute in stratagems
Of the spirit. This, in sight and memory,
Must take its place, as what is possible
Replaces what is not. The resounding cry
Is like ten thousand tumblers tumbling down

To share the day. The trumpet supposes that
A mind exists, aware of division, aware
Of its cry as clarion, its diction's way
As that of a personage in a multitude:
Man's mind grown venerable in the unreal.

IX

Fly low, cock bright, and stop on a bean pole. Let
Your brown breast redden, while you wait for
     warmth.
With one eye watch the willow, motionless.
The gardener's cat is dead, the gardener gone
And last year's garden grows salacious weeds.

A complex of emotions falls apart,
In an abandoned spot. Soft, civil bird,
The decay that you regard: of the arranged
And of the spirit of the arranged, *douceurs,*
Tristesses, the fund of life and death, suave bush

And polished beast, this complex falls apart.
And on your bean pole, it may be, you detect
Another complex of other emotions, not
So soft, so civil, and you make a sound,
Which is not part of the listener's own sense.

X

The personae of summer play the characters
Of an inhuman author, who meditates
With the gold bugs, in blue meadows, late at night.
He does not hear his characters talk. He sees
Them mottled, in the moodiest costumes,

377

Of blue and yellow, sky and sun, belted
And knotted, sashed and seamed, half pales of red,
Half pales of green, appropriate habit for
The huge decorum, the manner of the time,
Part of the mottled mood of summer's whole,

In which the characters speak because they want
To speak, the fat, the roseate characters,
Free, for a moment, from malice and sudden cry,
Complete in a completed scene, speaking
Their parts as in a youthful happiness.

❀◇

A PASTORAL NUN

Finally, in the last year of her age,
Having attained a present blessedness,
She said poetry and apotheosis are one.

This is the illustration that she used:
If I live according to this law I live
In an immense activity, in which

Everything becomes morning, summer, the hero,
The enraptured woman, the sequestered night,
The man that suffered, lying there at ease,

Without his envious pain in body, in mind,
The favorable transformations of the wind
As of a general being or human universe.

378

There was another illustration, in which
The two things compared their tight resemblances:
Each matters only in that which it conceives.

THE PASTOR CABALLERO

The importance of its hat to a form becomes
More definite. The sweeping brim of the hat
Makes of the form Most Merciful Capitan,

If the observer says so: grandiloquent
Locution of a hand in a rhapsody.
Its line moves quickly with the genius

Of its improvisation until, at length,
It enfolds the head in a vital ambiance,
A vital, linear ambiance. The flare

In the sweeping brim becomes the origin
Of a human evocation, so disclosed
That, nameless, it creates an affectionate name,

Derived from adjectives of deepest mine.
The actual form bears outwardly this grace,
An image of the mind, an inward mate,

Tall and unfretted, a figure meant to bear
Its poisoned laurels in this poisoned wood,
High in the height that is our total height.

The formidable helmet is nothing now.
These two go well together, the sinuous brim
And the green flauntings of the hours of peace.

<hr/>

NOTES TOWARD A SUPREME FICTION

To Henry Church

And for what, except for you, do I feel love?
Do I press the extremest book of the wisest man
Close to me, hidden in me day and night?
In the uncertain light of single, certain truth,
Equal in living changingness to the light
In which I meet you, in which we sit at rest,
For a moment in the central of our being,
The vivid transparence that you bring is peace.

It Must Be Abstract

I

Begin, ephebe, by perceiving the idea
Of this invention, this invented world,
The inconceivable idea of the sun.

You must become an ignorant man again
And see the sun again with an ignorant eye
And see it clearly in the idea of it.

380

Never suppose an inventing mind as source
Of this idea nor for that mind compose
A voluminous master folded in his fire.

How clean the sun when seen in its idea,
Washed in the remotest cleanliness of a heaven
That has expelled us and our images . . .

The death of one god is the death of all.
Let purple Phoebus lie in umber harvest,
Let Phoebus slumber and die in autumn umber,

Phoebus is dead, ephebe. But Phoebus was
A name for something that never could be named.
There was a project for the sun and is.

There is a project for the sun. The sun
Must bear no name, gold flourisher, but be
In the difficulty of what it is to be.

II

It is the celestial ennui of apartments
That sends us back to the first idea, the quick
Of this invention; and yet so poisonous

Are the ravishments of truth, so fatal to
The truth itself, the first idea becomes
The hermit in a poet's metaphors,

Who comes and goes and comes and goes all day.
May there be an ennui of the first idea?
What else, prodigious scholar, should there be?

The monastic man is an artist. The philosopher
Appoints man's place in music, say, today.
But the priest desires. The philosopher desires.

And not to have is the beginning of desire.
To have what is not is its ancient cycle.
It is desire at the end of winter, when

It observes the effortless weather turning blue
And sees the myosotis on its bush.
Being virile, it hears the calendar hymn.

It knows that what it has is what is not
And throws it away like a thing of another time,
As morning throws off stale moonlight and shabby
      sleep.

III

The poem refreshes life so that we share,
For a moment, the first idea . . . It satisfies
Belief in an immaculate beginning

And sends us, winged by an unconscious will,
To an immaculate end. We move between these
      points:
From that ever-early candor to its late plural

And the candor of them is the strong exhilaration
Of what we feel from what we think, of thought
Beating in the heart, as if blood newly came,

An elixir, an excitation, a pure power.
The poem, through candor, brings back a power
      again
That gives a candid kind to everything.

We say: At night an Arabian in my room,
With his damned hoobla-hoobla-hoobla-how,
Inscribes a primitive astronomy

Across the unscrawled fores the future casts
And throws his stars around the floor. By day
The wood-dove used to chant his hoobla-hoo

And still the grossest iridescence of ocean
Howls hoo and rises and howls hoo and falls.
Life's nonsense pierces us with strange relation.

IV

The first idea was not our own. Adam
In Eden was the father of Descartes
And Eve made air the mirror of herself,

Of her sons and of her daughters. They found them-
    selves
In heaven as in a glass; a second earth;
And in the earth itself they found a green—

The inhabitants of a very varnished green.
But the first idea was not to shape the clouds
In imitation. The clouds preceded us

There was a muddy centre before we breathed.
There was a myth before the myth began,
Venerable and articulate and complete.

From this the poem springs: that we live in a place
That is not our own and, much more, not ourselves
And hard it is in spite of blazoned days.

383

We are the mimics. Clouds are pedagogues
The air is not a mirror but bare board,
Coulisse bright-dark, tragic chiaroscuro

And comic color of the rose, in which
Abysmal instruments make sounds like pips
Of the sweeping meanings that we add to them.

v

The lion roars at the enraging desert,
Reddens the sand with his red-colored noise,
Defies red emptiness to evolve his match,

Master by foot and jaws and by the mane,
Most supple challenger. The elephant
Breaches the darkness of Ceylon with blares,

The glitter-goes on surfaces of tanks,
Shattering velvetest far-away. The bear,
The ponderous cinnamon, snarls in his mountain

At summer thunder and sleeps through winter snow.
But you, ephebe, look from your attic window,
Your mansard with a rented piano. You lie

In silence upon your bed. You clutch the corner
Of the pillow in your hand. You writhe and press
A bitter utterance from your writhing, dumb,

Yet voluble dumb violence. You look
Across the roofs as sigil and as ward
And in your centre mark them and are cowed . . .

These are the heroic children whom time breeds
Against the first idea—to lash the lion,
Caparison elephants, teach bears to juggle.

VI

Not to be realized because not to
Be seen, not to be loved nor hated because
Not to be realized. Weather by Franz Hals,

Brushed up by brushy winds in brushy clouds,
Wetted by blue, colder for white. Not to
Be spoken to, without a roof, without

First fruits, without the virginal of birds,
The dark-blown ceinture loosened, not relinquished.
Gay is, gay was, the gay forsythia

And yellow, yellow thins the Northern blue.
Without a name and nothing to be desired,
If only imagined but imagined well.

My house has changed a little in the sun.
The fragrance of the magnolias comes close,
False flick, false form, but falseness close to kin.

It must be visible or invisible,
Invisible or visible or both:
A seeing and unseeing in the eye.

The weather and the giant of the weather,
Say the weather, the mere weather, the mere air:
An abstraction blooded, as a man by thought.

385

It feels good as it is without the giant,
A thinker of the first idea. Perhaps
The truth depends on a walk around a lake,

A composing as the body tires, a stop
To see hepatica, a stop to watch
A definition growing certain and

A wait within that certainty, a rest
In the swags of pine-trees bordering the lake.
Perhaps there are times of inherent excellence,

As when the cock crows on the left and all
Is well, incalculable balances,
At which a kind of Swiss perfection comes

And a familiar music of the machine
Sets up its Schwärmerei, not balances
That we achieve but balances that happen,

As a man and woman meet and love forthwith.
Perhaps there are moments of awakening,
Extreme, fortuitous, personal, in which

We more than awaken, sit on the edge of sleep,
As on an elevation, and behold
The academies like structures in a mist.

VIII

Can we compose a castle-fortress-home,
Even with the help of Viollet-le-Duc,
And set the MacCullough there as major man?

386

The first idea is an imagined thing.
The pensive giant prone in violet space
May be the MacCullough, an expedient,

Logos and logic, crystal hypothesis,
Incipit and a form to speak the word
And every latent double in the word,

Beau linguist. But the MacCullough is MacCul-
    lough.
It does not follow that major man is man.
If MacCullough himself lay lounging by the sea,

Drowned in its washes, reading in the sound,
About the thinker of the first idea,
He might take habit, whether from wave or phrase,

Or power of the wave, or deepened speech,
Or a leaner being, moving in on him,
Of greater aptitude and apprehension,

As if the waves at last were never broken,
As if the language suddenly, with ease,
Said things it had laboriously spoken.

IX

The romantic intoning, the declaimed clairvoyance
Are parts of apotheosis, appropriate
And of its nature, the idiom thereof.

They differ from reason's click-clack, its applied
Enflashings. But apotheosis is not
The origin of the major man. He comes,

387

Compact in invincible foils, from reason,
Lighted at midnight by the studious eye,
Swaddled in revery, the object of

The hum of thoughts evaded in the mind,
Hidden from other thoughts, he that reposes
On a breast forever precious for that touch,

For whom the good of April falls tenderly,
Falls down, the cock-birds calling at the time.
My dame, sing for this person accurate songs.

He is and may be but oh! he is, he is,
This foundling of the infected past, so bright,
So moving in the manner of his hand.

Yet look not at his colored eyes. Give him
No names. Dismiss him from your images.
The hot of him is purest in the heart.

x

The major abstraction is the idea of man
And major man is its exponent, abler
In the abstract than in his singular,

More fecund as principle than particle,
Happy fecundity, flor-abundant force,
In being more than an exception, part,

Though an heroic part, of the commonal.
The major abstraction is the commonal,
The inanimate, difficult visage. Who is it?

388

What rabbi, grown furious with human wish,
What chieftain, walking by himself, crying
Most miserable, most victorious,

Does not see these separate figures one by one,
And yet see only one, in his old coat,
His slouching pantaloons, beyond the town,

Looking for what was, where it used to be?
Cloudless the morning. It is he. The man
In that old coat, those sagging pantaloons,

It is of him, ephebe, to make, to confect
The final elegance, not to console
Nor sanctify, but plainly to propound.

It Must Change

I

The old seraph, parcel-gilded, among violets
Inhaled the appointed odor, while the doves
Rose up like phantoms from chronologies.

The Italian girls wore jonquils in their hair
And these the seraph saw, had seen long since,
In the bandeaux of the mothers, would see again.

The bees came booming as if they had never gone,
As if hyacinths had never gone. We say
This changes and that changes. Thus the constant

Violets, doves, girls, bees and hyacinths
Are inconstant objects of inconstant cause
In a universe of inconstancy. This means

Night-blue is an inconstant thing. The seraph
Is satyr in Saturn, according to his thoughts.
It means the distaste we feel for this withered scene

Is that it has not changed enough. It remains,
It is a repetition. The bees come booming
As if—The pigeons clatter in the air.

An erotic perfume, half of the body, half
Of an obvious acid is sure what it intends
And the booming is blunt, not broken in subtleties.

II

The President ordains the bee to be
Immortal. The President ordains. But does
The body lift its heavy wing, take up,

Again, an inexhaustible being, rise
Over the loftiest antagonist
To drone the green phrases of its juvenal?

Why should the bee recapture a lost blague,
Find a deep echo in a horn and buzz
The bottomless trophy, new hornsman after old?

The President has apples on the table
And barefoot servants round him, who adjust
The curtains to a metaphysical t

And the banners of the nation flutter, burst
On the flag-poles in a red-blue dazzle, whack
At the halyards. Why, then, when in golden fury

Spring vanishes the scraps of winter, why
Should there be a question of returning or
Of death in memory's dream? Is spring a sleep?

This warmth is for lovers at last accomplishing
Their love, this beginning, not resuming, this
Booming and booming of the new-come bee.

III

The great statue of the General Du Puy
Rested immobile, though neighboring catafalques
Bore off the residents of its noble Place.

The right, uplifted foreleg of the horse
Suggested that, at the final funeral,
The music halted and the horse stood still.

On Sundays, lawyers in their promenades
Approached this strongly-heightened effigy
To study the past, and doctors, having bathed

Themselves with care, sought out the nerveless frame
Of a suspension, a permanence, so rigid
That it made the General a bit absurd,

Changed his true flesh to an inhuman bronze.
There never had been, never could be, such
A man. The lawyers disbelieved, the doctors

Said that as keen, illustrious ornament,
As a setting for geraniums, the General,
The very Place Du Puy, in fact, belonged

Among our more vestigial states of mind.
Nothing had happened because nothing had changed.
Yet the General was rubbish in the end.

IV

Two things of opposite natures seem to depend
On one another, as a man depends
On a woman, day on night, the imagined

On the real. This is the origin of change.
Winter and spring, cold copulars, embrace
And forth the particulars of rapture come.

Music falls on the silence like a sense,
A passion that we feel, not understand.
Morning and afternoon are clasped together

And North and South are an intrinsic couple
And sun and rain a plural, like two lovers
That walk away as one in the greenest body.

In solitude the trumpets of solitude
Are not of another solitude resounding;
A little string speaks for a crowd of voices.

The partaker partakes of that which changes him.
The child that touches takes character from the thing,
The body, it touches. The captain and his men

Are one and the sailor and the sea are one.
Follow after, O my companion, my fellow, my self,
Sister and solace, brother and delight.

V

On a blue island in a sky-wide water
The wild orange trees continued to bloom and to bear,
Long after the planter's death. A few limes remained,

Where his house had fallen, three scraggy trees
    weighted
With garbled green. These were the planter's turquoise
And his orange blotches, these were his zero green,

A green baked greener in the greenest sun.
These were his beaches, his sea-myrtles in
White sand, his patter of the long sea-slushes.

There was an island beyond him on which rested,
An island to the South, on which rested like
A mountain, a pineapple pungent as Cuban summer.

And là-bas, là-bas, the cool bananas grew,
Hung heavily on the great banana tree,
Which pierces clouds and bends on half the world.

He thought often of the land from which he came,
How that whole country was a melon, pink
If seen rightly and yet a possible red.

An unaffected man in a negative light
Could not have borne his labor nor have died
Sighing that he should leave the banjo's twang.

VI

Bethou me, said sparrow, to the crackled blade,
And you, and you, bethou me as you blow,
When in my coppice you behold me be.

Ah, ké! the bloody wren, the felon jay,
Ké-ké, the jug-throated robin pouring out,
Bethou, bethou, bethou me in my glade.

There was such idiot minstrelsy in rain,
So many clappers going without bells,
That these bethous compose a heavenly gong.

One voice repeating, one tireless chorister,
The phrases of a single phrase, ké-ké,
A single text, granite monotony,

One sole face, like a photograph of fate,
Glass-blower's destiny, bloodless episcopus,
Eye without lid, mind without any dream—

These are of minstrels lacking minstrelsy,
Of an earth in which the first leaf is the tale
Of leaves, in which the sparrow is a bird

Of stone, that never changes. Bethou him, you
And you, bethou him and bethou. It is
A sound like any other. It will end.

VII

After a lustre of the moon, we say
We have not the need of any paradise,
We have not the need of any seducing hymn.

It is true. Tonight the lilacs magnify
The easy passion, the ever-ready love
Of the lover that lies within us and we breathe

394

An odor evoking nothing, absolute.
We encounter in the dead middle of the night
The purple odor, the abundant bloom.

The lover sighs as for accessible bliss,
Which he can take within him on his breath,
Possess in his heart, conceal and nothing known.

For easy passion and ever-ready love
Are of our earthy birth and here and now
And where we live and everywhere we live,

As in the top-cloud of a May night-evening,
As in the courage of the ignorant man,
Who chants by book, in the heat of the scholar, who
    writes

The book, hot for another accessible bliss:
The fluctuations of certainty, the change
Of degrees of perception in the scholar's dark.

VIII

On her trip around the world, Nanzia Nunzio
Confronted Ozymandias. She went
Alone and like a vestal long-prepared.

I am the spouse. She took her necklace off
And laid it in the sand. As I am, I am
The spouse. She opened her stone-studded belt.

I am the spouse, divested of bright gold,
The spouse beyond emerald or amethyst,
Beyond the burning body that I bear.

I am the woman stripped more nakedly
Than nakedness, standing before an inflexible
Order, saying I am the contemplated spouse.

Speak to me that, which spoken, will array me
In its own only precious ornament.
Set on me the spirit's diamond coronal.

Clothe me entire in the final filament,
So that I tremble with such love so known
And myself am precious for your perfecting.

Then Ozymandias said the spouse, the bride
Is never naked. A fictive covering
Weaves always glistening from the heart and mind.

IX

The poem goes from the poet's gibberish to
The gibberish of the vulgate and back again.
Does it move to and fro or is it of both

At once? Is it a luminous flittering
Or the concentration of a cloudy day?
Is there a poem that never reaches words

And one that chaffers the time away?
Is the poem both peculiar and general?
There's a meditation there, in which there seems

To be an evasion, a thing not apprehended or
Not apprehended well. Does the poet
Evade us, as in a senseless element?

Evade, this hot, dependent orator,
The spokesman at our bluntest barriers,
Exponent by a form of speech, the speaker

Of a speech only a little of the tongue?
It is the gibberish of the vulgate that he seeks.
He tries by a peculiar speech to speak

The peculiar potency of the general,
To compound the imagination's Latin with
The lingua franca et jocundissima.

x

A bench was his catalepsy, Theatre
Of Trope. He sat in the park. The water of
The lake was full of artificial things,

Like a page of music, like an upper air,
Like a momentary color, in which swans
Were seraphs, were saints, were changing essences.

The west wind was the music, the motion, the force
To which the swans curveted, a will to change,
A will to make iris frettings on the blank.

There was a will to change, a necessitous
And present way, a presentation, a kind
Of volatile world, too constant to be denied,

The eye of a vagabond in metaphor
That catches our own. The casual is not
Enough. The freshness of transformation is

The freshness of a world. It is our own,
It is ourselves, the freshness of ourselves,
And that necessity and that presentation

Are rubbings of a glass in which we peer.
Of these beginnings, gay and green, propose
The suitable amours. Time will write them down.

It Must Give Pleasure

I

To sing jubilas at exact, accustomed times,
To be crested and wear the mane of a multitude
And so, as part, to exult with its great throat,

To speak of joy and to sing of it, borne on
The shoulders of joyous men, to feel the heart
That is the common, the bravest fundament,

This is a facile exercise. Jerome
Begat the tubas and the fire-wind strings,
The golden fingers picking dark-blue air:

For companies of voices moving there,
To find of sound the bleakest ancestor,
To find of light a music issuing

Whereon it falls in more than sensual mode.
But the difficultest rigor is forthwith,
On the image of what we see, to catch from that

Irrational moment its unreasoning,
As when the sun comes rising, when the sea
Clears deeply, when the moon hangs on the wall

Of heaven-haven. These are not things transformed.
Yet we are shaken by them as if they were.
We reason about them with a later reason.

II

The blue woman, linked and lacquered, at her win-
    dow
Did not desire that feathery argentines
Should be cold silver, neither that frothy clouds

Should foam, be foamy waves, should move like
    them,
Nor that the sexual blossoms should repose
Without their fierce addictions, nor that the heat

Of summer, growing fragrant in the night,
Should strengthen her abortive dreams and take
In sleep its natural form. It was enough

For her that she remembered: the argentines
Of spring come to their places in the grape leaves
To cool their ruddy pulses; the frothy clouds

Are nothing but frothy clouds; the frothy blooms
Waste without puberty; and afterward,
When the harmonious heat of August pines

Enters the room, it drowses and is the night.
It was enough for her that she remembered.
The blue woman looked and from her window
    named

399

The corals of the dogwood, cold and clear,
Cold, coldly delineating, being real,
Clear and, except for the eye, without intrusion.

III

A lasting visage in a lasting bush,
A face of stone in an unending red,
Red-emerald, red-slitted-blue, a face of slate,

An ancient forehead hung with heavy hair,
The channel slots of rain, the red-rose-red
And weathered and the ruby-water-worn,

The vines around the throat, the shapeless lips,
The frown like serpents basking on the brow,
The spent feeling leaving nothing of itself,

Red-in-red repetitions never going
Away, a little rusty, a little rouged,
A little roughened and ruder, a crown

The eye could not escape, a red renown
Blowing itself upon the tedious ear.
An effulgence faded, dull cornelian

Too venerably used. That might have been.
It might and might have been. But as it was,
A dead shepherd brought tremendous chords from
    hell

And bade the sheep carouse. Or so they said.
Children in love with them brought early flowers
And scattered them about, no two alike.

We reason of these things with later reason
And we make of what we see, what we see clearly
And have seen, a place dependent on ourselves.

There was a mystic marriage in Catawba,
At noon it was on the mid-day of the year
Between a great captain and the maiden Bawda.

This was their ceremonial hymn: Anon
We loved but would no marriage make. Anon
The one refused the other one to take,

Foreswore the sipping of the marriage wine.
Each must the other take not for his high,
His puissant front nor for her subtle sound,

The shoo-shoo-shoo of secret cymbals round.
Each must the other take as sign, short sign
To stop the whirlwind, balk the elements.

The great captain loved the ever-hill Catawba
And therefore married Bawda, whom he found there,
And Bawda loved the captain as she loved the sun.

They married well because the marriage-place
Was what they loved. It was neither heaven nor hell.
They were love's characters come face to face.

V

We drank Meursault, ate lobster Bombay with
    mango
Chutney. Then the Canon Aspirin declaimed
Of his sister, in what a sensible ecstasy

She lived in her house. She had two daughters, one
Of four, and one of seven, whom she dressed
The way a painter of pauvred color paints.

But still she painted them, appropriate to
Their poverty, a gray-blue yellowed out
With ribbon, a rigid statement of them, white,

With Sunday pearls, her widow's gayety.
She hid them under simple names. She held
Them closelier to her by rejecting dreams.

The words they spoke were voices that she heard.
She looked at them and saw them as they were
And what she felt fought off the barest phrase.

The Canon Aspirin, having said these things,
Reflected, humming an outline of a fugue
Of praise, a conjugation done by choirs.

Yet when her children slept, his sister herself
Demanded of sleep, in the excitements of silence
Only the unmuddled self of sleep, for them.

VI

When at long midnight the Canon came to sleep
And normal things had yawned themselves away,
The nothingness was a nakedness, a point,

Beyond which fact could not progress as fact.
Thereon the learning of the man conceived
Once more night's pale illuminations, gold

Beneath, far underneath, the surface of
His eye and audible in the mountain of
His ear, the very material of his mind.

So that he was the ascending wings he saw
And moved on them in orbits' outer stars
Descending to the children's bed, on which

They lay. Forth then with huge pathetic force
Straight to the utmost crown of night he flew.
The nothingness was a nakedness, a point

Beyond which thought could not progress as thought.
He had to choose. But it was not a choice
Between excluding things. It was not a choice

Between, but of. He chose to include the things
That in each other are included, the whole,
The complicate, the amassing harmony.

VII

He imposes orders as he thinks of them,
As the fox and snake do. It is a brave affair.
Next he builds capitols and in their corridors,

Whiter than wax, sonorous, fame as it is,
He establishes statues of reasonable men,
Who surpassed the most literate owl, the most
    erudite

Of elephants. But to impose is not
To discover. To discover an order as of
A season, to discover summer and know it,

403

To discover winter and know it well, to find,
Not to impose, not to have reasoned at all,
Out of nothing to have come on major weather,

It is possible, possible, possible. It must
Be possible. It must be that in time
The real will from its crude compoundings come,

Seeming, at first, a beast disgorged, unlike,
Warmed by a desperate milk. To find the real,
To be stripped of every fiction except one,

The fiction of an absolute—Angel,
Be silent in your luminous cloud and hear
The luminous melody of proper sound.

VIII

What am I to believe? If the angel in his cloud,
Serenely gazing at the violent abyss,
Plucks on his strings to pluck abysmal glory,

Leaps downward through evening's revelations, and
On his spredden wings, needs nothing but deep
      space,
Forgets the gold centre, the golden destiny,

Grows warm in the motionless motion of his flight,
Am I that imagine this angel less satisfied?
Are the wings his, the lapis-haunted air?

Is it he or is it I that experience this?
Is it I then that keep saying there is an hour
Filled with expressible bliss, in which I have

No need, am happy, forget need's golden hand,
Am satisfied without solacing majesty,
And if there is an hour there is a day,

There is a month, a year, there is a time
In which majesty is a mirror of the self:
I have not but I am and as I am, I am.

These external regions, what do we fill them with
Except reflections, the escapades of death,
Cinderella fulfilling herself beneath the roof?

IX

Whistle aloud, too weedy wren. I can
Do all that angels can. I enjoy like them,
Like men besides, like men in light secluded,

Enjoying angels. Whistle, forced bugler,
That bugles for the mate, nearby the nest,
Cock bugler, whistle and bugle and stop just short,

Red robin, stop in your preludes, practicing
Mere repetitions. These things at least comprise
An occupation, an exercise, a work,

A thing final in itself and, therefore, good:
One of the vast repetitions final in
Themselves and, therefore, good, the going round

And round and round, the merely going round,
Until merely going round is a final good,
The way wine comes at a table in a wood.

405

And we enjoy like men, the way a leaf
Above the table spins its constant spin,
So that we look at it with pleasure, look

At it spinning its eccentric measure. Perhaps,
The man-hero is not the exceptional monster,
But he that of repetition is most master.

x

Fat girl, terrestrial, my summer, my night,
How is it I find you in difference, see you there
In a moving contour, a change not quite completed?

You are familiar yet an aberration.
Civil, madam, I am, but underneath
A tree, this unprovoked sensation requires

That I should name you flatly, waste no words,
Check your evasions, hold you to yourself.
Even so when I think of you as strong or tired,

Bent over work, anxious, content, alone,
You remain the more than natural figure. You
Become the soft-footed phantom, the irrational

Distortion, however fragrant, however dear.
That's it: the more than rational distortion,
The fiction that results from feeling. Yes, that.

They will get it straight one day at the Sorbonne.
We shall return at twilight from the lecture
Pleased that the irrational is rational,

406

Until flicked by feeling, in a gildered street,
I call you by name, my green, my fluent mundo.
You will have stopped revolving except in crystal.

―――――

Soldier, there is a war between the mind
And sky, between thought and day and night. It is
For that the poet is always in the sun,

Patches the moon together in his room
To his Virgilian cadences, up down,
Up down. It is a war that never ends.

Yet it depends on yours. The two are one.
They are a plural, a right and left, a pair,
Two parallels that meet if only in

The meeting of their shadows or that meet
In a book in a barrack, a letter from Malay.
But your war ends. And after it you return

With six meats and twelve wines or else without
To walk another room . . . Monsieur and comrade,
The soldier is poor without the poet's lines,

His petty syllabi, the sounds that stick,
Inevitably modulating, in the blood.
And war for war, each has its gallant kind.

How simply the fictive hero becomes the real;
How gladly with proper words the soldier dies,
If he must, or lives on the bread of faithful speech.

THE AURORAS OF AUTUMN

THE AURORAS OF AUTUMN

I

This is where the serpent lives, the bodiless.
His head is air. Beneath his tip at night
Eyes open and fix on us in every sky.

Or is this another wriggling out of the egg,
Another image at the end of the cave,
Another bodiless for the body's slough?

This is where the serpent lives. This is his nest,
These fields, these hills, these tinted distances,
And the pines above and along and beside the sea.

This is form gulping after formlessness,
Skin flashing to wished-for disappearances
And the serpent body flashing without the skin.

This is the height emerging and its base
These lights may finally attain a pole
In the midmost midnight and find the serpent there,

In another nest, the master of the maze
Of body and air and forms and images,
Relentlessly in possession of happiness.

This is his poison: that we should disbelieve
Even that. His meditations in the ferns,
When he moved so slightly to make sure of sun,

Made us no less as sure. We saw in his head,
Black beaded on the rock, the flecked animal,
The moving grass, the Indian in his glade.

II

Farewell to an idea . . . A cabin stands,
Deserted, on a beach. It is white,
As by a custom or according to

An ancestral theme or as a consequence
Of an infinite course. The flowers against the wall
Are white, a little dried, a kind of mark

Reminding, trying to remind, of a white
That was different, something else, last year
Or before, not the white of an aging afternoon,

Whether fresher or duller, whether of winter cloud
Or of winter sky, from horizon to horizon.
The wind is blowing the sand across the floor.

Here, being visible is being white,
Is being of the solid of white, the accomplishment
Of an extremist in an exercise . . .

The season changes. A cold wind chills the beach.
The long lines of it grow longer, emptier,
A darkness gathers though it does not fall

And the whiteness grows less vivid on the wall.
The man who is walking turns blankly on the sand.
He observes how the north is always enlarging the
    change,

412

With its frigid brilliances, its blue-red sweeps
And gusts of great enkindlings, its polar green,
The color of ice and fire and solitude.

III

Farewell to an idea . . . The mother's face,
The purpose of the poem, fills the room.
They are together, here, and it is warm,

With none of the prescience of oncoming dreams,
It is evening. The house is evening, half dissolved.
Only the half they can never possess remains,

Still-starred. It is the mother they possess,
Who gives transparence to their present peace.
She makes that gentler that can gentle be.

And yet she too is dissolved, she is destroyed.
She gives transparence. But she has grown old.
The necklace is a carving not a kiss.

The soft hands are a motion not a touch.
The house will crumble and the books will burn.
They are at ease in a shelter of the mind

And the house is of the mind and they and time,
Together, all together. Boreal night
Will look like frost as it approaches them

And to the mother as she falls asleep
And as they say good-night, good-night. Upstairs
The windows will be lighted, not the rooms.

A wind will spread its windy grandeurs round
And knock like a rifle-butt against the door.
The wind will command them with invincible sound.

IV

Farewell to an idea . . . The cancellings,
The negations are never final. The father sits
In space, wherever he sits, of bleak regard,

As one that is strong in the bushes of his eyes.
He says no to no and yes to yes. He says yes
To no; and in saying yes he says farewell.

He measures the velocities of change.
He leaps from heaven to heaven more rapidly
Than bad angels leap from heaven to hell in flames.

But now he sits in quiet and green-a-day.
He assumes the great speeds of space and flutters
        them
From cloud to cloudless, cloudless to keen clear

In flights of eye and ear, the highest eye
And the lowest ear, the deep ear that discerns,
At evening, things that attend it until it hears

The supernatural preludes of its own,
At the moment when the angelic eye defines
Its actors approaching, in company, in their masks.

Master O master seated by the fire
And yet in space and motionless and yet
Of motion the ever-brightening origin,

414

Profound, and yet the king and yet the crown,
Look at this present throne. What company,
In masks, can choir it with the naked wind?

v

The mother invites humanity to her house
And table. The father fetches tellers of tales
And musicians who mute much, muse much, on the
     tales.

The father fetches negresses to dance,
Among the children, like curious ripenesses
Of pattern in the dance's ripening.

For these the musicians make insidious tones,
Clawing the sing-song of their instruments.
The children laugh and jangle a tinny time.

The father fetches pageants out of air,
Scenes of the theatre, vistas and blocks of woods
And curtains like a naive pretence of sleep.

Among these the musicians strike the instinctive
     poem.
The father fetches his unherded herds,
Of barbarous tongue, slavered and panting halves

Of breath, obedient to his trumpet's touch.
This then is Chatillon or as you please.
We stand in the tumult of a festival.

What festival? This loud, disordered mooch?
These hospitaliers? These brute-like guests?
These musicians dubbing at a tragedy,

415

A-dub, a-dub, which is made up of this:
That there are no lines to speak? There is no play.
Or, the persons act one merely by being here.

VI

It is a theatre floating through the clouds,
Itself a cloud, although of misted rock
And mountains running like water, wave on wave,

Through waves of light. It is of cloud transformed
To cloud transformed again, idly, the way
A season changes color to no end,

Except the lavishing of itself in change,
As light changes yellow into gold and gold
To its opal elements and fire's delight,

Splashed wide-wise because it likes magnificence
And the solemn pleasures of magnificent space.
The cloud drifts idly through half-thought-of forms.

The theatre is filled with flying birds,
Wild wedges, as of a volcano's smoke, palm-eyed
And vanishing, a web in a corridor

Or massive portico. A capitol,
It may be, is emerging or has just
Collapsed. The denouement has to be postponed . . .

This is nothing until in a single man contained,
Nothing until this named thing nameless is
And is destroyed. He opens the door of his house

On flames. The scholar of one candle sees
An Arctic effulgence flaring on the frame
Of everything he is. And he feels afraid.

VII

Is there an imagination that sits enthroned
As grim as it is benevolent, the just
And the unjust, which in the midst of summer stops

To imagine winter? When the leaves are dead,
Does it take its place in the north and enfold itself,
Goat-leaper, crystalled and luminous, sitting

In highest night? And do these heavens adorn
And proclaim it, the white creator of black, jetted
By extinguishings, even of planets as may be,

Even of earth, even of sight, in snow,
Except as needed by way of majesty,
In the sky, as crown and diamond cabala?

It leaps through us, through all our heavens leaps,
Extinguishing our planets, one by one,
Leaving, of where we were and looked, of where

We knew each other and of each other thought,
A shivering residue, chilled and foregone,
Except for that crown and mystical cabala.

But it dare not leap by chance in its own dark.
It must change from destiny to slight caprice.
And thus its jetted tragedy, its stele

417

And shape and mournful making move to find
What must unmake it and, at last, what can,
Say, a flippant communication under the moon.

VIII

There may be always a time of innocence.
There is never a place. Or if there is no time,
If it is not a thing of time, nor of place,

Existing in the idea of it, alone,
In the sense against calamity, it is not
Less real. For the oldest and coldest philosopher,

There is or may be a time of innocence
As pure principle. Its nature is its end,
That it should be, and yet not be, a thing

That pinches the pity of the pitiful man,
Like a book at evening beautiful but untrue,
Like a book on rising beautiful and true.

It is like a thing of ether that exists
Almost as predicate. But it exists,
It exists, it is visible, it is, it is.

So, then, these lights are not a spell of light,
A saying out of a cloud, but innocence.
An innocence of the earth and no false sign

Or symbol of malice. That we partake thereof,
Lie down like children in this holiness,
As if, awake, we lay in the quiet of sleep,

418

As if the innocent mother sang in the dark
Of the room and on an accordion, half-heard,
Created the time and place in which we breathed . . .

IX

And of each other thought—in the idiom
Of the work, in the idiom of an innocent earth,
Not of the enigma of the guilty dream.

We were as Danes in Denmark all day long
And knew each other well, hale-hearted landsmen,
For whom the outlandish was another day

Of the week, queerer than Sunday. We thought alike
And that made brothers of us in a home
In which we fed on being brothers, fed

And fattened as on a decorous honeycomb.
This drama that we live—We lay sticky with sleep.
This sense of the activity of fate—

The rendezvous, when she came alone,
By her coming became a freedom of the two,
An isolation which only the two could share.

Shall we be found hanging in the trees next spring?
Of what disaster is this the imminence:
Bare limbs, bare trees and a wind as sharp as salt?

The stars are putting on their glittering belts.
They throw around their shoulders cloaks that flash
Like a great shadow's last embellishment.

419

It may come tomorrow in the simplest word,
Almost as part of innocence, almost,
Almost as the tenderest and the truest part.

x

An unhappy people in a happy world—
Read, rabbi, the phases of this difference.
An unhappy people in an unhappy world—

Here are too many mirrors for misery.
A happy people in an unhappy world—
It cannot be. There's nothing there to roll

On the expressive tongue, the finding fang.
A happy people in a happy world—
Buffo! A ball, an opera, a bar.

Turn back to where we were when we began:
An unhappy people in a happy world.
Now, solemnize the secretive syllables.

Read to the congregation, for today
And for tomorrow, this extremity,
This contrivance of the spectre of the spheres,

Contriving balance to contrive a whole,
The vital, the never-failing genius,
Fulfilling his meditations, great and small.

In these unhappy he meditates a whole,
The full of fortune and the full of fate,
As if he lived all lives, that he might know,

In hall harridan, not hushful paradise,
To a haggling of wind and weather, by these lights
Like a blaze of summer straw, in winter's nick.

⊙⊦

PAGE FROM A TALE

In the hard brightness of that winter day
The sea was frozen solid and Hans heard,
By his drift-fire, on the shore, the difference
Between loud water and loud wind, between that
Which has no accurate syllables and that
Which cries *so blau* and cries again *so lind*
Und so lau, between sound without meaning and
    speech,
Of clay and wattles made as it ascends
And *hear it* as it falls *in the deep heart's core.*
A steamer lay near him, foundered in the ice.

So blau, so blau . . . Hans listened by the fire.
New stars that were a foot across came out
And shone. *And a small cabin build there.*
So lind. The wind blazed as they sang. *So lau.*
The great ship, Balayne, lay frozen in the sea.
The one-foot stars were couriers of its death
To the wild limits of its habitation.
These were not tepid stars of torpid places
But bravest at midnight and in lonely spaces,
They looked back at Hans' look with savage faces.

421

The wet weed sputtered, the fire died down, the cold
Was like a sleep. The sea was a sea he dreamed.
Yet Hans lay wide awake. *And live alone*
In the bee-loud glade. Lights on the steamer moved.
Men would be starting at dawn to walk ashore.
They would be afraid of the sun: what it might be,
Afraid of the country angels of those skies,
The finned flutterings and gaspings of the ice,
As if whatever in water strove to speak
Broke dialect in a break of memory.

The sun might rise and it might not and if
It rose, ashen and red and yellow, each
Opaque, in orange circlet, nearer than it
Had ever been before, no longer known,
No more that which most of all brings back the known,
But that which destroys it completely by this light
For that, or a motion not in the astronomies,
Beyond the habit of sense, anarchic shape
Afire—it might and it might not in that
Gothic blue, speed home its portents to their ends.

It might become a wheel spoked red and white
In alternate stripes converging at a point
Of flame on the line, with a second wheel below,
Just rising, accompanying, arranged to cross,
Through weltering illuminations, humps
Of billows, downward, toward the drift-fire shore.
It might come bearing, out of chaos, kin
Smeared, smoked, and drunken of thin potencies,
Lashing at images in the atmosphere,
Ringed round and barred, with eyes held in their
        hands,

422

And capable of incapably evil thought:
Slight gestures that could rend the palpable ice,
Or melt Arcturus to ingots dropping drops,
Or spill night out in brilliant vanishings,
Whirlpools of darkness in whirlwinds of light . . .
The miff-maff-muff of water, the vocables
Of the wind, the glassily-sparkling particles
Of the mind—They would soon climb down the side of
    the ship.
They would march single file, with electric lamps, alert
For a tidal undulation underneath.

✦✦✦✦✦✦✦✦✦✦✦✦✦✦✦✦✦✦✦✦✦✦✦✦✦✦✦✦✦✦✦✦✦✦✦✦✦✦

LARGE RED MAN READING

There were ghosts that returned to earth to hear his phrases,
As he sat there reading, aloud, the great blue tabulae.
They were those from the wilderness of stars that had expected
    more.

There were those that returned to hear him read from the
    poem of life,
Of the pans above the stove, the pots on the table, the tulips
    among them.
They were those that would have wept to step barefoot into
    reality,

That would have wept and been happy, have shivered in the
    frost
And cried out to feel it again, have run fingers over leaves
And against the most coiled thorn, have seized on what was
    ugly

And laughed, as he sat there reading, from out of the purple
    tabulae,
The outlines of being and its expressings, the syllables of its
    law:
Poesis, poesis, the literal characters, the vatic lines,

Which in those ears and in those thin, those spended hearts,
Took on color, took on shape and the size of things as they are
And spoke the feeling for them, which was what they had
    lacked.

❀❖

THIS SOLITUDE OF CATARACTS

He never felt twice the same about the flecked river,
Which kept flowing and never the same way twice, flowing

Through many places, as if it stood still in one,
Fixed like a lake on which the wild ducks fluttered,

Ruffling its common reflections, thought-like Monadnocks.
There seemed to be an apostrophe that was not spoken.

424

There was so much that was real that was not real at all.
He wanted to feel the same way over and over.

He wanted the river to go on flowing the same way,
To keep on flowing. He wanted to walk beside it,

Under the buttonwoods, beneath a moon nailed fast.
He wanted his heart to stop beating and his mind to rest

In a permanent realization, without any wild ducks
Or mountains that were not mountains, just to know how it
     would be,

Just to know how it would feel, released from destruction,
To be a bronze man breathing under archaic lapis,

Without the oscillations of planetary pass-pass,
Breathing his bronzen breath at the azury centre of time.

⊙⊱

IN THE ELEMENT OF ANTAGONISMS

    If it is a world without a genius,
    It is most happily contrived. Here, then,

    We ask which means most, for us, all the genii
    Or one man who, for us, is greater than they,

On his gold horse striding, like a conjured beast,
Miraculous in its panache and swish?

Birds twitter pandemoniums around
The idea of the chevalier of chevaliers,

The well-composed in his burnished solitude,
The tower, the ancient accent, the wintry size.

And the north wind's mighty buskin seems to fall
In an excessive corridor, alas!

IN A BAD TIME

How mad would he have to be to say, "He beheld
An order and thereafter he belonged
To it"? He beheld the order of the northern sky.

But the beggar gazes on calamity
And thereafter he belongs to it, to bread
Hard found, and water tasting of misery.

For him cold's glacial beauty is his fate.
Without understanding, he belongs to it
And the night, and midnight, and after, where it is.

What has he? What he has he has. But what?
It is not a question of captious repartee.
What has he that becomes his heart's strong core?

426

He has his poverty and nothing more.
His poverty becomes his heart's strong core—
A forgetfulness of summer at the pole.

Sordid Melpomene, why strut bare boards,
Without scenery or lights, in the theatre's bricks,
Dressed high in heliotrope's inconstant hue,

The muse of misery? Speak loftier lines.
Cry out, "I am the purple muse." Make sure
The audience beholds you, not your gown.

✿◈✿

THE BEGINNING

So summer comes in the end to these few stains
And the rust and rot of the door through which she
    went.

The house is empty. But here is where she sat
To comb her dewy hair, a touchless light,

Perplexed by its darker iridescences.
This was the glass in which she used to look

At the moment's being, without history,
The self of summer perfectly perceived,

And feel its country gayety and smile
And be surprised and tremble, hand and lip.

This is the chair from which she gathered up
Her dress, the carefulest, commodious weave

Inwoven by a weaver to twelve bells . . .
The dress is lying, cast-off, on the floor.

Now, the first tutoyers of tragedy
Speak softly, to begin with, in the eaves.

THE COUNTRYMAN

Swatara, Swatara, black river,
Descending, out of the cap of midnight,
Toward the cape at which
You enter the swarthy sea,

Swatara, Swatara, heavy the hills
Are, hanging above you, as you move,
Move blackly and without crystal.
A countryman walks beside you.

He broods of neither cap nor cape,
But only of your swarthy motion,
But always of the swarthy water,
Of which Swatara is the breathing,

The name. He does not speak beside you.
He is there because he wants to be
And because being there in the heavy hills
And along the moving of the water—

Being there is being in a place,
As of a character everywhere,
The place of a swarthy presence moving,
Slowly, to the look of a swarthy name.

THE ULTIMATE POEM IS ABSTRACT

This day writhes with what? The lecturer
On This Beautiful World Of Ours composes himself
And hems the planet rose and haws it ripe,

And red, and right. The particular question—here
The particular answer to the particular question
Is not in point—the question is in point.

If the day writhes, it is not with revelations.
One goes on asking questions. That, then, is one
Of the categories. So said, this placid space

Is changed. It is not so blue as we thought. To be blue,
There must be no questions. It is an intellect
Of windings round and dodges to and fro,

Writhings in wrong obliques and distances,
Not an intellect in which we are fleet: present
Everywhere in space at once, cloud-pole

Of communication. It would be enough
If we were ever, just once, at the middle, fixed
In This Beautiful World Of Ours and not as now,

Helplessly at the edge, enough to be
Complete, because at the middle, if only in sense,
And in that enormous sense, merely enjoy.

❖❖❖❖❖❖❖❖❖❖❖❖❖❖❖❖❖❖❖❖❖❖❖❖❖❖❖❖❖❖❖❖❖❖❖❖

BOUQUET OF ROSES IN SUNLIGHT

Say that it is a crude effect, black reds,
Pink yellows, orange whites, too much as they are
To be anything else in the sunlight of the room,

Too much as they are to be changed by metaphor,
Too actual, things that in being real
Make any imaginings of them lesser things.

And yet this effect is a consequence of the way
We feel and, therefore, is not real, except
In our sense of it, our sense of the fertilest red,

Of yellow as first color and of white,
In which the sense lies still, as a man lies,
Enormous, in a completing of his truth.

Our sense of these things changes and they change,
Not as in metaphor, but in our sense
Of them. So sense exceeds all metaphor.

It exceeds the heavy changes of the light.
It is like a flow of meanings with no speech
And of as many meanings as of men.

We are two that use these roses as we are,
In seeing them. This is what makes them seem
So far beyond the rhetorician's touch.

THE OWL IN THE SARCOPHAGUS

I

Two forms move among the dead, high sleep
Who by his highness quiets them, high peace
Upon whose shoulders even the heavens rest,

Two brothers. And a third form, she that says
Good-by in the darkness, speaking quietly there,
To those that cannot say good-by themselves.

These forms are visible to the eye that needs,
Needs out of the whole necessity of sight.
The third form speaks, because the ear repeats,

Without a voice, inventions of farewell.
These forms are not abortive figures, rocks,
Impenetrable symbols, motionless. They move

About the night. They live without our light,
In an element not the heaviness of time,
In which reality is prodigy.

There sleep the brother is the father, too,
And peace is cousin by a hundred names
And she that in the syllable between life

And death cries quickly, in a flash of voice,
Keep you, keep you, I am gone, oh keep you as
My memory, is the mother of us all,

The earthly mother and the mother of
The dead. Only the thought of those dark three
Is dark, thought of the forms of dark desire.

II

There came a day, there was a day—one day
A man walked living among the forms of thought
To see their lustre truly as it is

And in harmonious prodigy to be,
A while, conceiving his passage as into a time
That of itself stood still, perennial,

Less time than place, less place than thought of place
And, if of substance, a likeness of the earth,
That by resemblance twanged him through and
    through,

Releasing an abysmal melody,
A meeting, an emerging in the light,
A dazzle of remembrance and of sight.

III

There he saw well the foldings in the height
Of sleep, the whiteness folded into less,
Like many robings, as moving masses are,

As a moving mountain is, moving through day
And night, colored from distances, central
Where luminous agitations come to rest,

In an ever-changing, calmest unity,
The unique composure, harshest streakings joined
In a vanishing-vanished violet that wraps round

The giant body the meanings of its folds,
The weaving and the crinkling and the vex,
As on water of an afternoon in the wind

After the wind has passed. Sleep realized
Was the whiteness that is the ultimate intellect,
A diamond jubilance beyond the fire,

That gives its power to the wild-ringed eye.
Then he breathed deeply the deep atmosphere
Of sleep, the accomplished, the fulfilling air.

433

There peace, the godolphin and fellow, estranged,
    estranged,
Hewn in their middle as the beam of leaves,
The prince of shither-shade and tinsel lights,

Stood flourishing the world. The brilliant height
And hollow of him by its brilliance calmed,
Its brightness burned the way good solace seethes.

This was peace after death, the brother of sleep,
The inhuman brother so much like, so near,
Yet vested in a foreign absolute,

Adorned with cryptic stones and sliding shines,
An immaculate personage in nothingness,
With the whole spirit sparkling in its cloth,

Generations of the imagination piled
In the manner of its stitchings, of its thread,
In the weaving round the wonder of its need,

And the first flowers upon it, an alphabet
By which to spell out holy doom and end,
A bee for the remembering of happiness.

Peace stood with our last blood adorned, last mind,
Damasked in the originals of green,
A thousand begettings of the broken bold.

This is that figure stationed at our end,
Always, in brilliance, fatal, final, formed
Out of our lives to keep us in our death,

To watch us in the summer of Cyclops
Underground, a king as candle by our beds
In a robe that is our glory as he guards.

v

But she that says good-by losing in self
The sense of self, rosed out of prestiges
Of rose, stood tall in self not symbol, quick

And potent, an influence felt instead of seen.
She spoke with backward gestures of her hand.
She held men closely with discovery,

Almost as speed discovers, in the way
Invisible change discovers what is changed,
In the way what was has ceased to be what is.

It was not her look but a knowledge that she had.
She was a self that knew, an inner thing,
Subtler than look's declaiming, although she moved

With a sad splendor, beyond artifice,
Impassioned by the knowledge that she had,
There on the edges of oblivion.

O exhalation, O fling without a sleeve
And motion outward, reddened and resolved
From sight, in the silence that follows her last word—

VI

This is the mythology of modern death
And these, in their mufflings, monsters of elegy,
Of their own marvel made, of pity made,

435

Compounded and compounded, life by life,
These are death's own supremest images,
The pure perfections of parental space,

The children of a desire that is the will,
Even of death, the beings of the mind
In the light-bound space of the mind, the floreate
     flare . . .

It is a child that sings itself to sleep,
The mind, among the creatures that it makes,
The people, those by which it lives and dies.

◈◈◈◈◈◈◈◈◈◈◈◈◈◈◈◈◈◈◈◈◈◈◈◈◈◈◈◈◈◈◈◈

SAINT JOHN AND THE BACK–ACHE

The Back-Ache
    The mind is the terriblest force in the world, father,
    Because, in chief, it, only, can defend
    Against itself. At its mercy, we depend
        Upon it.
Saint John
              The world is presence and not force.
    Presence is not mind.
The Back-Ache
               Presence is *Kinder-Scenen.*
Saint John
    It fills the being before the mind can think.
    The effect of the object is beyond the mind's

436

Extremest pinch and, easily, as in
A sudden color on the sea. But it is not
That big-brushed green. Or in a tragic mode,
As at the moment of the year when, tick,
Autumn howls upon half-naked summer. But
It is not the unravelling of her yellow shift.
Presence is not the woman, come upon,
Not yet accustomed, yet, at sight, humane
To most incredible depths. I speak below
The tension of the lyre. My point is that
These illustrations are neither angels, no,
Nor brilliant blows thereof, ti-rill-a-roo,
Nor all one's luck at once in a play of strings.
They help us face the dumbfoundering abyss
Between us and the object, external cause,
The little ignorance that is everything,
The possible nest in the invisible tree,
Which in a composite season, now unknown,
Denied, dismissed, may hold a serpent, loud
In our captious hymns, erect and sinuous,
Whose venom and whose wisdom will be one.
Then the stale turtle will grow limp from age.
We shall be heavy with the knowledge of that day.

The Back-Ache

It may be, may be. It is possible.
Presence lies far too deep, for me to know
Its irrational reaction, as from pain.

CELLE QUI FÛT HÉAULMIETTE

Out of the first warmth of spring,
And out of the shine of the hemlocks,
Among the bare and crooked trees,
She found a helping from the cold,

Like a meaning in nothingness,
Like the snow before it softened
And dwindled into patches,
Like a shelter not in an arc

But in a circle, not in the arc
Of winter, in the unbroken circle
Of summer, at the windy edge,
Sharp in the ice shadow of the sky,

Blue for all that and white and hard,
And yet with water running in the sun,
Entinselled and gilderlinged and gone,
Another American vulgarity.

Into that native shield she slid,
Mistress of an idea, child
Of a mother with vague severed arms
And of a father bearded in his fire.

438

IMAGO

Who can pick up the weight of Britain,
Who can move the German load
Or say to the French here is France again?
Imago. Imago. Imago.

It is nothing, no great thing, nor man
Of ten brilliancies of battered gold
And fortunate stone. It moves its parade
Of motions in the mind and heart,

A gorgeous fortitude. Medium man
In February hears the imagination's hymns
And sees its images, its motions
And multitude of motions

And feels the imagination's mercies,
In a season more than sun and south wind,
Something returning from a deeper quarter,
A glacier running through delirium,

Making this heavy rock a place,
Which is not of our lives composed . . .
Lightly and lightly, O my land,
Move lightly through the air again.

439

A PRIMITIVE LIKE AN ORB

I

The essential poem at the centre of things,
The arias that spiritual fiddlings make,
Have gorged the cast-iron of our lives with good
And the cast-iron of our works. But it is, dear sirs,
A difficult apperception, this gorging good,
Fetched by such slick-eyed nymphs, this essential
    gold,
This fortune's finding, disposed and re-disposed
By such slight genii in such pale air.

II

We do not prove the existence of the poem.
It is something seen and known in lesser poems.
It is the huge, high harmony that sounds
A little and a little, suddenly,
By means of a separate sense. It is and it
Is not and, therefore, is. In the instant of speech,
The breadth of an accelerando moves,
Captives the being, widens—and was there.

III

What milk there is in such captivity,
What wheaten bread and oaten cake and kind,
Green guests and table in the woods and songs
At heart, within an instant's motion, within
A space grown wide, the inevitable blue

Of secluded thunder, an illusion, as it was,
Oh as, always too heavy for the sense
To seize, the obscurest as, the distant was . . .

IV

One poem proves another and the whole,
For the clairvoyant men that need no proof:
The lover, the believer and the poet.
Their words are chosen out of their desire,
The joy of language, when it is themselves.
With these they celebrate the central poem,
The fulfillment of fulfillments, in opulent,
Last terms, the largest, bulging still with more,

V

Until the used-to earth and sky, and the tree
And cloud, the used-to tree and used-to cloud,
Lose the old uses that they made of them,
And they: these men, and earth and sky, inform
Each other by sharp informations, sharp,
Free knowledges, secreted until then,
Breaches of that which held them fast. It is
As if the central poem became the world,

VI

And the world the central poem, each one the mate
Of the other, as if summer was a spouse,
Espoused each morning, each long afternoon,
And the mate of summer: her mirror and her look,
Her only place and person, a self of her
That speaks, denouncing separate selves, both one.
The essential poem begets the others. The light
Of it is not a light apart, up-hill.

VII

The central poem is the poem of the whole,
The poem of the composition of the whole,
The composition of blue sea and of green,
Of blue light and of green, as lesser poems,
And the miraculous multiplex of lesser poems,
Not merely into a whole, but a poem of
The whole, the essential compact of the parts,
The roundness that pulls tight the final ring

VIII

And that which in an altitude would soar,
A vis, a principle or, it may be,
The meditation of a principle,
Or else an inherent order active to be
Itself, a nature to its natives all
Beneficence, a repose, utmost repose,
The muscles of a magnet aptly felt,
A giant, on the horizon, glistening,

IX

And in bright excellence adorned, crested
With every prodigal, familiar fire,
And unfamiliar escapades: whirroos
And scintillant sizzlings such as children like,
Vested in the serious folds of majesty,
Moving around and behind, a following,
A source of trumpeting seraphs in the eye,
A source of pleasant outbursts on the ear.

X

It is a giant, always, that is evolved,
To be in scale, unless virtue cuts him, snips

Both size and solitude or thinks it does,
As in a signed photograph on a mantelpiece.
But the virtuoso never leaves his shape,
Still on the horizon elongates his cuts,
And still angelic and still plenteous,
Imposes power by the power of his form.

XI

Here, then, is an abstraction given head,
A giant on the horizon, given arms,
A massive body and long legs, stretched out,
A definition with an illustration, not
Too exactly labelled, a large among the smalls
Of it, a close, parental magnitude,
At the centre on the horizon, concentrum, grave
And prodigious person, patron of origins.

XII

That's it. The lover writes, the believer hears,
The poet mumbles and the painter sees,
Each one, his fated eccentricity,
As a part, but part, but tenacious particle,
Of the skeleton of the ether, the total
Of letters, prophecies, perceptions, clods
Of color, the giant of nothingness, each one
And the giant ever changing, living in change.

METAPHOR AS DEGENERATION

If there is a man white as marble
Sits in a wood, in the greenest part,
Brooding sounds of the images of death,

So there is a man in black space
Sits in nothing that we know,
Brooding sounds of river noises;

And these images, these reverberations,
And others, make certain how being
Includes death and the imagination.

The marble man remains himself in space.
The man in the black wood descends unchanged.
It is certain that the river

Is not Swatara. The swarthy water
That flows round the earth and through the skies,
Twisting among the universal spaces,

Is not Swatara. It is being.
That is the flock-flecked river, the water,
The blown sheen—or is it air?

How, then, is metaphor degeneration,
When Swatara becomes this undulant river
And the river becomes the landless, waterless
    ocean?

444

Here the black violets grow down to its banks
And the memorial mosses hang their green
Upon it, as it flows ahead.

⬧⬦⬧⬦⬧⬦⬧⬦⬧⬦⬧⬦⬧⬦⬧⬦⬧⬦⬧⬦⬧⬦⬧⬦⬧⬦⬧⬦⬧⬦⬧⬦⬧⬦⬧⬦⬧

THE WOMAN IN SUNSHINE

It is only that this warmth and movement are like
The warmth and movement of a woman.

It is not that there is any image in the air
Nor the beginning nor end of a form:

It is empty. But a woman in threadless gold
Burns us with brushings of her dress

And a dissociated abundance of being,
More definite for what she is—

Because she is disembodied,
Bearing the odors of the summer fields,

Confessing the taciturn and yet indifferent,
Invisibly clear, the only love.

445

REPLY TO PAPINI

In all the solemn moments of
human history . . . poets rose
to sing the hymn of victory or
the psalm of supplication. . . .
Cease, then, from being the
astute calligraphers of con-
gealed daydreams, the hunters
of cerebral phosphorescences.
LETTER OF CELESTIN VI, POPE,
TO THE POETS
P.C.C. GIOVANNI PAPINI

1

Poor procurator, why do you ask someone else
To say what Celestin should say for himself?

He has an ever-living subject. The poet
Has only the formulations of midnight.

Is Celestin dislodged? The way through the world
Is more difficult to find than the way beyond it.

You know that the nucleus of a time is not
The poet but the poem, the growth of the mind

Of the world, the heroic effort to live expressed
As victory. The poet does not speak in ruins

Nor stand there making orotund consolations.
He shares the confusions of intelligence.

Giovanni Papini, by your faith, know how
He wishes that all hard poetry were true.

This pastoral of endurance and of death
Is of a nature that must be perceived

And not imagined. The removes must give,
Including the removes toward poetry.

II

Celestin, the generous, the civilized,
Will understand what it is to understand.

The world is still profound and in its depths
Man sits and studies silence and himself,

Abiding the reverberations in the vaults.
Now, once, he accumulates himself and time

For humane triumphals. But a politics
Of property is not an area

For triumphals. These are hymns appropriate to
The complexities of the world, when apprehended,

The intricacies of appearance, when perceived.
They become our gradual possession. The poet

Increases the aspects of experience,
As in an enchantment, analyzed and fixed

447

And final. This is the centre. The poet is
The angry day-son clanging at its make:

The satisfaction underneath the sense,
The conception sparkling in still obstinate thought.

❖❖❖❖❖❖❖❖❖❖❖❖❖❖❖❖❖❖❖❖❖❖❖❖❖❖❖❖❖❖❖❖❖❖❖❖❖

THE BOUQUET

I

Of medium nature, this farouche extreme
Is a drop of lightning in an inner world,
Suspended in temporary jauntiness.

The bouquet stands in a jar, as metaphor,
As lightning itself is, likewise, metaphor
Crowded with apparitions suddenly gone

And no less suddenly here again, a growth
Of the reality of the eye, an artifice,
Nothing much, a flitter that reflects itself.

II

One approaches, simply, the reality
Of the other eye. One enters, entering home,
The place of meta-men and para-things,

448

And yet still men though meta-men, still things
Though para-things; the meta-men for whom
The world has turned to the several speeds of glass,

For whom no blue in the sky prevents them, as
They understand, and take on potency,
By growing clear, transparent magistrates,

Bearded with chains of blue-green glitterings
And wearing hats of angular flick and fleck,
Cold with an under impotency that they know,

Now that they know, because they know. One comes
To the things of medium nature, as meta-men
Behold them, not choses of Provence, growing

In glue, but things transfixed, transpierced and well
Perceived: the white seen smoothly argentine
And plated up, dense silver shine, in a land

Without a god, O silver sheen and shape,
And movement of emotion through the air,
True nothing, yet accosted self to self.

Through the door one sees on the lake that the white
      duck swims
Away—and tells and tells the water tells
Of the image spreading behind it in idea.

The meta-men behold the idea as part
Of the image, behold it with exactness through beads
And dewy bearings of their light-locked beards.

449

The green bouquet comes from the place of the duck.
It is centi-colored and mille-flored and ripe,
Of dulce atmosphere, the fore of lofty scenes

But not of romance, the bitterest vulgar do
And die. It stands on a table at a window
Of the land, on a checkered cover, red and white.

The checkered squares, the skeleton of repose,
Breathe slightly, slightly move or seem to move
Toward a consciousness of red and white as one,

A vibrancy of petals, fallen, that still cling
By trivial filaments to the thing intact:
The recognizable, medium, central whole—

So near detachment, the cover's cornered squares,
And, when detached, so unimportantly gone,
So severed and so much forlorn debris.

Here the eye fastens intently to these lines
And crawls on them, as if feathers of the duck
Fell openly from the air to reappear

In other shapes, as if duck and tablecloth
And the eccentric twistings of the rapt bouquet
Exacted attention with attentive force.

A pack of cards is falling toward the floor.
The sun is secretly shining on a wall.
One remembers a woman standing in such a dress.

450

The rose, the delphinium, the red, the blue,
Are questions of the looks they get. The bouquet,
Regarded by the meta-men, is quirked

And queered by lavishings of their will to see.
It stands a sovereign of souvenirs
Neither remembered nor forgotten, nor old,

Nor new, nor in the sense of memory.
It is a symbol, a sovereign of symbols
In its interpretations voluble,

Embellished by the quicknesses of sight,
When in a way of seeing seen, an extreme,
A sovereign, a souvenir, a sign,

Of today, of this morning, of this afternoon,
Not yesterday, nor tomorrow, an appanage
Of indolent summer not quite physical

And yet of summer, the petty tones
Its colors make, the migratory daze,
The doubling second things, not mystical,

The infinite of the actual perceived,
A freedom revealed, a realization touched,
The real made more acute by an unreal.

IV

Perhaps, these colors, seen in insight, assume
In the eye a special hue of origin.
But if they do, they cast it widely round.

451

They cast deeply round a crystal crystal-white
And pallid bits, that tend to comply with blue,
A right red with its composites glutted full,

Like a monster that has everything and rests,
And yet is there, a presence in the way.
They cast closely round the facture of the thing

Turned para-thing, the rudiments in the jar,
The stalk, the weed, the grassy flourishes,
The violent disclosure trimly leafed,

Lean larkspur and jagged fern and rusting rue
In a stubborn literacy, an intelligence,
The prismatic sombreness of a torrent's wave.

The rudiments in the jar, farced, finikin,
Are flatly there, unversed except to be,
Made difficult by salt fragrance, intricate.

They are not splashings in a penumbra. They stand.
They are. The bouquet is a part of a dithering:
Cloud's gold, of a whole appearance that stands and is.

V

A car drives up. A soldier, an officer,
Steps out. He rings and knocks. The door is not
    locked.
He enters the room and calls. No one is there.

452

He bumps the table. The bouquet falls on its side.
He walks through the house, looks round him and
    then leaves.
The bouquet has slopped over the edge and lies on the
    floor.

✥✥✥✥✥✥✥✥✥✥✥✥✥✥✥✥✥✥✥✥✥✥✥✥✥✥✥✥✥✥✥✥

WORLD WITHOUT PECULIARITY

The day is great and strong—
But his father was strong, that lies now
In the poverty of dirt.

Nothing could be more hushed than the way
The moon moves toward the night.
But what his mother was returns and cries on his
    breast.

The red ripeness of round leaves is thick
With the spices of red summer.
But she that he loved turns cold at his light touch.

What good is it that the earth is justified,
That it is complete, that it is an end,
That in itself it is enough?

453

It is the earth itself that is humanity . . .
He is the inhuman son and she,
She is the fateful mother, whom he does not know.

She is the day, the walk of the moon
Among the breathless spices and, sometimes,
He, too, is human and difference disappears

And the poverty of dirt, the thing upon his breast,
The hating woman, the meaningless place,
Become a single being, sure and true.

OUR STARS COME FROM IRELAND

I

> *Tom McGreevy, in America,*
> *Thinks of Himself as a Boy*

Out of him that I loved,
Mal Bay I made,
I made Mal Bay
And him in that water.

Over the top of the Bank of Ireland,
The wind blows quaintly
Its thin-stringed music,
As he heard it in Tarbert.

These things were made of him
And out of myself.
He stayed in Kerry, died there.
I live in Pennsylvania.

Out of him I made Mal Bay
And not a bald and tasselled saint.
What would the water have been,
Without that that he makes of it?

The stars are washing up from Ireland
And through and over the puddles of
    Swatara
And Schuylkill. The sound of him
Comes from a great distance and is heard.

II

The Westwardness of Everything

These are the ashes of fiery weather,
Of nights full of the green stars from Ireland,
Wet out of the sea, and luminously wet,
Like beautiful and abandoned refugees.

The whole habit of the mind is changed by them,
These Gaeled and fitful-fangled darknesses
Made suddenly luminous, themselves a change,
An east in their compelling westwardness,

Themselves an issue as at an end, as if
There was an end at which in a final change,
When the whole habit of the mind was changed,
The ocean breathed out morning in one breath.

455

PUELLA PARVULA

Every thread of summer is at last unwoven.
By one caterpillar is great Africa devoured
And Gibraltar is dissolved like spit in the wind.

But over the wind, over the legends of its roaring,
The elephant on the roof and its elephantine blaring,
The bloody lion in the yard at night or ready to
      spring

From the clouds in the midst of trembling trees
Making a great gnashing, over the water wallows
Of a vacant sea declaiming with wide throat,

Over all these the mighty imagination triumphs
Like a trumpet and says, in this season of memory,
When the leaves fall like things mournful of the past,

Keep quiet in the heart, O wild bitch. O mind
Gone wild, be what he tells you to be: *Puella.*
Write *pax* across the window pane. And then

Be still. The *summarium in excelsis* begins . . .
Flame, sound, fury composed . . . Hear what he
      says,
The dauntless master, as he starts the human tale.

THE NOVEL

The crows are flying above the foyer of summer.
The winds batter it. The water curls. The leaves
Return to their original illusion.

The sun stands like a Spaniard as he departs,
Stepping from the foyer of summer into that
Of the past, the rodomontadean emptiness.

Mother was afraid I should freeze in the Parisian
  hotels.
She had heard of the fate of an Argentine writer. At
  night,
He would go to bed, cover himself with blankets—

Protruding from the pile of wool, a hand,
In a black glove, holds a novel by Camus. She begged
That I stay away. These are the words of José . . .

He is sitting by the fidgets of a fire,
The first red of red winter, winter-red,
The late, least foyer in a qualm of cold.

How tranquil it was at vividest Varadero,
While the water kept running through the mouth of
  the speaker,
Saying: *Olalla blanca en el blanco,*

457

Lol-lolling the endlessness of poetry.
But here tranquillity is what one thinks.
The fire burns as the novel taught it how.

The mirror melts and moulds itself and moves
And catches from nowhere brightly-burning breath.
It blows a glassy brightness on the fire

And makes flame flame and makes it bite the wood
And bite the hard-bite, barking as it bites.
The arrangement of the chairs is so and so,

Not as one would have arranged them for oneself,
But in the style of the novel, its tracing
Of an unfamiliar in the familiar room,

A *retrato* that is strong because it is like,
A second that grows first, a black unreal
In which a real lies hidden and alive.

Day's arches are crumbling into the autumn night.
The fire falls a little and the book is done.
The stillness is the stillness of the mind.

Slowly the room grows dark. It is odd about
That Argentine. Only the real can be
Unreal today, be hidden and alive.

It is odd, too, how that Argentine is oneself,
Feeling the fear that creeps beneath the wool,
Lies on the breast and pierces into the heart,

Straight from the Arcadian imagination,
Its being beating heavily in the veins,
Its knowledge cold within one as one's own;

And one trembles to be so understood and, at last,
To understand, as if to know became
The fatality of seeing things too well.

WHAT WE SEE IS WHAT WE THINK

At twelve, the disintegration of afternoon
Began, the return to phantomerei, if not
To phantoms. Till then, it had been the other way:

One imagined the violet trees but the trees stood
        green,
At twelve, as green as ever they would be.
The sky was blue beyond the vaultiest phrase.

Twelve meant as much as: the end of normal time,
Straight up, an élan without harrowing,
The imprescriptible zenith, free of harangue,

Twelve and the first gray second after, a kind
Of violet gray, a green violet, a thread
To weave a shadow's leg or sleeve, a scrawl

459

On the pedestal, an ambitious page dog-eared
At the upper right, a pyramid with one side
Like a spectral cut in its perception, a tilt

And its tawny caricature and tawny life,
Another thought, the paramount ado . . .
Since what we think is never what we see.

✿✧✿

A GOLDEN WOMAN IN A SILVER MIRROR

Suppose this was the root of everything.
Suppose it turned out to be or that it touched
An image that was mistress of the world.

For example: Au Château. Un Salon. A glass
The sun steps into, regards and finds itself;
Or: Gawks of hay . . . Augusta Moon, before

An attic glass, hums of the old Lutheran bells
At home; or: In the woods, belle Belle alone
Rattles with fear in unreflecting leaves.

Abba, dark death is the breaking of a glass.
The dazzled flakes and splinters disappear.
The seal is as relaxed as dirt, perdu.

But the images, disembodied, are not broken.
They have, or they may have, their glittering crown,
Sound-soothing pearl and omni-diamond,

460

Of the most beautiful, the most beautiful maid
And mother. How long have you lived and looked,
Ababba, expecting this king's queen to appear?

+O+O+O+O+O+O+O+O+O+O+O+O+O+O+O+O+O+O+O+O+O+O+O+O+

THE OLD LUTHERAN BELLS AT HOME

These are the voices of the pastors calling
In the names of St. Paul and of the halo-John
And of other holy and learned men, among them

Great choristers, propounders of hymns, trumpeters,
Jerome and the scrupulous Francis and Sunday
    women,
The nurses of the spirit's innocence.

These are the voices of the pastors calling
Much rough-end being to smooth Paradise,
Spreading out fortress walls like fortress wings.

Deep in their sound the stentor Martin sings.
Dark Juan looks outward through his mystic
    brow . . .
Each sexton has his sect. The bells have none.

These are the voices of the pastors calling
And calling like the long echoes in long sleep,
Generations of shepherds to generations of sheep.

Each truth is a sect though no bells ring for it.
And the bells belong to the sextons, after all,
As they jangle and dangle and kick their feet.

QUESTIONS ARE REMARKS

In the weed of summer comes this green sprout why.
The sun aches and ails and then returns halloo
Upon the horizon amid adult enfantillages.

Its fire fails to pierce the vision that beholds it,
Fails to destroy the antique acceptances,
Except that the grandson sees it as it is,

Peter the voyant, who says "Mother, what is that"—
The object that rises with so much rhetoric,
But not for him. His question is complete.

It is the question of what he is capable.
It is the extreme, the expert aetat. 2.
He will never ride the red horse she describes.

His question is complete because it contains
His utmost statement. It is his own array,
His own pageant and procession and display,

As far as nothingness permits . . . Hear him.
He does not say, "Mother, my mother, who are
      you,"
The way the drowsy, infant, old men do.

✿❀✿

STUDY OF IMAGES I

It does no good to speak of the big, blue bush
Of day. If the study of his images
Is the study of man, this image of Saturday,

This Italian symbol, this Southern landscape, is
      like
A waking, as in images we awake,
Within the very object that we seek,

Participants of its being. It is, we are.
He is, we are. Ah, bella! He is, we are,
Within the big, blue bush and its vast shade

At evening and at night. It does no good.
Stop at the terraces of mandolins,
False, faded and yet inextricably there,

The pulse of the object, the heat of the body
      grown cold
Or cooling in late leaves, not false except
When the image itself is false, a mere desire,

Not faded, if images are all we have.
They can be no more faded than ourselves.
The blood refreshes with its stale demands.

❀❁❀❁❀❁❀❁❀❁❀❁❀❁❀❁❀❁❀❁❀❁❀❁❀❁❀❁❀❁❀❁❀❁

STUDY OF IMAGES II

The frequency of images of the moon
Is more or less. The pearly women that drop
From heaven and float in air, like animals

Of ether, exceed the excelling witches, whence
They came. But, brown, the ice-bear sleeping in ice-
    month
In his cave, remains dismissed without a dream,

As if the centre of images had its
Congenial mannequins, alert to please,
Beings of other beings manifold—

The shadowless moon wholly composed of shade,
Women with other lives in their live hair,
Rose—women as half-fishes of salt shine,

As if, as if, as if the disparate halves
Of things were waiting in a bethrothal known
To none, awaiting espousal to the sound

464

Of right joining, a music of ideas, the burning
And breeding and bearing birth of harmony,
The final relation, the marriage of the rest.

◇◇

AN ORDINARY EVENING IN NEW HAVEN

I

The eye's plain version is a thing apart,
The vulgate of experience. Of this,
A few words, an and yet, and yet, and yet—

As part of the never-ending meditation,
Part of the question that is a giant himself:
Of what is this house composed if not of the sun,

These houses, these difficult objects, dilapidate
Appearances of what appearances,
Words, lines, not meanings, not communications,

Dark things without a double, after all,
Unless a second giant kills the first—
A recent imagining of reality,

Much like a new resemblance of the sun,
Down-pouring, up-springing and inevitable,
A larger poem for a larger audience,

465

As if the crude collops came together as one,
A mythological form, a festival sphere,
A great bosom, beard and being, alive with age.

II

Suppose these houses are composed of ourselves,
So that they become an impalpable town, full of
Impalpable bells, transparencies of sound,

Sounding in transparent dwellings of the self,
Impalpable habitations that seem to move
In the movement of the colors of the mind,

The far-fire flowing and the dim-coned bells
Coming together in a sense in which we are poised,
Without regard to time or where we are,

In the perpetual reference, object
Of the perpetual meditation, point
Of the enduring, visionary love,

Obscure, in colors whether of the sun
Or mind, uncertain in the clearest bells,
The spirit's speeches, the indefinite,

Confused illuminations and sonorities,
So much ourselves, we cannot tell apart
The idea and the bearer-being of the idea.

III

The point of vision and desire are the same.
It is to the hero of midnight that we pray
On a hill of stones to make beau mont thereof.

466

If it is misery that infuriates our love,
If the black of night stands glistening on beau
    mont,
Then, ancientest saint ablaze with ancientest truth,

Say next to holiness is the will thereto,
And next to love is the desire for love,
The desire for its celestial ease in the heart,

Which nothing can frustrate, that most secure,
Unlike love in possession of that which was
To be possessed and is. But this cannot

Possess. It is desire, set deep in the eye,
Behind all actual seeing, in the actual scene,
In the street, in a room, on a carpet or a wall,

Always in emptiness that would be filled,
In denial that cannot contain its blood,
A porcelain, as yet in the bats thereof.

IV

The plainness of plain things is savagery,
As: the last plainness of a man who has fought
Against illusion and was, in a great grinding

Of growling teeth, and falls at night, snuffed out
By the obese opiates of sleep. Plain men in plain
    towns
Are not precise about the appeasement they need.

They only know a savage assuagement cries
With a savage voice; and in that cry they hear
Themselves transposed, muted and comforted

In a savage and subtle and simple harmony,
A matching and mating of surprised accords,
A responding to a diviner opposite.

So lewd spring comes from winter's chastity.
So, after summer, in the autumn air,
Comes the cold volume of forgotten ghosts,

But soothingly, with pleasant instruments,
So that this cold, a children's tale of ice,
Seems like a sheen of heat romanticized.

v

Inescapable romance, inescapable choice
Of dreams, disillusion as the last illusion,
Reality as a thing seen by the mind,

Not that which is but that which is apprehended,
A mirror, a lake of reflections in a room,
A glassy ocean lying at the door,

A great town hanging pendent in a shade,
An enormous nation happy in a style,
Everything as unreal as real can be,

In the inexquisite eye. Why, then, inquire
Who has divided the world, what entrepreneur?
No man. The self, the chrysalis of all men

Became divided in the leisure of blue day
And more, in branchings after day. One part
Held fast tenaciously in common earth

468

And one from central earth to central sky
And in moonlit extensions of them in the mind
Searched out such majesty as it could find.

VI

Reality is the beginning not the end,
Naked Alpha, not the hierophant Omega,
Of dense investiture, with luminous vassals.

It is the infant A standing on infant legs,
Not twisted, stooping, polymathic Z,
He that kneels always on the edge of space

In the pallid perceptions of its distances.
Alpha fears men or else Omega's men
Or else his prolongations of the human.

These characters are around us in the scene.
For one it is enough; for one it is not;
For neither is it profound absentia,

Since both alike appoint themselves the choice
Custodians of the glory of the scene,
The immaculate interpreters of life.

But that's the difference: in the end and the way
To the end. Alpha continues to begin.
Omega is refreshed at every end.

VII

In the presence of such chapels and such schools,
The impoverished architects appear to be
Much richer, more fecund, sportive and alive.

469

The objects tingle and the spectator moves
With the objects. But the spectator also moves
With lesser things, with things exteriorized

Out of rigid realists. It is as if
Men turning into things, as comedy,
Stood, dressed in antic symbols, to display

The truth about themselves, having lost, as things,
That power to conceal they had as men,
Not merely as to depth but as to height

As well, not merely as to the commonplace
But, also, as to their miraculous,
Conceptions of new mornings of new worlds,

The tips of cock-cry pinked out pastily,
As that which was incredible becomes,
In misted contours, credible day again.

VIII

We fling ourselves, constantly longing, on this form.
We descend to the street and inhale a health of air
To our sepulchral hollows. Love of the real

Is soft in three-four cornered fragrances
From five-six cornered leaves, and green, the signal
To the lover, and blue, as of a secret place

In the anonymous color of the universe.
Our breath is like a desperate element
That we must calm, the origin of a mother tongue

470

With which to speak to her, the capable
In the midst of foreignness, the syllable
Of recognition, avowal, impassioned cry,

The cry that contains its converse in itself,
In which looks and feelings mingle and are part
As a quick answer modifies a question,

Not wholly spoken in a conversation between
Two bodies disembodied in their talk,
Too fragile, too immediate for any speech.

IX

We keep coming back and coming back
To the real: to the hotel instead of the hymns
That fall upon it out of the wind. We seek

The poem of pure reality, untouched
By trope or deviation, straight to the word,
Straight to the transfixing object, to the object

At the exactest point at which it is itself,
Transfixing by being purely what it is,
A view of New Haven, say, through the certain eye,

The eye made clear of uncertainty, with the sight
Of simple seeing, without reflection. We seek
Nothing beyond reality. Within it,

Everything, the spirit's alchemicana
Included, the spirit that goes roundabout
And through included, not merely the visible,

471

The solid, but the movable, the moment,
The coming on of feasts and the habits of saints,
The pattern of the heavens and high, night air.

x

It is fatal in the moon and empty there.
But, here, allons. The enigmatical
Beauty of each beautiful enigma

Becomes amassed in a total double-thing.
We do not know what is real and what is not.
We say of the moon, it is haunted by the man

Of bronze whose mind was made up and who, there-
    fore, died.
We are not men of bronze and we are not dead.
His spirit is imprisoned in constant change.

But ours is not imprisoned. It resides
In a permanence composed of impermanence,
In a faithfulness as against the lunar light,

So that morning and evening are like promises kept,
So that the approaching sun and its arrival,
Its evening feast and the following festival,

This faithfulness of reality, this mode,
This tendance and venerable holding-in
Make gay the hallucinations in surfaces.

XI

In the metaphysical streets of the physical town
We remember the lion of Juda and we save
The phrase . . . Say of each lion of the spirit

It is a cat of a sleek transparency
That shines with a nocturnal shine alone.
The great cat must stand potent in the sun.

The phrase grows weak. The fact takes up the
    strength
Of the phrase. It contrives the self-same evocations
And Juda becomes New Haven or else must.

In the metaphysical streets, the profoundest forms
Go with the walker subtly walking there.
These he destroys with wafts of wakening,

Free from their majesty and yet in need
Of majesty, of an invincible clou,
A minimum of making in the mind,

A verity of the most veracious men,
The propounding of four seasons and twelve months.
The brilliancy at the central of the earth.

XII

The poem is the cry of its occasion,
Part of the res itself and not about it.
The poet speaks the poem as it is,

Not as it was: part of the reverberation
Of a windy night as it is, when the marble statues
Are like newspapers blown by the wind. He speaks

By sight and insight as they are. There is no
Tomorrow for him. The wind will have passed by,
The statues will have gone back to be things about.

473

The mobile and the immobile flickering
In the area between is and was are leaves,
Leaves burnished in autumnal burnished trees

And leaves in whirlings in the gutters, whirlings
Around and away, resembling the presence of
    thought,
Resembling the presences of thoughts, as if,

In the end, in the whole psychology, the self,
The town, the weather, in a casual litter,
Together, said words of the world are the life of the
    world.

XIII

The ephebe is solitary in his walk.
He skips the journalism of subjects, seeks out
The perquisites of sanctity, enjoys

A strong mind in a weak neighborhood and is
A serious man without the serious,
Inactive in his singular respect.

He is neither priest nor proctor at low eve,
Under the birds, among the perilous owls,
In the big X of the returning primitive.

It is a fresh spiritual that he defines,
A coldness in a long, too-constant warmth,
A thing on the side of a house, not deep in a cloud,

A difficulty that we predicate:
The difficulty of the visible
To the nations of the clear invisible,

The actual landscape with its actual horns
Of baker and butcher blowing, as if to hear,
Hear hard, gets at an essential integrity.

XIV

The dry eucalyptus seeks god in the rainy cloud.
Professor Eucalyptus of New Haven seeks him
In New Haven with an eye that does not look

Beyond the object. He sits in his room, beside
The window, close to the ramshackle spout in which
The rain falls with a ramshackle sound. He seeks

God in the object itself, without much choice.
It is a choice of the commodious adjective
For what he sees, it comes in the end to that:

The description that makes it divinity, still speech
As it touches the point of reverberation—not grim
Reality but reality grimly seen

And spoken in paradisal parlance new
And in any case never grim, the human grim
That is part of the indifference of the eye

Indifferent to what it sees. The tink-tonk
Of the rain in the spout is not a substitute.
It is of the essence not yet well perceived.

XV

He preserves himself against the repugnant rain
By an instinct for a rainless land, the self
Of his self, come at upon wide delvings of wings.

The instinct for heaven had its counterpart:
The instinct for earth, for New Haven, for his room,
The gay tournamonde as of a single world

In which he is and as and is are one.
For its counterpart a kind of counterpoint
Irked the wet wallows of the water-spout.

The rain kept falling loudly in the trees
And on the ground. The hibernal dark that hung
In primavera, the shadow of bare rock,

Becomes the rock of autumn, glittering,
Ponderable source of each imponderable,
The weight we lift with the finger of a dream,

The heaviness we lighten by light will,
By the hand of desire, faint, sensitive, the soft
Touch and trouble of the touch of the actual hand.

XVI

Among time's images, there is not one
Of this present, the venerable mask above
The dilapidation of dilapidations.

The oldest-newest day is the newest alone.
The oldest-newest night does not creak by,
With lanterns, like a celestial ancientness.

Silently it heaves its youthful sleep from the sea—
The Oklahoman—the Italian blue
Beyond the horizon with its masculine,

Their eyes closed, in a young palaver of lips.
And yet the wind whimpers oldly of old age
In the western night. The venerable mask,

In this perfection, occasionally speaks
And something of death's poverty is heard.
This should be tragedy's most moving face.

It is a bough in the electric light
And exhalations in the eaves, so little
To indicate the total leaflessness.

XVII

The color is almost the color of comedy,
Not quite. It comes to the point and at the point,
It fails. The strength at the centre is serious.

Perhaps instead of failing it rejects
As a serious strength rejects pin-idleness.
A blank underlies the trials of device,

The dominant blank, the unapproachable.
This is the mirror of the high serious:
Blue verdured into a damask's lofty symbol,

Gold easings and ouncings and fluctuations of thread
And beetling of belts and lights of general stones,
Like blessed beams from out a blessed bush

Or the wasted figurations of the wastes
Of night, time and the imagination,
Saved and beholden, in a robe of rays.

These fitful sayings are, also, of tragedy:
The serious reflection is composed
Neither of comic nor tragic but of commonplace.

XVIII

It is the window that makes it difficult
To say good-by to the past and to live and to be
In the present state of things as, say, to paint

In the present state of painting and not the state
Of thirty years ago. It is looking out
Of the window and walking in the street and seeing,

As if the eyes were the present or part of it,
As if the ears heard any shocking sound,
As if life and death were ever physical.

The life and death of this carpenter depend
On a fuchsia in a can—and iridescences
Of petals that will never be realized,

Things not yet true which he perceives through truth,
Or thinks he does, as he perceives the present,
Or thinks he does, a carpenter's iridescences,

Wooden, the model for astral apprentices,
A city slapped up like a chest of tools,
The eccentric exterior of which the clocks talk.

XIX

The moon rose in the mind and each thing there
Picked up its radial aspect in the night,
Prostrate below the singleness of its will.

That which was public green turned private gray.
At another time, the radial aspect came
From a different source. But there was always one:

A century in which everything was part
Of that century and of its aspect, a personage,
A man who was the axis of his time,

An image that begot its infantines,
Imaginary poles whose intelligence
Streamed over chaos their civilities.

What is the radial aspect of this place,
This present colony of a colony
Of colonies, a sense in the changing sense

Of things? A figure like Ecclesiast,
Rugged and luminous, chants in the dark
A text that is an answer, although obscure.

xx

The imaginative transcripts were like clouds,
Today; and the transcripts of feeling, impossible
To distinguish. The town was a residuum,

A neuter shedding shapes in an absolute.
Yet the transcripts of it when it was blue remain;
And the shapes that it took in feeling, the persons
    that

It became, the nameless, flitting characters—
These actors still walk in a twilight muttering lines.
It may be that they mingle, clouds and men, in the
    air

479

Or street or about the corners of a man,
Who sits thinking in the corners of a room.
In this chamber the pure sphere escapes the impure

Because the thinker himself escapes. And yet
To have evaded clouds and men leaves him
A naked being with a naked will

And everything to make. He may evade
Even his own will and in his nakedness
Inhabit the hypnosis of that sphere.

XXI

But he may not. He may not evade his will,
Nor the wills of other men; and he cannot evade
The will of necessity, the will of wills—

Romanza out of the black shepherd's isle,
Like the constant sound of the water of the sea
In the hearing of the shepherd and his black forms;

Out of the isle, but not of any isle.
Close to the senses there lies another isle
And there the senses give and nothing take,

The opposite of Cythère, an isolation
At the centre, the object of the will, this place,
The things around—the alternate romanza

Out of the surfaces, the windows, the walls,
The bricks grown brittle in time's poverty,
The clear. A celestial mode is paramount,

If only in the branches sweeping in the rain:
The two romanzas, the distant and the near,
Are a single voice in the boo-ha of the wind.

XXII

Professor Eucalyptus said, "The search
For reality is as momentous as
The search for god." It is the philosopher's search

For an interior made exterior
And the poet's search for the same exterior made
Interior: breathless things broodingly abreath

With the inhalations of original cold
And of original earliness. Yet the sense
Of cold and earliness is a daily sense,

Not the predicate of bright origin.
Creation is not renewed by images
Of lone wanderers. To re-create, to use

The cold and earliness and bright origin
Is to search. Likewise to say of the evening star,
The most ancient light in the most ancient sky,

That it is wholly an inner light, that it shines
From the sleepy bosom of the real, re-creates,
Searches a possible for its possibleness.

XXIII

The sun is half the world, half everything,
The bodiless half. There is always this bodiless half,
This illumination, this elevation, this future

481

Or, say, the late going colors of that past,
Effete green, the woman in black cassimere.
If, then, New Haven is half sun, what remains,

At evening, after dark, is the other half,
Lighted by space, big over those that sleep,
Of the single future of night, the single sleep,

As of a long, inevitable sound,
A kind of cozening and coaxing sound,
And the goodness of lying in a maternal sound,

Unfretted by day's separate, several selves,
Being part of everything come together as one.
In this identity, disembodiments

Still keep occurring. What is, uncertainly,
Desire prolongs its adventure to create
Forms of farewell, furtive among green ferns.

XXIV
The consolations of space are nameless things.
It was after the neurosis of winter. It was
In the genius of summer that they blew up

The statue of Jove among the boomy clouds.
It took all day to quieten the sky
And then to refill its emptiness again,

So that at the edge of afternoon, not over,
Before the thought of evening had occurred
Or the sound of Incomincia had been set,

There was a clearing, a readiness for first bells,
An opening for outpouring, the hand was raised:
There was a willingness not yet composed,

A knowing that something certain had been pro-
      posed,
Which, without the statue, would be new,
An escape from repetition, a happening

In space and the self, that touched them both at once
And alike, a point of the sky or of the earth
Or of a town poised at the horizon's dip.

XXV

Life fixed him, wandering on the stair of glass,
With its attentive eyes. And, as he stood,
On his balcony, outsensing distances,

There were looks that caught him out of empty air.
C'est toujours la vie qui me regarde . . . This was
Who watched him, always, for unfaithful thought.

This sat beside his bed, with its guitar,
To keep him from forgetting, without a word,
A note or two disclosing who it was.

Nothing about him ever stayed the same,
Except this hidalgo and his eye and tune,
The shawl across one shoulder and the hat.

The commonplace became a rumpling of blazons.
What was real turned into something most unreal,
Bare beggar-tree, hung low for fruited red

483

In isolated moments—isolations
Were false. The hidalgo was permanent, abstract,
A hatching that stared and demanded an answering
    look.

XXVI

How facilely the purple blotches fell
On the walk, purple and blue, and red and gold,
Blooming and beaming and voluming colors out.

Away from them, capes, along the afternoon Sound,
Shook off their dark marine in lapis light.
The sea shivered in transcendent change, rose up

As rain and booming, gleaming, blowing, swept
The wateriness of green wet in the sky.
Mountains appeared with greater eloquence

Than that of their clouds. These lineaments were the
    earth,
Seen as inamorata, of loving fame
Added and added out of a fame-full heart . . .

But, here, the inamorata, without distance
And thereby lost, and naked or in rags,
Shrunk in the poverty of being close,

Touches, as one hand touches another hand,
Or as a voice that, speaking without form,
Gritting the ear, whispers humane repose.

484

XXVII

A scholar, in his Segmenta, left a note,
As follows, "The Ruler of Reality,
If more unreal than New Haven, is not

A real ruler, but rules what is unreal."
In addition, there were draftings of him, thus:
"He is the consort of the Queen of Fact.

Sunrise is his garment's hem, sunset is hers.
He is the theorist of life, not death,
The total excellence of its total book."

Again, "The sibilance of phrases is his
Or partly his. His voice is audible,
As the fore-meaning in music is." Again,

"This man abolishes by being himself
That which is not ourselves: the regalia,
The attributions, the plume and helmet-ho."

Again, "He has thought it out, he thinks it out,
As he has been and is and, with the Queen
Of Fact, lies at his ease beside the sea."

XXVIII

If it should be true that reality exists
In the mind: the tin plate, the loaf of bread on it,
The long-bladed knife, the little to drink and her

Misericordia, it follows that
Real and unreal are two in one: New Haven
Before and after one arrives or, say,

485

Bergamo on a postcard, Rome after dark,
Sweden described, Salzburg with shaded eyes
Or Paris in conversation at a café.

This endlessly elaborating poem
Displays the theory of poetry,
As the life of poetry. A more severe,

More harassing master would extemporize
Subtler, more urgent proof that the theory
Of poetry is the theory of life,

As it is, in the intricate evasions of as,
In things seen and unseen, created from nothingness,
The heavens, the hells, the worlds, the longed-for
    lands.

XXIX

In the land of the lemon trees, yellow and yellow
    were
Yellow-blue, yellow-green, pungent with citron-sap,
Dangling and spangling, the mic-mac of mocking
    birds.

In the land of the elm trees, wandering mariners
Looked on big women, whose ruddy-ripe images
Wreathed round and round the round wreath of
    autumn.

They rolled their r's, there, in the land of the citrons.
In the land of big mariners, the words they spoke
Were mere brown clods, mere catching weeds of
    talk.

When the mariners came to the land of the lemon
    trees,
At last, in that blond atmosphere, bronzed hard,
They said, "We are back once more in the land of
    the elm trees,

But folded over, turned round." It was the same,
Except for the adjectives, an alteration
Of words that was a change of nature, more

Than the difference that clouds make over a town.
The countrymen were changed and each constant
    thing.
Their dark-colored words had redescribed the
    citrons.

xxx

The last leaf that is going to fall has fallen.
The robins are là-bas, the squirrels, in tree-caves,
Huddle together in the knowledge of squirrels.

The wind has blown the silence of summer away.
It buzzes beyond the horizon or in the ground:
In mud under ponds, where the sky used to be re-
    flected.

The barrenness that appears is an exposing.
It is not part of what is absent, a halt
For farewells, a sad hanging on for remembrances.

It is a coming on and a coming forth.
The pines that were fans and fragrances emerge,
Staked solidly in a gusty grappling with rocks.

487

The glass of the air becomes an element—
It was something imagined that has been washed
    away.
A clearness has returned. It stands restored.

It is not an empty clearness, a bottomless sight.
It is a visibility of thought,
In which hundreds of eyes, in one mind, see at once.

XXXI

The less legible meanings of sounds, the little reds
Not often realized, the lighter words
In the heavy drum of speech, the inner men

Behind the outer shields, the sheets of music
In the strokes of thunder, dead candles at the
    window
When day comes, fire-foams in the motions of the
    sea,

Flickings from finikin to fine finikin
And the general fidget from busts of Constantine
To photographs of the late president, Mr. Blank,

These are the edgings and inchings of final form,
The swarming activities of the formulae
Of statement, directly and indirectly getting at,

Like an evening evoking the spectrum of violet,
A philosopher practicing scales on his piano,
A woman writing a note and tearing it up.

It is not in the premise that reality
Is a solid. It may be a shade that traverses
A dust, a force that traverses a shade.

❖◇

THINGS OF AUGUST

I

These locusts by day, these crickets by night
Are the instruments on which to play
Of an old and disused ambit of the soul
Or of a new aspect, bright in discovery—

A disused ambit of the spirit's way,
The sort of thing that August crooners sing,
By a pure fountain, that was a ghost, and is,
Under the sun-slides of a sloping mountain;

Or else a new aspect, say the spirit's sex,
Its attitudes, its answers to attitudes
And the sex of its voices, as the voice of one
Meets nakedly another's naked voice.

Nothing is lost, loud locusts. No note fails.
These sounds are long in the living of the ear.
The honky-tonk out of the somnolent grasses
Is a memorizing, a trying out, to keep.

489

II

We make, although inside an egg,
Variations on the words spread sail.

The morning-glories grow in the egg.
It is full of the myrrh and camphor of summer

And Adirondack glittering. The cat hawks it
And the hawk cats it and we say spread sail,

Spread sail, we say spread white, spread way.
The shell is a shore. The egg of the sea

And the egg of the sky are in shells, in walls, in skins
And the egg of the earth lies deep within an egg.

Spread outward. Crack the round dome. Break
    through.
Have liberty not as the air within a grave

Or down a well. Breathe freedom, oh, my native,
In the space of horizons that neither love nor hate.

III

High poetry and low:
Experience in perihelion
Or in the penumbra of summer night—

The solemn sentences,
Like interior intonations,
The speech of truth in its true solitude,
A nature that is created in what it says,
The peace of the last intelligence;

Or the same thing without desire,
He that in this intelligence
Mistakes it for a world of objects,
Which, being green and blue, appease him,
By chance, or happy chance, or happiness,
According to his thought, in the Mediterranean
Of the quiet of the middle of the night,
With the broken statues standing on the shore.

IV

The sad smell of the lilacs—one remembered it,
Not as the fragrance of Persephone,
Nor of a widow Dooley,
But as of an exhumation returned to earth,

The rich earth, of its own self made rich,
Fertile of its own leaves and days and wars,
Of its brown wheat rapturous in the wind,
The nature of its women in the air,

The stern voices of its necessitous men,
This chorus as of those that wanted to live.
The sentiment of the fatal is a part
Of filial love. Or is it the element,

An approximation of an element,
A little thing to think of on Sunday walks,
Something not to be mentioned to Mrs. Dooley,
An arrogant dagger darting its arrogance,

In the parent's hand, perhaps parental love?
One wished that there had been a season,
Longer and later, in which the lilacs opened
And spread about them a warmer, rosier odor.

491

V

We'll give the week-end to wisdom, to Weisheit, the
    rabbi,
Lucidity of his city, joy of his nation,
The state of circumstance.

The thinker as reader reads what has been written.
He wears the words he reads to look upon
Within his being,

A crown within him of crispest diamonds,
A reddened garment falling to his feet,
A hand of light to turn the page,

A finger with a ring to guide his eye
From line to line, as we lie on the grass and listen
To that which has no speech,

The voluble intentions of the symbols,
The ghostly celebrations of the picnic,
The secretions of insight.

VI

The world images for the beholder.
He is born the blank mechanic of the mountains,

The blank frere of fields, their matin laborer.
He is the possessed of sense not the possessor.

He does not change the sea from crumpled tinfoil
To chromatic crawler. But it is changed.

He does not raise the rousing of fresh light
On the still, black-slatted eastward shutters.

The woman is chosen but not by him,
Among the endlessly emerging accords.

The world? The inhuman as human? That which
    thinks not,
Feels not, resembling thought, resembling feeling?

It habituates him to the invisible,
By its faculty of the exceptional,

The faculty of ellipses and deviations,
In which he exists but never as himself.

VII

He turned from the tower to the house,
From the spun sky and the high and deadly view,
To the novels on the table,
The geraniums on the sill.

He could understand the things at home.
And being up high had helped him when up high,
As if on a taller tower
He would be certain to see

That, in the shadowless atmosphere,
The knowledge of things lay round but unperceived:
The height was not quite proper;
The position was wrong.

It was curious to have to descend
And, seated in the nature of his chair,
To feel the satisfactions
Of that transparent air.

493

VIII

When was it that the particles became
The whole man, that tempers and beliefs became
Temper and belief and that differences lost
Difference and were one? It had to be
In the presence of a solitude of the self,
An expanse and the abstraction of an expanse,
A zone of time without the ticking of clocks,
A color that moved us with forgetfulness.
When was it that we heard the voice of union?

Was it as we sat in the park and the archaic form
Of a woman with a cloud on her shoulder rose
Against the trees and then against the sky
And the sense of the archaic touched us at once
In a movement of the outlines of similarity?
We resembled one another at the sight.
The forgetful color of the autumn day
Was full of these archaic forms, giants
Of sense, evoking one thing in many men,
Evoking an archaic space, vanishing
In the space, leaving an outline of the size
Of the impersonal person, the wanderer,
The father, the ancestor, the bearded peer,
The total of human shadows bright as glass.

IX

A new text of the world,
A scribble of fret and fear and fate,
From a bravura of the mind,
A courage of the eye,

494

In which, for all the breathings
From the edge of night,
And for all the white voices
That were rosen once,

The meanings are our own—
It is a text that we shall be needing,
To be the footing of noon,
The pillar of midnight,

That comes from ourselves, neither from knowing
Nor not knowing, yet free from question,
Because we wanted it so
And it had to be,

A text of intelligent men
At the centre of the unintelligible,
As in a hermitage, for us to think,
Writing and reading the rigid inscription.

x

The mornings grow silent, the never-tiring wonder.
The trees are reappearing in poverty.

Without rain, there is the sadness of rain
And an air of lateness. The moon is a tricorn

Waved in pale adieu. The rex Impolitor
Will come stamping here, the ruler of less than men,

In less than nature. He is not here yet.
Here the adult one is still banded with fulgor,

495

Is still warm with the love with which she came,
Still touches solemnly with what she was

And willed. She has given too much, but not enough.
She is exhausted and a little old.

ⓈⓉⓈⓉⓈⓉⓈⓉⓈⓉⓈⓉⓈⓉⓈⓉⓈⓉⓈⓉⓈⓉⓈⓉⓈⓉⓈⓉⓈⓉⓈⓉ

ANGEL SURROUNDED BY PAYSANS

One of the countrymen:
                                          There is
      A welcome at the door to which no one comes?
The angel:
      I am the angel of reality,
      Seen for a moment standing in the door.

      I have neither ashen wing nor wear of ore
      And live without a tepid aureole,

      Or stars that follow me, not to attend,
      But, of my being and its knowing, part.

      I am one of you and being one of you
      Is being and knowing what I am and know.

      Yet I am the necessary angel of earth,
      Since, in my sight, you see the earth again,

496

Cleared of its stiff and stubborn, man-locked set,
And, in my hearing, you hear its tragic drone

Rise liquidly in liquid lingerings,
Like watery words awash; like meanings said

By repetitions of half-meanings. Am I not,
Myself, only half of a figure of a sort,

A figure half seen, or seen for a moment, a man
Of the mind, an apparition apparelled in

Apparels of such lightest look that a turn
Of my shoulder and quickly, too quickly, I am gone?

THE ROCK

THE BOOK

AN OLD MAN ASLEEP

The two worlds are asleep, are sleeping, now.
A dumb sense possesses them in a kind of solemnity.

The self and the earth—your thoughts, your feelings,
Your beliefs and disbeliefs, your whole peculiar plot;

The redness of your reddish chestnut trees,
The river motion, the drowsy motion of the river R.

THE IRISH CLIFFS OF MOHER

Who is my father in this world, in this house,
At the spirit's base?

My father's father, his father's father, his—
Shadows like winds

Go back to a parent before thought, before speech,
At the head of the past.

They go to the cliffs of Moher rising out of the mist,
Above the real,

Rising out of present time and place, above
The wet, green grass.

This is not landscape, full of the somnambulations
Of poetry

And the sea. This is my father or, maybe,
It is as he was,

A likeness, one of the race of fathers: earth
And sea and air.

❦❦❦❦❦❦❦❦❦❦❦❦❦❦❦❦❦❦❦❦❦❦❦❦❦❦❦❦❦

THE PLAIN SENSE OF THINGS

After the leaves have fallen, we return
To a plain sense of things. It is as if
We had come to an end of the imagination,
Inanimate in an inert savoir.

It is difficult even to choose the adjective
For this blank cold, this sadness without cause.
The great structure has become a minor house.
No turban walks across the lessened floors.

The greenhouse never so badly needed paint.
The chimney is fifty years old and slants to one side.
A fantastic effort has failed, a repetition
In a repetitiousness of men and flies.

Yet the absence of the imagination had
Itself to be imagined. The great pond,
The plain sense of it, without reflections, leaves,
Mud, water like dirty glass, expressing silence

Of a sort, silence of a rat come out to see,
The great pond and its waste of the lilies, all this
Had to be imagined as an inevitable knowledge,
Required, as a necessity requires.

<hr>

ONE OF THE INHABITANTS OF THE WEST

Our divinations,
Mechanisms of angelic thought,
The means of prophecy,

Alert us most
At evening's one star
And its pastoral text,

When the establishments
Of wind and light and cloud
Await an arrival,

A reader of the text,
A reader without a body,
Who reads quietly:

"Horrid figures of Medusa,
These accents explicate
The sparkling fall of night
On Europe, to the last Alp,
And the sheeted Atlantic.

These are not banlieus
Lacking men of stone,
In a well-rosed two-light
Of their own.
I am the archangel of evening and praise
This one star's blaze.
Suppose it was a drop of blood . . .
So much guilt lies buried
Beneath the innocence
Of autumn days."

❀✧❀◇

LEBENSWEISHEITSPIELEREI

Weaker and weaker, the sunlight falls
In the afternoon. The proud and the strong
Have departed.

Those that are left are the unaccomplished,
The finally human,
Natives of a dwindled sphere.

Their indigence is an indigence
That is an indigence of the light,
A stellar pallor that hangs on the threads.

Little by little, the poverty
Of autumnal space becomes
A look, a few words spoken.

Each person completely touches us
With what he is and as he is,
In the stale grandeur of annihilation.

THE HERMITAGE AT THE CENTER

The leaves on the macadam make a noise—
  How soft the grass on which the desired
  Reclines in the temperature of heaven—

Like tales that were told the day before yesterday—
  Sleek in a natural nakedness,
  She attends the tintinnabula—

And the wind sways like a great thing tottering—
  Of birds called up by more than the sun,
  Birds of more wit, that substitute—

Which suddenly is all dissolved and gone—
  Their intelligible twittering
  For unintelligible thought.

505

And yet this end and this beginning are one,
    And one last look at the ducks is a look
    At lucent children round her in a ring.

◆◇

THE GREEN PLANT

Silence is a shape that has passed.
Otu-bre's lion-roses have turned to paper
And the shadows of the trees
Are like wrecked umbrellas.

The effete vocabulary of summer
No longer says anything.
The brown at the bottom of red
The orange far down in yellow,

Are falsifications from a sun
In a mirror, without heat,
In a constant secondariness,
A turning down toward finality—

Except that a green plant glares, as you look
At the legend of the maroon and olive forest,
Glares, outside of the legend, with the barbar-
    ous green
Of the harsh reality of which it is part.

506

MADAME LA FLEURIE

Weight him down, O side-stars, with the great weightings of
    the end.
Seal him there. He looked in a glass of the earth and thought
    he lived in it.
Now, he brings all that he saw into the earth, to the waiting
    parent.
His crisp knowledge is devoured by her, beneath a dew.

Weight him, weight, weight him with the sleepiness of the
    moon.
It was only a glass because he looked in it. It was nothing he
    could be told.
It was a language he spoke, because he must, yet did not know.
It was a page he had found in the handbook of heartbreak.

The black fugatos are strumming the blacknesses of black . . .
The thick strings stutter the finial gutturals.
He does not lie there remembering the blue-jay, say the jay.
His grief is that his mother should feed on him, himself and
    what he saw,
In that distant chamber, a bearded queen, wicked in her dead
    light.

TO AN OLD PHILOSOPHER IN ROME

On the threshold of heaven, the figures in the street
Become the figures of heaven, the majestic movement
Of men growing small in the distances of space,
Singing, with smaller and still smaller sound,
Unintelligible absolution and an end—

The threshold, Rome, and that more merciful Rome
Beyond, the two alike in the make of the mind.
It is as if in a human dignity
Two parallels become one, a perspective, of which
Men are part both in the inch and in the mile.

How easily the blown banners change to wings . . .
Things dark on the horizons of perception,
Become accompaniments of fortune, but
Of the fortune of the spirit, beyond the eye,
Not of its sphere, and yet not far beyond,

The human end in the spirit's greatest reach,
The extreme of the known in the presence of the extreme
Of the unknown. The newsboys' muttering
Becomes another murmuring; the smell
Of medicine, a fragrantness not to be spoiled . . .

The bed, the books, the chair, the moving nuns,
The candle as it evades the sight, these are
The sources of happiness in the shape of Rome,

A shape within the ancient circles of shapes,
And these beneath the shadow of a shape

In a confusion on bed and books, a portent
On the chair, a moving transparence on the nuns,
A light on the candle tearing against the wick
To join a hovering excellence, to escape
From fire and be part only of that of which

Fire is the symbol: the celestial possible.
Speak to your pillow as if it was yourself.
Be orator but with an accurate tongue
And without eloquence, O, half-asleep,
Of the pity that is the memorial of this room,

So that we feel, in this illumined large,
The veritable small, so that each of us
Beholds himself in you, and hears his voice
In yours, master and commiserable man,
Intent on your particles of nether-do,

Your dozing in the depths of wakefulness,
In the warmth of your bed, at the edge of your chair, alive
Yet living in two worlds, impenitent
As to one, and, as to one, most penitent,
Impatient for the grandeur that you need

In so much misery; and yet finding it
Only in misery, the afflatus of ruin,
Profound poetry of the poor and of the dead,
As in the last drop of the deepest blood,
As it falls from the heart and lies there to be seen,

Even as the blood of an empire, it might be,
For a citizen of heaven though still of Rome.
It is poverty's speech that seeks us out the most.
It is older than the oldest speech of Rome.
This is the tragic accent of the scene.

And you—it is you that speak it, without speech,
The loftiest syllables among loftiest things,
The one invulnerable man among
Crude captains, the naked majesty, if you like,
Of bird-nest arches and of rain-stained-vaults.

The sounds drift in. The buildings are remembered.
The life of the city never lets go, nor do you
Ever want it to. It is part of the life in your room.
Its domes are the architecture of your bed.
The bells keep on repeating solemn names

In choruses and choirs of choruses,
Unwilling that mercy should be a mystery
Of silence, that any solitude of sense
Should give you more than their peculiar chords
And reverberations clinging to whisper still.

It is a kind of total grandeur at the end,
With every visible thing enlarged and yet
No more than a bed, a chair and moving nuns,
The immensest theatre, the pillared porch,
The book and candle in your ambered room,

Total grandeur of a total edifice,
Chosen by an inquisitor of structures

For himself. He stops upon this threshold,
As if the design of all his words takes form
And frame from thinking and is realized.

❖◇❖

VACANCY IN THE PARK

March . . . Someone has walked across the
    snow,
Someone looking for he knows not what.

It is like a boat that has pulled away
From a shore at night and disappeared.

It is like a guitar left on a table
By a woman, who has forgotten it.

It is like the feeling of a man
Come back to see a certain house.

The four winds blow through the rustic arbor,
Under its mattresses of vines.

THE POEM THAT TOOK THE PLACE
OF A MOUNTAIN

There it was, word for word,
The poem that took the place of a mountain.

He breathed its oxygen,
Even when the book lay turned in the dust of his table.

It reminded him how he had needed
A place to go to in his own direction,

How he had recomposed the pines,
Shifted the rocks and picked his way among clouds,

For the outlook that would be right,
Where he would be complete in an unexplained completion:

The exact rock where his inexactnesses
Would discover, at last, the view toward which they had edged,

Where he could lie and, gazing down at the sea,
Recognize his unique and solitary home.

TWO ILLUSTRATIONS THAT THE WORLD
IS WHAT YOU MAKE OF IT

I

The Constant Disquisition of the Wind
The sky seemed so small that winter day,
A dirty light on a lifeless world,
Contracted like a withered stick.

It was not the shadow of cloud and cold,
But a sense of the distance of the sun—
The shadow of a sense of his own,

A knowledge that the actual day
Was so much less. Only the wind
Seemed large and loud and high and strong.

And as he thought within the thought
Of the wind, not knowing that that thought
Was not his thought, nor anyone's,

The appropriate image of himself,
So formed, became himself and he breathed
The breath of another nature as his own,

But only its momentary breath,
Outside of and beyond the dirty light,
That never could be animal,

A nature still without a shape,
Except his own—perhaps, his own
In a Sunday's violent idleness.

II

The World Is Larger in Summer
He left half a shoulder and half a head
To recognize him in after time.

These marbles lay weathering in the grass
When the summer was over, when the change

Of summer and of the sun, the life
Of summer and of the sun, were gone.

He had said that everything possessed
The power to transform itself, or else,

And what meant more, to be transformed.
He discovered the colors of the moon

In a single spruce, when, suddenly,
The tree stood dazzling in the air

And blue broke on him from the sun,
A bullioned blue, a blue abulge,

Like daylight, with time's bellishings,
And sensuous summer stood full-height.

514

The master of the spruce, himself,
Became transformed. But his mastery

Left only the fragments found in the grass,
From his project, as finally magnified.

◇◇

PROLOGUES TO WHAT IS POSSIBLE

I

There was an ease of mind that was like being alone in a boat
    at sea,
A boat carried forward by waves resembling the bright backs
    of rowers,
Gripping their oars, as if they were sure of the way to their
    destination,
Bending over and pulling themselves erect on the wooden
    handles,
Wet with water and sparkling in the one-ness of their motion.

The boat was built of stones that had lost their weight and be-
    ing no longer heavy
Had left in them only a brilliance, of unaccustomed origin,
So that he that stood up in the boat leaning and looking be-
    fore him
Did not pass like someone voyaging out of and beyond the
    familiar.

515

He belonged to the far-foreign departure of his vessel and was
    part of it,
Part of the speculum of fire on its prow, its symbol, whatever
    it was,
Part of the glass-like sides on which it glided over the salt-
    stained water,
As he traveled alone, like a man lured on by a syllable without
    any meaning,
A syllable of which he felt, with an appointed sureness,
That it contained the meaning into which he wanted to enter,
A meaning which, as he entered it, would shatter the boat and
    leave the oarsmen quiet
As at a point of central arrival, an instant moment, much or
    little,
Removed from any shore, from any man or woman, and need-
    ing none.

II

The metaphor stirred his fear. The object with which he was
    compared
Was beyond his recognizing. By this he knew that likeness of
    him extended
Only a little way, and not beyond, unless between himself
And things beyond resemblance there was this and that in-
    tended to be recognized,
The this and that in the enclosures of hypotheses
On which men speculated in summer when they were half
    asleep.

What self, for example, did he contain that had not yet been
    loosed,
Snarling in him for discovery as his attentions spread,

As if all his hereditary lights were suddenly increased
By an access of color, a new and unobserved, slight dithering,
The smallest lamp, which added its puissant flick, to which he
    gave
A name and privilege over the ordinary of his commonplace—

A flick which added to what was real and its vocabulary,
The way some first thing coming into Northern trees
Adds to them the whole vocabulary of the South,
The way the earliest single light in the evening sky, in spring,
Creates a fresh universe out of nothingness by adding itself,
The way a look or a touch reveals its unexpected magnitudes.

❀◇

LOOKING ACROSS THE FIELDS AND
WATCHING THE BIRDS FLY

Among the more irritating minor ideas
Of Mr. Homburg during his visits home
To Concord, at the edge of things, was this:

To think away the grass, the trees, the clouds,
Not to transform them into other things,
Is only what the sun does every day,

Until we say to ourselves that there may be
A pensive nature, a mechanical
And slightly detestable *operandum*, free

517

From man's ghost, larger and yet a little like,
Without his literature and without his gods . . .
No doubt we live beyond ourselves in air,

In an element that does not do for us,
So well, that which we do for ourselves, too big,
A thing not planned for imagery or belief,

Not one of the masculine myths we used to make,
A transparency through which the swallow weaves,
Without any form or any sense of form,

What we know in what we see, what we feel in what
We hear, what we are, beyond mystic disputation,
In the tumult of integrations out of the sky,

And what we think, a breathing like the wind,
A moving part of a motion, a discovery
Part of a discovery, a change part of a change,

A sharing of color and being part of it.
The afternoon is visibly a source,
Too wide, too irised, to be more than calm,

Too much like thinking to be less than thought,
Obscurest parent, obscurest patriarch,
A daily majesty of meditation,

That comes and goes in silences of its own.
We think, then, as the sun shines or does not.
We think as wind skitters on a pond in a field

Or we put mantles on our words because
The same wind, rising and rising, makes a sound
Like the last muting of winter as it ends.

A new scholar replacing an older one reflects
A moment on this fantasia. He seeks
For a human that can be accounted for.

The spirit comes from the body of the world,
Or so Mr. Homburg thought: the body of a world
Whose blunt laws make an affectation of mind,

The mannerism of nature caught in a glass
And there become a spirit's mannerism,
A glass aswarm with things going as far as they can.

❀❀❀❀❀❀❀❀❀❀❀❀❀❀❀❀❀❀❀❀❀❀❀❀❀❀

SONG OF FIXED ACCORD

Rou-cou spoke the dove,
Like the sooth lord of sorrow,
Of sooth love and sorrow,
And a hail-bow, hail-bow,
To this morrow.

She lay upon the roof,
A little wet of wing and woe,
And she rou-ed there,
Softly she piped among the suns
And their ordinary glare,

519

The sun of five, the sun of six,
Their ordinariness,
And the ordinariness of seven,
Which she accepted,
Like a fixed heaven,

Not subject to change . . .
Day's invisible beginner,
The lord of love and of sooth sorrow,
Lay on the roof
And made much within her.

<hr>

THE WORLD AS MEDITATION

*J'ai passé trop de temps à
travailler mon violon, à voyager. Mais l'exercice essentiel
du compositeur—la méditation
—rien ne l'a jamais suspendu
en moi . . . Je vis un rêve
permanent, qui ne s'arrête ni
nuit ni jour.*
GEORGES ENESCO

Is it Ulysses that approaches from the east,
The interminable adventurer? The trees are mended.
That winter is washed away. Someone is moving

On the horizon and lifting himself up above it.
A form of fire approaches the cretonnes of Penelope,
Whose mere savage presence awakens the world in which
    she dwells.

She has composed, so long, a self with which to welcome
    him,
Companion to his self for her, which she imagined,
Two in a deep-founded sheltering, friend and dear friend.

The trees had been mended, as an essential exercise
In an inhuman meditation, larger than her own.
No winds like dogs watched over her at night.

She wanted nothing he could not bring her by coming
    alone.
She wanted no fetchings. His arms would be her necklace
And her belt, the final fortune of their desire.

But was it Ulysses? Or was it only the warmth of the sun
On her pillow? The thought kept beating in her like her
    heart.
The two kept beating together. It was only day.

It was Ulysses and it was not. Yet they had met,
Friend and dear friend and a planet's encouragement.
The barbarous strength within her would never fail.

She would talk a little to herself as she combed her hair,
Repeating his name with its patient syllables,
Never forgetting him that kept coming constantly so near.

LONG AND SLUGGISH LINES

It makes so little difference, at so much more
Than seventy, where one looks, one has been there
    before.

Wood-smoke rises through trees, is caught in an upper
    flow
Of air and whirled away. But it has been often so.

The trees have a look as if they bore sad names
And kept saying over and over one same, same thing,

In a kind of uproar, because an opposite, a contradic-
    tion,
Has enraged them and made them want to talk it down.

What opposite? Could it be that yellow patch, the side
Of a house, that makes one think the house is laughing;

Or these—escent—issant pre-personae: first fly,
A comic infanta among the tragic drapings,

Babyishness of forsythia, a snatch of belief,
The spook and makings of the nude magnolia?

. . . Wanderer, this is the pre-history of February.
The life of the poem in the mind has not yet begun.

You were not born yet when the trees were crystal
Nor are you now, in this wakefulness inside a sleep.

A QUIET NORMAL LIFE

His place, as he sat and as he thought, was not
In anything that he constructed, so frail,
So barely lit, so shadowed over and naught,

As, for example, a world in which, like snow,
He became an inhabitant, obedient
To gallant notions on the part of cold.

It was here. This was the setting and the time
Of year. Here in his house and in his room,
In his chair, the most tranquil thought grew peaked

And the oldest and the warmest heart was cut
By gallant notions on the part of night—
Both late and alone, above the crickets' chords,

Babbling, each one, the uniqueness of its sound.
There was no fury in transcendent forms.
But his actual candle blazed with artifice.

FINAL SOLILOQUY OF THE INTERIOR PARAMOUR

Light the first light of evening, as in a room
In which we rest and, for small reason, think
The world imagined is the ultimate good.

This is, therefore, the intensest rendezvous.
It is in that thought that we collect ourselves,
Out of all the indifferences, into one thing:

Within a single thing, a single shawl
Wrapped tightly round us, since we are poor, a
        warmth,
A light, a power, the miraculous influence.

Here, now, we forget each other and ourselves.
We feel the obscurity of an order, a whole,
A knowledge, that which arranged the rendezvous.

Within its vital boundary, in the mind.
We say God and the imagination are one . . .
How high that highest candle lights the dark.

Out of this same light, out of the central mind,
We make a dwelling in the evening air,
In which being there together is enough.

THE ROCK

I

Seventy Years Later

It is an illusion that we were ever alive,
Lived in the houses of mothers, arranged ourselves
By our own motions in a freedom of air.

Regard the freedom of seventy years ago.
It is no longer air. The houses still stand,
Though they are rigid in rigid emptiness.

Even our shadows, their shadows, no longer re-
      main.
The lives these lived in the mind are at an end.
They never were . . . The sounds of the guitar

Were not and are not. Absurd. The words spoken
Were not and are not. It is not to be believed.
The meeting at noon at the edge of the field seems
      like

An invention, an embrace between one desperate
      clod
And another in a fantastic consciousness,
In a queer assertion of humanity:

A theorem proposed between the two—
Two figures in a nature of the sun,
In the sun's design of its own happiness,

As if nothingness contained a métier,
A vital assumption, an impermanence
In its permanent cold, an illusion so desired

That the green leaves came and covered the high
    rock,
That the lilacs came and bloomed, like a blindness
    cleaned,
Exclaiming bright sight, as it was satisfied,

In a birth of sight. The blooming and the musk
Were being alive, an incessant being alive,
A particular of being, that gross universe.

II

The Poem as Icon

It is not enough to cover the rock with leaves.
We must be cured of it by a cure of the ground
Or a cure of ourselves, that is equal to a cure

Of the ground, a cure beyond forgetfulness.
And yet the leaves, if they broke into bud,
If they broke into bloom, if they bore fruit,

And if we ate the incipient colorings
Of their fresh culls might be a cure of the ground.
The fiction of the leaves is the icon

Of the poem, the figuration of blessedness,
And the icon is the man. The pearled chaplet of
    spring,
The magnum wreath of summer, time's autumn
    snood,

Its copy of the sun, these cover the rock.
These leaves are the poem, the icon and the man.
These are a cure of the ground and of ourselves,

In the predicate that there is nothing else.
They bud and bloom and bear their fruit without
    change.
They are more than leaves that cover the barren
    rock

They bud the whitest eye, the pallidest sprout,
New senses in the engenderings of sense,
The desire to be at the end of distances,

The body quickened and the mind in root.
They bloom as a man loves, as he lives in love.
They bear their fruit so that the year is known,

As if its understanding was brown skin,
The honey in its pulp, the final found,
The plenty of the year and of the world.

In this plenty, the poem makes meanings of the
    rock,
Of such mixed motion and such imagery
That its barrenness becomes a thousand things

And so exists no more. This is the cure
Of leaves and of the ground and of ourselves.
His words are both the icon and the man.

Forms of the Rock in a Night-Hymn

The rock is the gray particular of man's life,
The stone from which he rises, up—and—ho,
The step to the bleaker depths of his descents . . .

The rock is the stern particular of the air,
The mirror of the planets, one by one,
But through man's eye, their silent rhapsodist,

Turquoise the rock, at odious evening bright
With redness that sticks fast to evil dreams;
The difficult rightness of half-risen day.

The rock is the habitation of the whole,
Its strength and measure, that which is near,
    point A
In a perspective that begins again

At B: the origin of the mango's rind.
It is the rock where tranquil must adduce
Its tranquil self, the main of things, the mind,

The starting point of the human and the end,
That in which space itself is contained, the gate
To the enclosure, day, the things illumined

By day, night and that which night illumines,
Night and its midnight-minting fragrances,
Night's hymn of the rock, as in a vivid sleep.

528

ST. ARMORER'S CHURCH FROM
THE OUTSIDE

St. Armorer's was once an immense success.
It rose loftily and stood massively; and to lie
In its church-yard, in the province of St. Armorer's,
Fixed one for good in geranium-colored day.

What is left has the foreign smell of plaster,
The closed-in smell of hay. A sumac grows
On the altar, growing toward the lights, inside.
Reverberations leak and lack among holes . . .

Its chapel rises from Terre Ensevelie,
An ember yes among its cindery noes,
His own: a chapel of breath, an appearance made
For a sign of meaning in the meaningless,

No radiance of dead blaze, but something seen
In a mystic eye, no sign of life but life,
Itself, the presence of the intelligible
In that which is created as its symbol.

It is like a new account of everything old,
Matisse at Vence and a great deal more than that,
A new-colored sun, say, that will soon change forms
And spread hallucinations on every leaf.

The chapel rises, his own, his period,
A civilization formed from the outward blank,

A sacred syllable rising from sacked speech,
The first car out of a tunnel en voyage

Into lands of ruddy-ruby fruits, achieved
Not merely desired, for sale, and market things
That press, strong peasants in a peasant world,
Their purports to a final seriousness—

Final for him, the acceptance of such prose,
Time's given perfections made to seem like less
Than the need of each generation to be itself,
The need to be actual and as it is.

St. Armorer's has nothing of this present,
This *vif*, this dizzle-dazzle of being new
And of becoming, for which the chapel spreads out
Its arches in its vivid element,

In the air of newness of that element,
In an air of freshness, clearness, greenness, blueness,
That which is always beginning because it is part
Of that which is always beginning, over and over.

The chapel underneath St. Armorer's walls,
Stands in a light, its natural light and day,
The origin and keep of its health and his own.
And there he walks and does as he lives and likes.

NOTE ON MOONLIGHT

The one moonlight, in the simple-colored night,
Like a plain poet revolving in his mind
The sameness of his various universe,
Shines on the mere objectiveness of things.

It is as if being was to be observed,
As if, among the possible purposes
Of what one sees, the purpose that comes first,
The surface, is the purpose to be seen,

The property of the moon, what it evokes.
It is to disclose the essential presence, say,
Of a mountain, expanded and elevated almost
Into a sense, an object the less; or else

To disclose in the figure waiting on the road
An object the more, an undetermined form
Between the slouchings of a gunman and a lover,
A gesture in the dark, a fear one feels

In the great vistas of night air, that takes this form,
In the arbors that are as if of Saturn-star.
So, then, this warm, wide, weatherless quietude
Is active with a power, an inherent life,

In spite of the mere objectiveness of things,
Like a cloud-cap in the corner of a looking-glass,

A change of color in the plain poet's mind,
Night and silence disturbed by an interior sound,

The one moonlight, the various universe, intended
So much just to be seen—a purpose, empty
Perhaps, absurd perhaps, but at least a purpose,
Certain and ever more fresh. Ah! Certain, for
    sure . . .

THE PLANET ON THE TABLE

Ariel was glad he had written his poems.
They were of a remembered time
Or of something seen that he liked.

Other makings of the sun
Were waste and welter
And the ripe shrub writhed.

His self and the sun were one
And his poems, although makings of his self,
Were no less makings of the sun.

It was not important that they survive.
What mattered was that they should bear
Some lineament or character,

532

Some affluence, if only half-perceived,
In the poverty of their words,
Of the planet of which they were part.

‹›

THE RIVER OF RIVERS IN CONNECTICUT

There is a great river this side of Stygia,
Before one comes to the first black cataracts
And trees that lack the intelligence of trees.

In that river, far this side of Stygia,
The mere flowing of the water is a gayety,
Flashing and flashing in the sun. On its banks,

No shadow walks. The river is fateful,
Like the last one. But there is no ferryman.
He could not bend against its propelling force.

It is not to be seen beneath the appearances
That tell of it. The steeple at Farmington
Stands glistening and Haddam shines and sways.

It is the third commonness with light and air,
A curriculum, a vigor, a local abstraction . . .
Call it, once more, a river, an unnamed flowing,

Space-filled, reflecting the seasons, the folk-lore
Of each of the senses; call it, again and again,
The river that flows nowhere, like a sea.

533

NOT IDEAS ABOUT THE THING
BUT THE THING ITSELF

At the earliest ending of winter,
In March, a scrawny cry from outside
Seemed like a sound in his mind.

He knew that he heard it,
A bird's cry, at daylight or before,
In the early March wind.

The sun was rising at six,
No longer a battered panache above snow . . .
It would have been outside.

It was not from the vast ventriloquism
Of sleep's faded papier-mâché . . .
The sun was coming from outside.

That scrawny cry—it was
A chorister whose c preceded the choir.
It was part of the colossal sun,

Surrounded by its choral rings,
Still far away. It was like
A new knowledge of reality.

534

INDEX OF TITLES OF POEMS

i

111

iv

A NOTE ON THE TYPE

This book is set in Electra, a Linotype face designed by W. A. Dwiggins. This face cannot be classified as either modern or old-style. It is not based on any historical model, nor does it echo any particular period or style. It avoids the extreme contrast between thick and thin elements that marks most modern faces, and attempts to give a feeling of fluidity, power, and speed.

The typography and binding were designed by W. A. Dwiggins.

The book was composed by The Plimpton Press, Norwood, Mass., and printed and bound by Kingsport Press, Inc., Kingsport, Tennessee.